I0032116

# FUTURE?
# CHINA!

How the New Superpower
is Changing the West

# FUTURE?
# CHINA!

How the New Superpower
is Changing the West

Frank Sieren

**World Scientific**

NEW JERSEY · LONDON · SINGAPORE · BEIJING · SHANGHAI · HONG KONG · TAIPEI · CHENNAI · TOKYO

*Published by*

World Scientific Publishing Co. Pte. Ltd.

5 Toh Tuck Link, Singapore 596224

*USA office:* 27 Warren Street, Suite 401-402, Hackensack, NJ 07601

*UK office:* 57 Shelton Street, Covent Garden, London WC2H 9HE

**Library of Congress Cataloging-in-Publication Data**
Names: Sieren, Frank, 1967–    author.
Title: Future? China! : how the new superpower is changing the West / Frank Sieren.
Other titles: Zukunft? China! English
Description: Hackensack, NJ : World Scientific, [2023]
Identifiers: LCCN 2022037856 | ISBN 9789811264238 (hardcover) |
    ISBN 9789811264672 (paperback)
Subjects: LCSH: China--Foreign economic relations--21st century. | China--Commerce--Europe. |
    Europe--Commerce--China. | International economic integration.
Classification: LCC HF1604.Z4 E85613 2023 | DDC 382.30951--dc23/eng/20221014
LC record available at https://lccn.loc.gov/2022037856

**British Library Cataloguing-in-Publication Data**
A catalogue record for this book is available from the British Library.

Original title: Zukunft? China! Wie die neue Supermacht unser Leben, unsere Politik, unsere
Wirtschaft verändert, by Frank Sieren
© 2018 by Penguin Verlag,
a division of Penguin Random House Verlagsgruppe GmbH, München, Germany.
following the English language copyright note in every edition without further prompting from the
PROPRIETOR.

Copyright © 2023 by World Scientific Publishing Co. Pte. Ltd.

*All rights reserved. This book, or parts thereof, may not be reproduced in any form or by any means,
electronic or mechanical, including photocopying, recording or any information storage and retrieval
system now known or to be invented, without written permission from the publisher.*

For photocopying of material in this volume, please pay a copying fee through the Copyright Clearance
Center, Inc., 222 Rosewood Drive, Danvers, MA 01923, USA. In this case permission to photocopy
is not required from the publisher.

For any available supplementary material, please visit
https://www.worldscientific.com/worldscibooks/10.1142/13081#t=suppl

Desk Editors: Soundararajan Raghuraman/Nicole Ong

Typeset by Stallion Press
Email: enquiries@stallionpress.com

*For Leo and Tim,*
*who can already read their names, but not yet the book.*

# About the Author

**Frank Sieren** is one of Germany's leading China experts.

The journalist, book author, and documentary filmmaker has lived in Beijing since 1994 — longer than any other Western business journalist. He has experienced the rise of the new world power firsthand. During his 3 decades in China, Sieren has been a correspondent for the *Süddeutsche Zeitung, WirtschaftsWoche, Die Zeit, Handelsblatt* and *Tagesspiegel*. He now also works for the startup "China.Table," the first and only German-language daily business briefing focusing on China.

Sieren has already published several China bestsellers.

# Contents

# Introduction

*We now have the strength to take our rightful place in the world.*

Xi Jinping, China's State and Party Leader

*We now have to fight for our future ourselves. As Europeans, for our destiny.*

Angela Merkel, German Chancellor

*I want to bring my soldiers back from Asia.*

Donald Trump, US President

When I arrived in Beijing in August 1994, I came to a country that had already been shaped by the opening policy of the reformer Deng Xiaoping. Nevertheless, I could not have imagined the breathtaking speed at which China would develop. If I had written down 15 or 20 years ago what China would look like in 2018, I would have been considered a crank who had lost all traction. Hardly anyone in the West foresaw China's successful development as it has taken place. For too long, China seemed to be a colossus with feet of clay. But now the country is bursting with strength. In 2017, it sold more products worth 420 billion US dollars than it had to import.

The range of products extends from jeans to smartphones to airplanes. China is no longer just the world's factory bank. In the meantime, they also have the world's best high-speed trains, and most of the world's electric cars and e-buses are on the country's roads. Together with the USA, China is a leader in the future technology of artificial intelligence (AI), which will turn our familiar world upside down. The Chinese are already world leaders in online retailing and smartphone payments. And investments in start-ups are already higher than in the USA. The world's most expensive "unicorn," as startups worth more than a billion U.S. dollars are called, comes from China. It is dedicated to facial recognition, another area in which China is now the world leader. At the same time, China is investing on all continents for the first time in its 3,500-year history. It's all about key industries, mineral resources, and infrastructure. Beijing is now building railroads, dams, and power plants of a quality that satisfies even the strict World Bank, where the West still calls the shots. The project that outshines everything else is the exciting New Silk Road, which reaches as far as Germany, Panama, and Senegal. It is the largest infrastructure project in the world since the Great Wall was built in the 7th century.

More and more countries are siding with the Chinese not only because they are investing generously in them but also because these countries want to become like China that is self-determined and independent. China is a country that does not allow itself to be dictated to by the West, it determines its own path, at its own pace, with its own political system. A country that now wants to rebalance the world and, if that is not possible with existing global institutions, is now powerful enough to create new ones. Like the Asian Infrastructure Investment Bank (AIIB), the counterweight to the U.S.-dominated World Bank. So China is forming new alliances with other emerging countries that hope to finally make their voices heard in the international concert of the powerful. This also means that they are free to decide in which currency they want to trade. The yuan is now the world's reserve currency, along with the U.S. dollar and the euro. From the good old days, the British pound and the Japanese yen are also still around.

What is also remarkable about China's rise is the fact that the country has no foreign debt. Furthermore, Beijing has a savings book with the largest foreign exchange reserves in the world. In terms of purchasing power, the People's Republic has been the world's largest economy for several years. GDP is still smaller in nominal terms, but the following chart shows the potential of China.

Germany
USA
China
EU

84 tr.

42 tr.

19.4 tr.
15.3 tr.
12 tr.
3.7 tr.

19.4 tr.
15.3 tr.
3.7 tr.

19.4 tr.
15.3 tr.
3.7 tr.

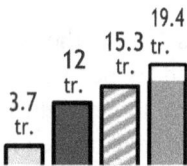

**The World today:**
The nominal level of GDP of Germany, China, Europe, and the USA. Figures in trillion US dollars.

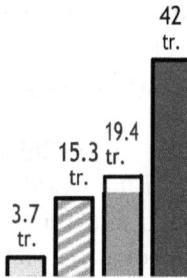

**Tomorrow's world:**
The nominal level of GDP in comparison once China has reached half the labor productivity of the USA.

**The world of the day after tomorrow:** The nominal level of GDP in comparison once China has reached the labor productivity of the USA.

So while Beijing itself is meticulously careful not to become financially dependent, it is also the Americans' biggest creditor. This is an instrument that should not be underestimated in the trade dispute with the USA.

In the meantime, China is also no longer focusing on growth at any price but has risen to become the biggest environmentalist on earth. The largest hydroelectric power plants and the most windmills in the world are located in China. In 2017, China installed nearly ten times as many gigawatts of solar panels as all of Europe combined. China is also setting standards in Industry 4.0 — with fully automated, self-learning factories. Technology companies, such as Alibaba, Tencent, and China Mobile, are leading the way and are now among the world's largest stock corporations.

And even in terms of soft power, China is catching up. The tea-drinking Master Wu already exists as a Lego figure. Art Basel Hong Kong is now more important than its counterpart in Miami. And former Louvre director Henri Loyrette recently admitted, "In truth, the Louvre is not a universal museum." "It is," he said, "a museum of the West." But now times are changing. The 2,500-year-old game of Go, which originated in China, is competing with chess. The largest film studios in the world are now located in China. Most of the world's cinemas are owned by Chinese, including a large number of American cinemas. Even one of the major Hollywood studios is already in Chinese hands. No Hollywood film can be calculated without the income from Chinese cinemas. Today, a top actor like Matt Damon plays a mercenary in a Chinese-American Hollywood production who is humbly apprenticed to clever Chinese fighters.

Even in terms of poverty alleviation, China ranks first in the world. No major country in the history of the world has lifted its people out of poverty as quickly as China. That's something you have to get right first. And it has previously wriggled out of a crisis that would have broken most other countries. In the 18th century, China still accounted for 30 percent of the world economy; at the time of the cultural revolution under Mao, the figure was only two percent. Now, it was 15 percent again. China is back, but still has room for improvement. The annual per capita income of the Chinese is just under 9,000 U.S. dollars. In the U.S. it is over 60,000. There is nothing to prevent China from reaching this level one day. And there is little to say that China's GDP will not be twice as high as America's in the future. Disposable household income grows by an average of around six percent every year. And that will continue for quite some time.

This growth and the many new opportunities that are emerging, especially through digitization, artificial intelligence, and e-mobility, make it comparatively easy for a large part of the population to overlook the restrictions on personal freedoms, the human rights situation, and the lack of democratic co-determination. The majority of Chinese support the authoritarian system, even if it seems suspicious to us. And this system is gaining more and more supporters, especially in the developing countries of the world. In many regions of Asia or Africa, stability and prosperity initially seem more important to people than comprehensive co-determination and a diverse civil society. The great advantages of democracy, as we see them, are not obvious to them. Especially since a look at Europe shows how paralyzed the democracies there are and how strong the political fringes are becoming, in other words, how unstable this system that was considered so secure has become. And a look at America shows that elections can bring unlikely bullies to power — because people are dissatisfied and are looking for simple solutions in complicated times, even if these cannot exist in reality.

Since we in the West are increasingly preoccupied with ourselves, this creates a vacuum into which China is only too happy to push. The Chinese are resolutely opening up new markets, investing in infrastructure projects and mineral resources, and thus not only doing something geopolitically and economically but systematically shifting the old, familiar power structure. Gone are the days when the West set the standards and declared the rest to be folklore.

Future? China!

Of course, China also has problems, and not too few. The legal system is non-transparent and sometimes politically controlled. There are still people in prison who are not even allowed to see their lawyer. Sentences are pronounced that were already determined before the trial. People are wiretapped, persecuted, or immediately imprisoned because of their political opinions. The media cannot write and broadcast what they want. Party cells must be installed in every company, including Western ones. Beijing has been announcing the opening of its markets for years, but in fact it is only opening at a snail's pace. In some areas, protectionism has even increased. Entire industrial sectors are protected from foreign competition. In others, Western companies are forced to transfer technology in order to be allowed to enter the Chinese market at all. Piracy and patent infringements still exist.

Add to that corruption and scandals like the recent one in July 2018. Hundreds of thousands of infants received ineffective and possibly harmful vaccinations. The pharmaceutical company admitted that it had acted out of greed. The real scandal, however, was that the regulatory authority discovered the fraud but did not inform the public about it until almost a year later. China must finally "scrape this poison off its bones," as President Xi Jinping demanded. But that is easier said than done. Some party cadres see the opening of the country as the root of all evil, introducing temptations of capitalism — even Chinese-style capitalism.

There are also difficulties on other fronts, the gap between rich and poor is widening and China is no exception. Water in the country is scarce and polluted, the government has to fight for every liter. This is expensive and time-consuming. The population of 1.4 billion must be fed, urbanization must be pursued with a sense of proportion and energy and resource consumption must be reduced. Beijing is aware of all these challenges. It is tackling them with decisiveness and consistency that is only possible in an authoritarian system.

It acts with similar determination and, at times, frightening arrogance, for example, in the showdown in the South China Sea or in its dealings with its neighbors. Even governments that suffer from China's impositions admire Beijing's strength at the same time, for there is a rift running through the world in terms of assessments of China's strengths and weaknesses. In the West, but also in Asian rivals India and Japan, the weaknesses tend to be overrated (this cannot go well, the resource theft, human rights, what about the democratization process, the real opening of the market ...). While in the rest of the world, the strengths play a much greater role (we want to be there, China is our role model). Are some possibly wise and far-sighted, others naive and short-sighted? This book intends to discover that.

It is already obvious that the West is playing an increasingly minor role in the world. The rulers in Beijing, as well as the leadership of the countries with which China cooperates, have long since ceased to be accountable to the West. They do not even have to consult with us. They have their own ideas about what the world should look like in the future. In the West, one reads that the world order has been upset by the rise of China. The world order in which the West set the tone. I hear from the Chinese, on the other hand, that everything is finally coming into order. The world will be rebalanced and become fairer. We hear similar things in Africa and Central Asia.

In fact, China is not only self-confident about its role but is increasingly determining the global rules of the game. In writing this book, it has become even clearer to me that China's direct influence on our lives is already much greater than I had thought. On the one hand, China is an opportunity for the world to renew itself. But it is also a danger for us if we do not accept the challenge. If we believe that *we don't* have to change, but only others do.

To put it in a nutshell; we cannot change the *fact that* China is rising to become a world power. We can hardly influence even *how* China rises. But we can adjust to it and choose a clever strategy that will enable us to defend our interests. This is not easy. It is certainly not pleasant, because we have always believed that we, as the minority that the West is, can permanently determine the rules of the game in the world. As democratic as we are in our country, we tend to behave undemocratically in international relations. Competition is indispensable, we have long preached to the Chinese. Now they are competing with us. And now we don't like it anymore. For just as long, we demanded that China open up, politically, but above all economically. We wanted to open up this huge market for ourselves and are now disgruntled that the Chinese flood ours with their products and have long since overtaken us on emerging markets in many areas.

These are just two of many examples of the West's double standards. And in doing so, it is demonstrating one thing above all — its fear of losing power. We have a massive problem with the fact that, for the first time in hundreds of years, the direction is being set by a non-Western power. Accepting this or coming up with a concept to counter it, is a major challenge. No one can see into the future. But after all, that is already apparent. No other country in the world will determine our future — the future of Germany and Europe — more than China in the coming decades.

And, yes, China will also push back the influence of the entire Western Hemisphere globally. That means we have to compromise and give up some power. It also means we have to try harder and be cleverer when it comes to anchoring our ideas globally. And that's what we want, right? Our values are important to us. We want them to endure in the global order.

In many areas, however, China has long since freed itself from its former dependence on the West. Our raised forefinger is losing its persuasive power. We can hardly attach conditions to our know-how anymore. After all, we need the Chinese market more urgently than they need our know-how. Despite some weaknesses, Beijing has managed to rise wisely so far, all in all, and is now setting the next course step-by-step on its way to becoming a big player on the world stage.

I was always convinced that China would not collapse. The facts were against it. So was my gut feeling. However, I was far too cautious in my assessment of the speed and success of the rise. Why was that? Probably what I learned about communism at school during the Cold War and what seemed to be confirmed after the fall of the Berlin Wall shaped me more than I realize in retrospect. One message was repeated like a prayer in school: Communism is far inferior to capitalism, and dictatorships have short legs. In the long run, people won't put up with it. That is all true. But it has only a limited connection with China.

My view has been additionally clouded by specific Chinese clichés that, as we now know, proved to be false, e.g., they can't do more than copy; they can obey, but they can't develop anything; a uniform mass, albeit a very large one, without creative minds; there's not enough to be more than the factory of the world.

But then, not everything was centrally controlled. Beijing actually succeeded in awakening the ambition and initiative of young people in particular. In this respect, the government was obviously convincing. After all, the fact that people are curious and creative, quick, amazingly well organized, and willing to work hard only succeeds if they trust the politicians that it pays to get involved. I didn't believe for a long time that Beijing could succeed in this.

So, it is rather our own ideological conditioning that clouds our view and gives rise to deep-seated prejudices. This is also why we can hardly believe that the long unimaginable has become part of everyday life today. And that is also why we still find it so difficult to react appropriately.

In recent years, the Chinese Communists have largely proved to be not only powerful but also peace-loving, far-sighted, and pragmatic. I am almost reluctant to write down such a sentence. Everything I have learned resists it. Nevertheless, the sentence is correct. They have opened up the country with its huge market potential — albeit with restrictions — and they have brought growth and increasing prosperity for the population, and we should be happy about that first of all. For the people there and for us. As an export nation, Germany benefits from this more than almost any other country. Almost 40 percent of the German automotive industry's profits are generated in China. For that, I say, Thank you, China!

Nevertheless, I am still convinced that our political as well as our social value system has many advantages and strengths that we have developed and refined over centuries. And I do not want them to be lost in the course of China's rise. Our individual freedom, the diversity of civil society with its citizens' initiatives and co-determination, and our legal and social system, at least in its original idea. Yes, co-determination is cumbersome, lengthy, and can be incredibly annoying, but it can be worked on. Then there is freedom of religion, freedom of the press, environmental protection, and data protection, which at least tries to preserve our privacy. These are strengths that we are far from having developed to the end. And they need constant attention. These values should be an integral part of the new world order. But unfortunately, that doesn't happen by itself. We need power to enforce them. Can we still do that? We are experiencing an erosion of democracy not only at the core of Europe but also at its edges, fueled, among other things, by nationalism that has unfortunately become an integral part of European politics. With Donald

Trump at the helm of the United States, we are witnessing the systematic disintegration of the structures and institutions on which the West was founded for decades. We are realizing far too slowly that we have perhaps made ourselves a little too comfortable.

How else could it happen that 16,000 electric buses are already running in Shenzhen in southern China alone, while we in Germany, the land of the energy transition, can't manage an e-bus fleet worth mentioning in a single city? To take a comparatively simple example, how could it happen that we rank so far behind in e-governance, even in Europe? Not to mention nationwide broadband expansion. Why do our politicians in Berlin and Brussels only "drive by sight" and no longer develop long-term strategies? This book will also discuss how competitive our social order really still is.

Listening to some China critics, one is reminded of the song of the 68er political activist Franz Josef Degenhardt: "Don't play with the muck-rakers, don't sing their songs. Why don't you go to the upper city, do it like your brothers?" We can hardly imagine that these grubby kids will be — and in some cases already are — the global upper class of tomorrow. And we don't want them to be. Actually, it is not only a virtue of a businessman to overestimate rather than underestimate his competitors. We have forgotten this virtue, and China has seized its opportunity. The Chinese are now more self-confident and stronger than ever before. They are convinced of their path. You could even say that this applies to a certain extent to the whole of Asia. 60 percent of the world's population lives in Asia. We, on the other hand, the Germans, the Europeans, and indeed the West as a whole, only account for 15 percent of the world's population (of which around seven percent live in the EU), and the trend is downward. The Chinese alone, a significant 18 percent of the world's population, outweigh the entire West.

As already mentioned, we as a minority have long determined the rules of the game in the world. Liberty, equality, and fraternity, belonged to us. For Asians, South Americans, and Africans, we had for a long time only a club, a whip, or even a rifle bullet. We came to their countries to exploit them. We exploited their labor and robbed them of their natural resources. In many places, the brutal colonial era left countries reeling politically and economically and dependent on the West's often meager drip of development aid.

Fortunate historical circumstances gave the West the opportunity to suppress China as well. In the 19th century, the Chinese committed a big mistake that should be a warning to us today. They thought they were the navel of the world. When the British politely asked whether China was not willing to reduce its trade surplus with England, they slammed the door in their face and closed themselves off. In their arrogance, the Chinese had overlooked the fact that thanks to the industrial revolution, the Europeans were now much more advanced than China. They actually thought they were playing outside the competition. The British, who had been snubbed, returned in 1839 with gunboats and colonized the main Chinese ports. The French, the Portuguese, the Americans, and even the Germans followed them. A great humiliation for China.

It would take 110 years before Communist leader Mao Zedong succeeded in driving the colonial powers back from mainland China in the early 1950s. The final withdrawal, however, was only a good 20 years ago — the British returned Hong Kong in 1997 and Portugal Macau in 1999. To this day, the Americans point weapons at China from neighboring South Korea. And the West still believes it has the core competence to tell people in other countries how they should live. Our supposedly superior system is supposed to bring prosperity, freedom, and democracy, if necessary with military force. For historical reasons, we Germans find the latter somewhat more difficult, but we see ourselves morally all the more obliged to protect the values of the Western world. The reason for this seems obvious; we failed morally under Hitler, so we are now doubly vigilant and protect even those who do not want to be protected. From our point of view, this is a great good; it is not for nothing that Chancellor Angela Merkel was ennobled by the Western media as the last guardian of the free world. In other countries, however, this interference is definitely met with skepticism. "Why here, of all places?" is the counter-question. People want to decide for themselves what they think is right and what they think is wrong. That, too, is a concept of freedom. A freedom that we are still all too happy to stand in the way of when it doesn't benefit us.

Just one example: "Why is China's environment so polluted?" is what the Chinese have to hear from Westerners time and again. In the meantime, they answer confidently: "Because we Chinese were not too shy to do the dirty work for the West as the factory of the world." We, the West, wanted to pay as little as possible for our jeans. The fact that dyes and chemicals are untreated and were discharged into Chinese rivers, who among us cared? After all, that was far away. The Chinese took the dirty job anyway because it was the only way for them to get wealth. That's why they allowed us to outsource "our" pollution, so to speak.

The Chinese will no longer put up with us pointing the finger at China and criticizing the environmental damage. It is quite possible that the government will one day levy an environmental tax. Beijing has already taken the first step in this direction — since January 2018, China no longer buys foreign waste for recycling. The world's garbage dump is now closed. The EU Commission's attempts to negotiate a transition period of several years were shot down by Beijing. Now, we have a major problem. Almost 90 percent of Europe's plastic waste went to China. This is what the new global justice looks like.

The Chinese have long since developed their own ideas of how global interaction could look like in the future. Knowing what Beijing wants is more helpful than ever when it comes to having a say. To this day, many in the West assume they can be both referee and player. Now, they are astonished and a little annoyed to discover that the other players no longer want to do this. This is also what this book is about.

In Chapter 1, I look at how Beijing is winning over disaffected EU countries and thereby undermining Europe. Already today, Brussels is no longer able to speak with a unified voice to China. And while we cannot really weaken the Russians with ever stricter sanctions, at the same time we are driving them further and further into the arms of the Chinese. Beijing is amused by so much European shortsightedness.

In Chapter 2, we will see the speed at which China is becoming increasingly innovative. Artificial intelligence is the biggest focus in China.

The globalization process in which the Chinese are preparing to overtake the West in the fourth industrial revolution will change the world dramatically. And whoever is at the forefront will play a decisive role in determining the rules of the new technological world order. In Germany, too.

In Chapter 3, I describe how this new technological world order affects us, the country of car companies, and the German "hidden champions." With the development of the electric car, the Chinese are now taking the lead in key German technology for the first time. The German auto industry is now facing the greatest challenge in the history of the Federal Republic. Since China wants it that way, nothing in Germany will remain as it was.

In Chapter 4, I analyze how China's President Xi Jinping, as a key figure, is simultaneously opening up China's economy and harassing civil society, fiercely fighting corruption and expanding his grip on power, advancing environmental protection, and perfecting the surveillance of the masses. Whether we like it or not, Xi is not only shaping China's future. While we analyze and criticize him, he is also changing Germany.

In Chapter 5, I explain how China could fundamentally go from being the world's workbench to an inventor's workshop. The days of copying are coming to an end, and the progress in creativity and innovation, in research and development, is enormous. The Chinese are thus attacking the core of the German economic miracle. China is once again on its way to becoming the innovation world power it once was centuries ago. A powerful new competitor is making life difficult for German SMEs.

In Chapter 6, I travel along the New Silk Road. With this project, Beijing wants to move closer to Europe, the rest of Asia, and Africa and, of course, systematically open up new growth markets — at the expense of the USA. But Brussels does not grasp the outstretched hand.

Chapter 7 deals with the North Korean conflict and China's provocations in the South China Sea. Even more than Syria and Ukraine, North Korea is one of the world's biggest trouble spots, even if the situation there may, surprisingly, be easing after all. Without China, nothing works there anymore. This also applies to the disputed islands in the South China Sea. Nowhere is Beijing showing its new power more blatantly than there. But although China's neighbors are coming under pressure, they are not calling on us for help; instead, they have their own ideas about how to survive in China's shadow.

Chapter 8 is about how China, as a rising world power, is playing off the still incumbent world power, the USA, with increasing skill. It is the great geostrategic power struggle of the early 21st century. Whereas in the past, wars were waged to fight the battles, today the conflicts are fought out in the economic sphere: with trade and patent wars, company takeovers, currency rivalries, and the bidding war for mineral resources. It is astonishing that the Chinese have long had a good plan and all the time in the world, while the West acts hectically and haphazardly.

Chapter 9 deals with nothing less than the world's last great growth market: Africa, whose economic boom is being fueled to a large extent by China. While we are still thinking about building wells and distributing development aid according to the watering can principle, China sees a continent about to leap into the 21st century. It is already clear that Europe will have a hard time without Africa.

One thing I had to learn during my years in China — and I only slowly realized how little this is taken for granted in the West — is that every country looks at the world from a different perspective. Every perspective has its justification. When viewed from Beijing, it is obvious that China and the West have much less in common than we in the West believe.

Frank Sieren
*September 2018*

# Chapter 1

# China, Russia and Europe: Annoying Neighbors

## How Beijing Is Creepily Undermining Europe and We Drive Putin Into the Arms of the Chinese

*We have to have something, we have to be able to do something that China needs.*

Martin Brudermüller, Chairman of the Board
of Executive Directors BASF

From a distance, the *Xing Guang* looks as if it has sunk in the port of Piraeus. Only the white superstructure as high as a house and the aquamarine bow still peek out of the water. The long hull and the stern shimmer faintly green under the waves. Behind them rises the picturesque backdrop of Piraeus. But the ship has not been wrecked. The *Xing Guang* is a heavy transporter. The largest of the Chinese and the second largest in the world. A ship that can even transport not only entire ships dry but also oil platforms or — as in this case — a floating dock from China with two bright red cranes on top. It bears the Greek name "ΠΕΙΡΑΙΑΣ III" — "Piraeus III." For loading and unloading, the hull lowers underwater, releasing the dock until it floats under its own power and can later accommodate vessels up to 240 meters long for repair.

The dock is the latest achievement of the once sleepy, backward port. The Chinese have invested almost 500 million euros here. 55 million for the new dock alone. Not without reason — Piraeus is the first port after the Suez Canal for ships sailing from Asia. The largest contribution was made by the Chinese shipping company COSCO in 2016, which invested around 280 million euro to buy 51 percent of the state-owned Greek port company PPA and now operates several container, car, and passenger terminals here until 2052. A lucrative business.

The Chinese owe the opportunity to acquire the port to Brussels, of all people. Since Greece was so heavily in debt, the EU and the International Monetary Fund demanded that Athens privatize its state-owned enterprises. They certainly didn't think of China first and foremost. The world's largest shipping company can get another 15 percent of the port company from the Greek state if the group sticks to its investment plan. The Chinese are to invest 350 million euros directly to port facilities by 2026. Another 200 million euros will be used, for example, to convert old warehouse buildings into luxury hotels, offices, and apartments, similar to what has been done in Hamburg.

COSCO has been operating two container terminals in Piraeus since 2009, and they have developed very well since then. Since the Chinese have been taking care of the port, three times as many goods have been handled here as before. Five million containers are expected in 2018. In 2017, around nine million containers were handled in Hamburg, although container throughput there has been stagnating for a number of years. Piraeus, on the other hand, is the fastest growing port in the world, with an annual increase of 30 percent. The fact that Hamburg is stagnating is also due to Piraeus. What will things look like once the Chinese have really developed their port concept? They are in the process of building a rail line from Piraeus to Budapest. Then, it will be cheaper not only for Hungary but also for Austria and southern Germany to unload goods in Piraeus instead of having to sail around Europe to Hamburg for another week, only to have to take another train into the heart of Europe. If you look at the map, you wonder why it took the Chinese to implement something so obvious and not the EU itself. It is like drawing a line with a ruler towards the North: from Piraeus and Athens across to Macedonia and Skopje via Belgrade to Budapest. The Chinese are already building the first section of the planned train route between the two capitals: 350 kilometers for around 2.6 billion euros. Travel time between Budapest and Belgrade will be reduced from eight to three hours.

The project is part of the New Silk Road (see Chapter 6). The new friends in Greece and Hungary are grateful and are becoming increasingly cheeky against Brussels, which is trying in vain to bring the rebellious leaders Alexis Tsipras and Viktor Orbán to heel. The Hungarian Prime Minister counters again and again, "Central Europe needs money for new roads and pipelines. If Europe is not able to provide enough capital, we'll get it from China." And his Foreign Minister, Péter Szijjártó, adds, "We in this region see China's major role in the new world order as an opportunity rather than a threat." Greece's Prime Minister Tsipras puts it more simply, "China is helping us. Why shouldn't we accept the help?"

Tsipras and Orbán also seem to know exactly what they and China are guilty of. When Brussels wanted to rebuke Beijing in the summer of 2016 for its policy in the South China Sea (see Chapter 7), Greece and Hungary stopped a joint resolution. Both countries are just the difficult children of the EU; some in Brussels reassured themselves. There, as well as in Berlin, however, the question should be asked whether the policy of the strong EU states has not brought about the stubbornness of these countries in the first place and thus opened the door to Beijing.

In the meantime, at least, the two are no longer the only ones. Back in August 2015, Czech President Miloš Zeman was the only president of an EU country to travel to Beijing for the celebrations marking the 70th anniversary of Japan's surrender. The strong order from Brussels was different; they did not want to be harnessed to the cart of an anti-Japanese campaign.

In 2017, Athens prevented the EU from unanimously criticizing China's human rights record. A short time later, Athens again objected to stricter rules for investments by Chinese companies in Europe. And when it came to criticizing the awarding practices of One Belt, One Road Initiative (OBOR) contracts in the spring of 2018 — that is, the New Silk Road — the Hungarians did not go along. "There are no teachers and students," Prime Minister Orbán said. Hungary and China would not reprimand each other. Brussels is fighting back as best its influence allows. The EU has announced that it will review the awarding of a Silk Road project in Hungary because there was no public tender, as required by European guidelines for such projects. However, nothing has come of the investigation so far.

The mood in the EU with regard to such Chinese influence is bad. The powerful EU countries think that China is undermining European unity. Even the usually level-headed German chancellor is so annoyed by the issue that she slipped out a clear sentence in an interview with *Wirtschaftswoche*: "Seen from Beijing, Europe is more like an Asian peninsula."

Yet, it could be so simple in the current global political situation. Trump is at odds with Europe. Trump is at odds with China. Trump is bickering with Russia. So, Europe is moving closer together. At the same time, Europe, China, and Russia are converging. The Eurasian continent, the world's largest landmass, is exploring common interests without leveling differences. Unfortunately, however, it is not that simple. Europeans disagree more than ever on what their common goals are. Great Britain is the first large country to leave the EU. The two remaining big countries — France and Germany — are fighting for supremacy. The rich countries feel exploited by the poor. The poor feel patronized by the rich. Some mourn the loss of the transatlantic alliance. Others are already hanging on China's coat-tails. At the same time, many in Brussels believe they can educate the Russians. And because of their European defiance, Russia has no choice but to work ever more closely with the Chinese.

The port of Piraeus is a mirror of this complicated situation. The Italians, who, like the Germans in Hamburg, are also losing business because of Piraeus, are making serious accusations against the Greeks and indirectly against the Chinese. Criminal organizations can import goods tax-free via the port operated by the Chinese state contractor COSCO. The imports are often counterfeit brand-name clothing. By using false delivery addresses, the true recipients avoid paying VAT. In addition, the gangs underdeclare the value of the goods in order to avoid import duties. Rome was outraged to learn that Italy had already suffered considerable damage. On the trail to Piraeus, the Italians had arrived at the end of 2017 through forged invoices. The EU's anti-fraud authority has launched joint investigations with Italy. The Greek port operator and its Chinese partner COSCO deny the allegations. Greek politicians are also practicing defensiveness. "While the Europeans are acting like medieval leeches toward Greece, the Chinese are continuously bringing money," says Costas Douzinas, chairman of the Defense and International Affairs Committee. Douzinas belongs to the ruling Syriza party.

In January 2015, people in Beijing were still holding their breath. This was the case when Greeks voted the left-wing Syriza party into power and its leader Alexis Tsipras became prime minister. During the election campaign, Tsipras had promised to oppose Brussels' austerity measures and to stop privatizations such as that of the port of Piraeus. Tsipras had barely taken office when Prime Minister Li Keqiang spoke to him on the phone. He informed Tsipras about what Beijing had already invested and still planned to invest. The Greek prime minister then announced that he would intensify relations with Beijing in the future. The EU experienced this first hand when it came to the human rights situation in China and the attempt to enforce stricter rules for Chinese investors in Europe. Greece did not play along. Merkel was annoyed.

"When you're on the ground and someone slaps you and someone else reaches out to you," Douzinas says, "and then when you're asked for a favor by either of them, who do you favor? The one who slapped you or the one who helped you?" A rhetorical question. And so it was clear what Tsipras would do when three Chinese military frigates entered the port of Piraeus. Tsipras paced the honor formation and promised, "Greece remains China's gateway to Europe." But it is not the only gateway. In some countries of Eastern Europe — not only EU members — the doors are also wide open.

In spring 2017, Serbia's President Tomislav Nikolić traveled to Beijing. Serbia is home to just under nine million people, not even half as many as Beijing. Nevertheless, Nikolić got the full program; President Xi Jinping as well as Premier Li Keqiang and the Chairman of the National People's Congress, Zhang Dejiang, rolled out the red carpet for him. He was even made an honorary citizen of Beijing and provided with contacts to companies, including the communications technology group Huawei, who has their eye on the Serbian market. The Chinese have long been active in other areas. For example, they are building the European Road 763, which will run from Belgrade to Bijelo Polje in Montenegro. President Xi was in Serbia in the summer of 2017 specifically to sign the contract. In the same year, it was also announced that the RTB Bor copper mine and a factory for smelting the raw material were sold to a Chinese company. There is also a new industrial park, and the country's largest steel mill in Smederevo was acquired by the Chinese steel giant HBIS. And Chinese investors have pledged over 200 million euros for a highway around Belgrade.

All this shows that China's interest in investing in Serbian infrastructure is great. But progress is also being made at other levels. Citizens of both countries no longer need to apply for a visa for trips lasting less than 30 days. There is no relaxation of this regulation between Germany and China. The new Serbian Prime Minister Aleksandar Vučić also hopes for a direct flight between Belgrade and Beijing. And he is fighting for the largest foreign investment to date — Chinese tire manufacturer Linglong wants to invest 400 million euros in a factory in Serbia. It is to produce 10 million passenger car tires and two million bus and truck tires per year.

The Chinese involvement painfully exposes Brussels' dilemma. No one would deny that Serbia belongs to Europe. At least rather than to China. But Brussels is reluctant to admit more countries. Europe is difficult enough to manage as it is. Serbia's government applied for EU membership in 2009, and since 2012 Serbia has officially been considered a candidate country. Finally, in February 2018, the EU Commission announced that it wanted to "accelerate" the accession of six Western Balkan states. The countries in question are Serbia, Montenegro, Macedonia, Bosnia-Herzegovina, Albania, and Kosovo. In the view of the EU Commission, Serbia could join the Union as early as 2025. It would then have taken Serbia 13 years to go from candidate country to EU member. Until then, however, the Serbs still have to carry out extensive reforms. There seems to be a small ray of hope for the candidates; the Commission wants to ensure that the EU is allowed to make more decisions by majority vote instead of unanimously.

Another country in the EU waiting loop is Albania, since 2017 a candidate country. The country is located on the southern coast of the Adriatic Sea, just 40 kilometers from the heel of the Italian boot. It borders Greece to the south. It is growing at 3.4 percent and, according to the International Monetary Fund, the government in Tirana is making good progress with its reforms. However, the legal system is still weak, organized crime is too strong, and Albania is the largest illegal cannabis producer in Europe — in the U.S., by the way, it is now the fastest growing industry.

Brussels is cautious here, too, and most Germans take Albania for granted. In Beijing, however, a good 7,000 kilometers away, people see things differently. The small country with three million inhabitants, an ancient history, and beautiful port cities is considered strategically favorable. It is located so far north that it is easy to supply Eastern Europe via its ports, but so far south that a ship can just pass the Italian boot and reach

Tunisia without having to make a turn, so to speak. And, if you want to get to the Adriatic, you have to pass Albania. So it's a worthwhile destination for Beijing. That's why the Chinese have acquired the concession for Tirana airport, initially until 2025. They are considering expanding the port and are building a new road from Albania to Macedonia for 200 million euros. For almost 450 million euros, they have bought two oil fields that Shell is exploiting. Albania's farmers receive a 1.3 million euro loan to buy new machinery. A trans-Adriatic oil and gas pipeline, in which Shell is the largest investor with a 20 percent stake, has also been built. And the Chinese IT network specialist Huawei is helping to modernize the country's electricity network. But that's not all; China is now Albania's second-largest trading partner. Not least because of the large Chinese investments, Albania is now rated a B+ by Standard & Poor's. The EU, on the other hand, has invested only about one billion euros in 27 years. It's bizarre that Beijing is making Albania fit for the EU. The Albanians will not forget what the Chinese have done.

Similar developments are taking place in Croatia and Bosnia-Herzegovina. There, the Chinese company China Shandong International is building a toll road between Banja Luka and the Croatian border for $382 million. In addition, CSI is planning a new rail line for just under $290 million. And Europe? Of course, there are various pots of funding from which the countries on the periphery are served. But what is missing is a long-term strategy. And that is what Beijing has in Eastern Europe. Vladimir Putin has already noticed this. First, China's President Xi Jinping celebrated the end of World War II with Putin and then in May 2015, he set off from Moscow directly to Belarus, where he met with the head of state Alexander Lukashenko. It was the first visit by a Chinese president in 14 years. And Xi made no secret of what he wanted from Lukashenko — more economic cooperation. The result was a new contract for the Chinese–Belarusian industrial park Great Stone. If Xi has his way, the park will become a "pearl" of the New Silk Road. The visit was a clear signal to Moscow — we work closely with you and are happy to buy your gas and oil, but we have our own interests in Eastern Europe.

Brussels leaves the field open to Beijing. A bridge project co-financed by the EU to connect Croatia's southernmost tip with the rest of the country shows that it is possible to work together. When completed, the Pelješac Bridge will connect the popular tourist destination of Dubrovnik with the rest of Croatia. Until now, travelers have had to cross a few kilometers of Bosnia-Herzegovina territory to get there. Time-consuming controls at the borders of the non-EU member state will be eliminated in the future, an important aspect also for the transit of goods. The EU has pledged over 350 million euros for the construction of the bridge. That is around 85 percent of the costs. The Croatian public procurement authority has awarded the contract to a Chinese company. It is to not only build the bridge but also access roads and tunnels. In January 2018, however, the project had to be halted. One co-bidder, an Italian–Turkish consortium, claimed that the China Road and Bridge Corporation (CRBC) was supported by the state. An Austrian company also criticized CRBC for violating EU investment and procurement rules. However, the Croatian authorities rejected both complaints. As planned, the construction is now to be completed by 2022.

Chinese investments in Eastern Europe are not always successful. In 2017, the car plant of the Chinese manufacturer Great Wall in Bulgaria had to file for bankruptcy after only six years. The 2015 agreement with Romania to build two new nuclear power plants has not yet materialized, and the Slovaks are also still waiting for a major project. In the meantime, however, the Chinese have even developed their own political format for cooperation with Eastern Europe, without even asking Brussels. It is called 16+1 and means 16 Eastern European countries plus China. The group has been meeting regularly since 2012. It was only two years later that the Western Balkans Summit was launched on the initiative of Angela Merkel. However, the forum suffers from the fact that there is not so much money in its pocket and Beijing is — let's say — more nimble when it comes to allocating funds.

Even before Premier Li Keqiang attended the German–Chinese meeting in Sofia, he met with the heads of the 16 Eastern European states. Beijing was somewhat surprised at the tone of the Polish president. He complained that nothing had happened in Poland so far except for big announcements.

The fact that the Chinese do make trouble at times cannot be overlooked. However, Andrzej Duda did not allow himself to be carried away by public criticism of China. Premier Li even invited Angela Merkel to this last meeting of the 16+1 group in Sofia in July 2018. The chancellor reacted skillfully when Li extended the invitation to her in Beijing.

"Have you coordinated this with the other countries?" she asked the prime minister. "I will still do that," Li replied. Merkel did not want to hear more, she canceled, and no one was sent by proxy.

Conversely, at the Sino-German intergovernmental consultations in Berlin, which also took place in July, a German minister asked his Chinese counterpart in the presence of Premier Li and Chancellor Merkel, "How would you react if we were to develop such a format with some of your provinces?" — "Interesting," the minister replied, "So you see EU members as your provinces?" It was one to one.

The meetings of the 16+1 are viewed critically by Brussels. The participating states show a little bad conscience when they justify themselves, "This format aims to strengthen Europe, not to divide it," said Bulgaria's head of government Boyko Borisov in a placating tone at the start of the meeting in Sofia. And Premier Li Keqiang countered criticism of the forum thus, "China supports the integration of Europe. We need a strong Europe with a strong euro." The problem for Brussels and Merkel is that Li can say this sentence with great conviction, because in fact each of the projects financed here by China contributes to the integration of Europe because it reduces development gaps. The 16+1 cooperation promotes "not only the development of the EU but more market diversity; that's a good thing," he added. Li is beating us at our own game. Haven't we always told the Chinese how important competition is? According to him, he adheres to EU law. And, "whether you agree or not Mrs. Merkel, we also take up contact with companies," Li said, adding that it's a good thing for Eastern and Central Europe, for the entire world population.

Foreign Minister Wang Yi also reiterated that he did not want to divide the EU and even suggested trilateral cooperation with Germany on specific projects in the region. "Other EU partners are, of course, also welcome," said Wang, thus passing the buck to Brussels. It now almost seems as if the EU is refusing to face up to Europe's future.

What is happening on a small scale in Eastern Europe is happening on a large scale in Russia. In this case, it is not Brussels' negligence but the West's mistaken belief that sanctions can bring a country like Russia to its senses. However, the sanctions have one main effect: The West is driving Russia politically, militarily, and economically into the arms of the Chinese.

If a ship was, in the beginning, the symbol of relations between the EU and China, ships could also become the symbol of relations between Moscow and Beijing:

The gray Chinese destroyer *Hefei* slowly enters the port of Kaliningrad in a light drizzle. It is followed by the frigate *Yuncheng* with a helicopter on board and special units. A third ship can be seen in the distance. Kaliningrad, formerly Königsberg, now lies in a Russian enclave between the two EU states of Poland and Lithuania. The enclave is separated from Russia by Belarus and can only be reached directly via the Baltic Sea. It is there, of all places, that the Russians and Chinese are staging a joint maneuver for the first time. When the world's second- and third-largest armies join forces, many in the West feel uneasy. It is a good 600 kilometers from Kaliningrad to Berlin. The Polish and Lithuanian EU borders are just 100 kilometers away.

On the other hand, the Americans have for decades regularly held much larger naval maneuvers with South Korea and other partners similarly close to the Chinese border in the South China Sea. In comparison, the three Chinese ships that are now almost timidly venturing into the Baltic Sea look like a school trip. Nevertheless, the first maneuver shows one thing: China and Russia are moving ever closer together under the pressure of the sanctions. The sanctions against Russia, which have been continuously tightened, have been in place since March 2014 because Moscow annexed Ukraine's Crimea. The new U.S. national security strategy sees China and Russia as "revisionist powers" that "challenge America's power, influence, and interests and seek to undermine U.S. security and well-being."

China and Russia are making the most of it. Back in May 2014, the two countries signed a contract for gas supplies worth $400 billion. In it, the Russian Gazprom Group undertakes to supply up to 38 billion cubic meters of gas annually. In November 2016, China Development Bank lent Russia's Vnesheconombank (VEB) about $1 billion in yuan. The loan runs for 15 years. Never before has VEB received a loan with such a long term. The borrowed money will be used to build a new infrastructure that will link China and Russia even more closely. "But the Chinese are also interested in timber, agriculture, mines, and non-ferrous metals," explains VEB CEO Sergei Gorkov. In June 2018, Beijing once again increased VEB's credit leeway to the equivalent of 8 billion U.S. dollars. The money is to be used to finance infrastructure projects, including sections of the high-speed rail line between Moscow and Beijing, for which the

Europeans will gain nothing (see Chapter 6). When the loan agreement was signed, there was talk of 70 joint projects. And there is still plenty of room for improvement; China's share of Russia's foreign debt was only 6 percent in 2017, and Russia still owes most of its debt to Europe.

Beijing is also offering that the Chinese payment service provider UnionPay could step in if the U.S. market leader Visa is politically forced to withdraw from Russia. And China is supplying more and more fresh food to the neighboring country; food that previously came from Europe. The Chinese oil company Sinopec and the Silk Road Fund each have a 10 percent stake in Russia's largest petrochemical company Sibur. The two hold a total of 29.9 percent in Russia's largest liquefied natural gas project, Yamal LNG. Together, the Russians and Chinese are building a wide-body jet and nuclear power plants. Four plants worth $3.6 billion are already under construction. The jointly developed C929 wide-body jet is scheduled to take off for the first time in 2023. It is expected to be cheaper to buy and cheaper to operate than the Boeing 777 of about the same size, at a cost of $20 billion. Final assembly will take place in China. For the Chinese, this can only be an advantage because so far they have not been able to produce their own engines. Together with the Russians, they could finally succeed in doing so.

Already in 2017, Russia had surpassed Saudi Arabia as the most important oil supplier.

Almost a quarter of Russia's oil exports now flow to China. But Beijing wants more because they pay Gazprom comparatively little — another consequence of the sanctions. In December 2019, the new "Power of Siberia" gas pipeline to China will be ready. It will cost 55 billion U.S. dollars. Engineers are struggling with an 80-degree temperature difference. Geopolitically, the project is also a challenge, especially to the West. When gas flows through the pipeline in 2019, the world's largest gas importer and the world's largest gas exporter will be directly connected for the first time, thanks to Western sanctions. For 30 years, 38 billion cubic meters of gas will then be pumped into China annually. That is significantly less than Germany (53 billion cubic meters per year) but considerably more than Turkey, Gazprom's second-largest customer to date.

Gazprom and Beijing negotiated without results for more than 10 years until they finally signed the gas supply contract. Some Chinese say that Beijing let Russia flounder, only to strike just when the Russians felt the Western sanctions most painfully. The Russians, on the other hand, emphasize that China has not abandoned Russia in difficult times. The fact is that China's partnership makes Russia more independent of the West. The West has maneuvered itself into a quandary. For this reason, but also for lack of alternatives, the EU imported more Russian gas in 2017 than ever before — despite the sanctions. An increase of over 8 percent compared to the previous year. The largest EU consumer of Russian gas is and remains Germany. The Russians want to achieve one goal with the help of the Chinese — that they can turn off the tap to the Europeans without hurting themselves. That is possible.

However, many projects are not moving ahead fast enough. The chemistry between the Chinese and the Russians is sometimes not quite right. There is a great deal of mistrust in Russia that they will be overrun by the Chinese. The Chinese, in turn, are worried that their projects will get bogged down in the Russian quagmire of corruption and inefficiency. But since U.S. President Donald Trump has been in power, the pressure to cooperate has increased. The first summit between Putin and Trump in July 2018 did not escalate the situation, but neither did it ease tensions. Each accuses the other of violating the rules of the game: The Russians blame the Americans and Europeans for taking action in Ukraine, even though they promised the opposite in 1990, after the collapse of the Soviet Union and the Warsaw Pact. The West resents Putin for taking back Crimea by force and holding parts of Ukraine in a headlock. Putin counters that Communist Party leader Nikita Khrushchev gave Crimea to Ukraine in 1954 — a symbolic gesture, nothing more. In fact, there was nothing about it in the Western press at the time; it was obviously taken for granted, and even in the Soviet press, there were at best a few scanty half-sentences. For Khrushchev, the Russians, and, incidentally, the West, it was inconceivable that Ukraine would one day become independent. Even today, many Russians feel that it was a historical injustice that Ukraine became independent in 1991. Not only was there the shame of the collapse of the proud Soviet empire but Crimea with its legendary spa hotels and the star's palace in Yalta were also lost to Russia. In terms of domestic politics, Putin had little choice but to take back Crimea after the West had at least supported, if not promoted, an anti-Russian coup in Ukraine. Experts in Brussels and Berlin had warned their politicians of the risks.

It was equally clear that the West viewed the annexation of Crimea as unacceptable and that Russia would be considered to be in breach of international law and would be subject to sanctions. Nevertheless, Russia is now more powerful than ever in global politics. This was also evident when the West tried to interfere in the Syrian conflict. Traditionally, this has been the sphere of influence of the Russians, who have maintained the only base on the Mediterranean for their Black Sea fleet since 1971. China and Russia played together — Russia militarily and China diplomatically — and were able to prevail.

Cooperation is also going well in other respects; Russia is a founding member of the BRICS countries, which include Brazil, India, China, and South Africa. Russia is also part of the Shanghai Co-operation Organization (SCO), which counts all of Central Asia, India, and Pakistan among its members. The SCO is an alliance that deals with political and economic as well as security issues in the region. All these countries are not at odds with Russia. The fact that NATO countries alone are sticking together is no longer enough to bring Moscow to its knees.

Europe in particular has suffered great economic damage as a result of the sanctions against Russia, without even being able to derive any political benefit from them. The winners in this power game are once again the Chinese, while the biggest loser is Germany. China replaced Germany as Russia's most important trading partner in 2017. Germany is now responsible for only 8.6 percent of Russia's foreign trade. China comes in at just under 15 percent. "The ice has been broken with China," said Russian Deputy Prime Minister Igor Shuvalov, "We have learned to talk to them, they now understand us better and we understand them too." An elegant way of admitting that there were difficulties.

Of course, there is still a lot of catching up to do. The EU's lead is still high, with a 45 percent import share, even if the trend is strongly downward. As far as Germany is concerned, exports to Russia are just half the volume of China's, at $48 billion. The German economy could accept this if something came out of it politically. In fact, Germany and the EU are losing economic ground to China every day for nothing. Meanwhile, the Russians are forced to offer their raw materials below cost to Beijing. China, the laughing third. "The fact that raw materials are flowing to the East cannot be in the interest of the West," says BASF CEO Martin Brudermüller, who will have more to say later.

"Russia is and will remain an important player in the international community of states. Those who think they can exclude the Russians are wrong. Russia is important for Europe. We should talk about how we can work together."

Moscow had to make concessions not only on commodity prices but also on weapons. After the outbreak of the Ukraine crisis, Beijing finally managed to buy modern Russian weapons, such as the S-400 air defense system and 24 fighter jets. The S-400 defense system can strike aircraft, drones, and cruise missiles at a range of up to 380 kilometers. China plans to station the system along its coast to control much of the airspace near Taiwan and around disputed islands in the South China Sea. Washington is concerned.

Nevertheless, Beijing does not just do what Moscow wants. The Chinese have lent Kiev three billion US dollars to modernize its agricultural economy. The sum is to be repaid over 15 years with grain deliveries. Of all countries, crisis-ridden Ukraine is now the world's largest grain supplier to China. The Russians are hardly buying anymore. And the Europeans need nothing. Ukraine has replaced the U.S., traditionally China's largest grain supplier — one less dependence on the U.S. again.

Kiev is also the largest arms supplier to the Chinese so far, and it intends to keep it that way. The Chinese have not only bought hundreds of Russian aircraft engines and the world's largest military landing craft from Ukraine — and even had them produced under license — but also an aircraft carrier. The first ever for China but now not the only one.

Even though trade between China and Ukraine grew by 18 percent in 2018, the Chinese still rank third behind the Russians and the EU. However, Beijing also has a lot planned for Kiev — a metro is to be built for 1.1 billion U.S. dollars, and 500 million is available for low-cost home loans. A train line connecting Kiev with Boryspil International Airport is being built for 400 million. A ring road around Kiev city is planned. The Chinese have already developed Ukraine's largest port. Two more are to follow. And Beijing is having two Ukrainian aircraft built in China, the Antonov An-225, the largest and heaviest aircraft in the world since 1988. This pleases neither the West nor the Russians. Beijing insists that is not the case. They are happy to point out that they still have a lot of plans with the Russians.

The most important strategic project for the future in this area is the Polar Silk Road. In its "First White Paper on the Arctic," the Chinese government, known for its long-term strategies, has presented plans that it would like to implement together with the Russians. "As a result of global warming, the Arctic shipping routes are expected to become important transport routes for international trade," the paper states. The sea routes could be ice-free as early as the mid-21st century, significantly shortening the transport of goods between Asia and Europe. The routes are safe, with no pirates or failed states on their shores. Beijing wants to open up the new "shipping route network" with Moscow. After all, Russia is one of the five Arctic riparian states, along with Greenland (Denmark), Norway, Canada, and the United States. Between 2005 and June 2017, China invested around 90 billion US dollars in infrastructure, energy production, and financial cooperation in the Arctic regions. It sees itself as a "stakeholder" in the Arctic, the new white paper states confidently. With the *Xuelong*, "snow dragon," China has a 167-meter-long, 21,000-ton icebreaker ship that is already on its eighth Arctic expedition. An even more powerful ship, built entirely in China, was scheduled to be launched in 2019. This would give the country as many icebreakers as the United States. The Americans have a bad hand if China and Russia join forces. Moscow is the top dog with its 44 icebreakers and Beijing has the money.

Of course, Beijing is also concerned with mineral resources in the Arctic. American geologists estimate that up to 30 percent of the known natural gas reserves and 13 percent of the oil are located under the Arctic ice. The estimated value is over 30 trillion euros. In this area, too, Beijing is seeking the expertise of Russia, which can deal with extreme temperatures like no other nation.

"China's government is already discussing this with Moscow," says China's Vice Foreign Minister Kong Xuanyu. This does not look good for the divided Europe.

At least the Russians, Chinese, and Europeans are still working closely together in one area — together they are keeping the nuclear agreement with Iran, which Donald Trump abandoned. Never before have Beijing and Berlin, as well as the Russians, cooperated as closely as they did in this case, when it came to convincing then President Obama that a deal with Iran was good for world stability. Donald Trump, however, does not want that. It divides the West in the process, and Beijing doesn't even have to say thank you.

Europe must get out of the sanctions policy because sanctions are not effective as long as there are powerful players like China on the other side. The Europeans should not stubbornly leave the game to the Chinese but approach Vladimir Putin. That is possible because, culturally, Russia does not belong to China but to Europe. Furthermore, Putin has a weak spot that could be addressed — he wants to be appreciated by Europeans, especially Germans. If there were progress in this regard, he would certainly be willing to make compromises. And of course, it would be better to talk turkey with a Putin who belongs to the European family behind closed doors, then he wouldn't have to constantly prove to his people how tough he is.

We should face reality: The EU needs Eastern Europe. And Europe needs Russia to be able to meet the big players like China and the USA on an equal footing. Europe must decide: Does it want to be in a powerful position vis-à-vis China or would it prefer to harass Russia in vain? Unfortunately, it can't do both. In short, Europe is incomplete without Russia. And Russia can better develop its full power alongside Europe. Although the China–Russia issue is actually much more important, because it involves a greater level of power, we talk more extensively about the question of how we deal with Chinese investments in Europe and especially in Germany. The dilemma is that on the one hand, we don't want to lose the know-how for which Germany is world famous. On the other hand, we have to closely dovetail with the most important growth market. The waves were particularly high when the Augsburg-based robot manufacturer Kuka was sold to the Chinese group Midea for 4.5 billion euros in the fall of 2016. The *FAZ* complained that the Chinese were "securing the pearls of German industry." And *Die Zeit* even ran the headline: "Buy up and cannibalize — China is buying us up." Kuka is the fourth-largest robot manufacturer in the world, swallowed up by, of all things, China's leading manufacturer of air conditioners and household appliances, which has no expertise in automation. Rarely have the chancellor's office and the economics ministry led then by SPD chairman Sigmar Gabriel been in such agreement. Hand in hand, they want to prevent Kuka from falling into Chinese hands. Siemens CEO Joe Kaeser receives a call from Chancellor Merkel, who wants to know whether he could still stop the sale to the Far East by buying into Kuka. Kaeser rejects the chancellor's request. The company man does not fit into Siemens' portfolio.

In fact, no one can be found who wants the company except the Chinese. And from Kuka's point of view, there is no point in snubbing the Chinese. Without access to the Chinese market, the company has no chance of even maintaining its market position, defends Kuka CEO Till Reuter. EU Digital Commissioner Günther Oettinger intervenes: The question must be considered whether "an entry of other European companies might be a better solution." Oettinger is hoping for the Zurich-based ABB Group, itself one of the market leaders in robot construction. But their interest is also low — especially since this would also be a problem under antitrust law. In addition, IG Metall is opposed to the idea because it fears that too many German jobs would be lost if the two robotics divisions were merged. Oettinger's idea leads to a dead end.

In addition to the Chancellor and the EU Digital Commissioner, even the Office for the Protection of the Constitution warns against Chinese investments. "You don't need to carry out an espionage attack anymore if you can buy out the company," says the president of the Federal Office for the Protection of the Constitution, Hans-Georg Maaßen. The takeover of Kuka by Midea makes the problem clear. That's because every Chinese company is obliged to cooperate with the intelligence service, he said. Kuka CEO Reuter counters, "Midea opens up a gigantic market for us. Our goal is to become number one in China in the next few years."

In the end, neither the German government nor the EU has any legal means to stop the sale. The fact that Kuka has received 15 million euros in subsidies from the EU over the past 10 years is not enough. The company will go to the Chinese at the end of 2016. Only the Americans are still setting conditions. Kuka had to sell part of the company that worked for Boeing to an American company.

2016 is the big year for takeovers. German companies worth 11 billion euros are sold. One year later, the total amount is even higher, but the number of individual transactions is lower. In 2018, Chinese investments in majority stakes or takeovers decrease again. The first big wave is over. Still, Germans are not comfortable with investors being Chinese. If we simply sell everything, there is a great chance of participating in the growth of the Chinese market, but at the same time, there is a high risk that we will lose our know-how altogether and thus become less attractive to the Chinese. If we close ourselves off, we will retain our know-how, but we will sell too little to remain competitive internationally. The best solution would be to take a middle course, for example, only owning 49 percent of a company.

But the Chinese are not interested in that. And neither are many of the German SMEs. Many of the hidden champions are only available because the owners cannot find a successor for their business within the family. They want to get rid of everything — and at the best possible price. It is true that they are interested in selling to someone who will deal with the company and its employees in a sustainable manner. But if no suitable domestic or European investor can be found, well, then it's the Chinese — especially since they act much more sustainably than some Anglo-Saxon financial investors.

The absurdity of this discussion is that in the vast majority of cases, it is about companies that have long since ceased to be in German hands. In January 2016, for example, the Munich-based plastics machinery manufacturer Krauss Maffei was sold to the chemical giant ChemChina for 950 million euros. The seller was the Canadian financial investor Onex. A month later, the Helmstadt-based waste company EEW Energy from Waste was sold to China for 1.4 billion euros. The seller was the Swedish consortium EQT. In the summer of 2016, China's Three Gorges acquired the offshore wind farm "Meereswind" north of Helgoland for 1.2 billion euros. Until then, the 80 percent majority was held by the American group Blackstone. The list could be continued.

In the spring of 2018, sensitive Germans were once again particularly shocked: Chinese automaker Geely acquired a 9 percent stake in Daimler for nine billion U.S. dollars. Although not the majority stakeholder, this makes Geely the largest foreign shareholder. It was Geely that opened the round of major investments in Europe — with the takeover of Volvo in 2010 for 1.4 billion euros. The hapless owner before that was not the Swedish founders but the U.S. company Ford.

And the world's most expensive Chinese acquisition also took place in the heart of Europe. In the spring of 2017, ChemChina acquired the Swiss company Syngenta, the largest manufacturer of crop protection products and one of the most important suppliers of seeds, for a good 43 billion US dollars. The deal came about primarily because it is hardly possible under antitrust law for a Western private company to merge with another Western private company from the same industry. A merger with the American competitor Monsanto did not work out for precisely these reasons. This was the main reason why a Chinese state-owned company came into the picture. In a sense, the West has tricked itself.

The acquisition has not yet given rise to celebration in China. Syngenta's sales fell by 1 percent in 2017. The company made a net loss of almost 100 million dollars, after making a profit of 1.18 billion dollars the year before. The reason is provisions. There are 4,500 lawsuits in the USA because Syngenta sold genetically modified seeds to American farmers that had not yet been approved for China. The farmers were there-fore not allowed to export the corn to China and sued. This is another irony of the economic history between the West and China — American farmers sue a now Chinese company for not playing by the Chinese rules. In this case, Beijing has scored its own goal for a change. The list of the many companies that have been sold may be disconcerting. However, it is not the Chinese who are the biggest investors in Germany but the USA with just under 25 percent, followed by Switzerland with just over 11 percent and Great Britain with around 10 percent. Nevertheless, the debate about Chinese investments is particularly tense here in Germany. After all, almost everyone who has been intensely involved with the issue outside of politics and on the front pages of newspapers is now giving the all-clear.

For example, a position paper by the Federation of German Industries, BDI, states that "The statistical data available to date on Chinese investments in Germany do not indicate that concerns about a loss of competitiveness and technology outflow are justified."

Christian Specht, a takeover expert at the auditing firm KPMG, also says that the reservations in Germany about Chinese investors are unfounded: "There is the spectre that the Chinese will rip off the know-how and suck the companies dry. But that is not the case," he says. "They generally continue their corporate activities and business model in peace."

The trade union-affiliated Hans Böckler Foundation has examined 42 companies that have been taken over by the Chinese. The study's findings are also positive — the buyers adhere to collective bargaining agreements, do not cut jobs, and are long-term investors. As a rule, they are not interested in making a quick profit. They are also not interested in selling the companies again quickly — unlike many Anglo-Saxon investment companies.

Of course, there are exceptions and not every takeover is immediately successful. In the case of Osram LED lighting manufacturer Ledvance, for example, things are not looking good. Just six months after the 500-million-euro takeover in the fall of 2017 by the Chinese consortium MLS, the clouds darkened. The Chinese want to cut 650 jobs. The traditional plant in Augsburg is to be closed by the end of 2018. Long-time Managing Director Jes Munk Hansen left the company in the beginning of December 2017. At least IG Metall is satisfied with the severance payments the Chinese are paying. However, the company is not out of the woods yet. The Chinese want to cut 1,400 to 2,000 more jobs in the coming years. One thing must not be forgotten — Osram has never hidden the fact that its light bulb business, which the Chinese bought, is loss-making. The company is losing money because the EU has already blown out the lights on the classic incandescent bulb. Halogen bulbs have been banned since 2018. In China, however, they will continue to glow for a long time. The now backward German technology is still valuable — but only in China.

The fact that jobs are being cut in this sector in Germany is no surprise to anyone. It is not fair to blame the Chinese for this. What is much more important is that another division may be able to close the gap in the long term. Osram wants to focus on LED technology and lucrative specialty lighting for cars in the future. Good news. High-tech will continue to be manufactured in Germany.

All in all, the takeover of German companies cannot be considered as the Chinese destroying jobs nor selling off German industry across the board. In other words, the Chinese are neither destroying jobs nor selling off German industry across the board. Even if it cannot be denied that the Chinese choose the companies they buy very carefully from a strategic point of view. But you can't blame them for that. Nevertheless, the Germans are not comfortable with this, and fear of China is rife. And so there was no peace after the sale of Kuka. How could we allow our silverware to be sold off like that? Especially since Germany's "economic powerhouse" is slowly running out of silverware.

The fact that the situation is more complicated than it looks at first glance can also be seen in the example of Kuka. Kuka is undoubtedly a showpiece of German mechanical engineering. But Kuka is only in ungrateful fourth place in the world market. Two Japanese companies Fanuc and Yaskawa lead the ranking — in terms of sales for industrial robots — followed by ABB. The only way for the Augsburg-based company to get out of this position was to join forces with a partner in the strongest growth market. China has the largest growth demand in the robotics sector at over 58 percent. In the USA, the figure was 6 percent, and in Germany, the leader in Europe, only 8 percent. It was therefore a sensible business decision to be taken over by a Chinese company. This, especially since the German shareholders of Kuka — none other than the Heidenheim-based family-owned company Voith — received considerably more money than the share price indicated. The Voith Group had a 25.1 percent stake in Kuka. Money that the engineering group can well reinvest.

One of the critics' arguments was that in the Kuka case, both the Augsburg site and the company's know-how were at risk. The proponents' response was that, especially in the case of high-tech company takeovers, the risk lies primarily with the buyer. The seller gets the money and the buyer gets know-how if the researchers and developers don't run away. They can't all be forced to stay with the company. That's why the new owners have to take care of the employees. In the case of Kuka, this is how it worked: About a year after the takeover, company CEO Reuter announced that the Chinese wanted to invest more than 100 million euros in Augsburg, where the company is still headquartered. A new production hall, a training center, and a parking garage are to be built by 2025. In addition, more money is to be put into research. "In Germany alone, we employ about 800 developers and will continue to hire more in the future," says Reuter. "Innovation and development are part of Kuka's DNA. In 2009,we had 250 developers, since then we've grown considerably." In China, only 100 developers work for Kuka, the same number as in Hungary.

"This announcement is the best location insurance you can imagine," sums up Augsburg's IG Metall head Michael Leppek, who is also deputy chairman of the company's supervisory board. However, the Chinese guarantee the Augsburg location for the Kuka patents only until 2025. Critics consider this to be a very short period of time. Midea defends itself by saying that it cannot look much further into the future. The fact that Kuka is growing more in China than in Germany is also undeniable. This is because the Chinese market in this industry is expanding faster and is significantly larger. However, this also means that more is supplied from Germany.

At the end of 2017, it was already clear that the joint future was promising; group sales increased by 18 percent. The Robotics division was able to increase its operating result by almost a third to 133.1 million euros and excelled with a margin of 11.1 percent. That is good for Germany as a business location. And Kuka could not have done it alone.

Politicians, however, are not deterred. It is urgently necessary to create appropriate regulations "in order to effectively counter takeover fantasies and the outflow of technology and know-how," said Matthias Machnig, State Secretary in the Federal Ministry of Economics under Sigmar Gabriel, as recently as spring 2018. In the summer of 2017, Gabriel had the Foreign Trade and Payments Act tightened up during the German election campaign. If Germany and Europe wanted to remain economically successful and innovative in the future, he said, the government must be able to scrutinize and, if necessary, prohibit state-led, strategic acquisitions of companies by other countries. Indeed, there is nothing to be said against this. A proposal to this effect has now been agreed to by France and Italy. But because some EU countries cooperate very well bilaterally with China, it is difficult to find a majority of control at the EU level. So, at the end of May 2018, a "soft solution" emerged that has a chance of being accepted by both the EU Council with the country representatives and the members of the Chinese Parliament before the end of the year. The most important, non-negotiable point for an EU solution to be possible is that the individual states decide for themselves, what they sell to whom, rather than Brussels. But they will exchange ideas and consider objections. A very soft formulation that the Hungarians and Greeks can also live with.

In August 2018, that time had come. For the first time, the German government prohibits the takeover of a German company. The Westphalian special machinery manufacturer Leifeld Metal Spinning is not allowed to sell to the Chinese. The Ahlen-based company employs around 200 people and is a technology leader in high-strength materials (which are) used in the aerospace industry and the nuclear sector. "As soon as the Chinese enter the German market as investors, Father State stands in front of the girls' room like the strict father of a youth hostel and says: This far and no further," says Gabor Steingart in his Morning Briefing.

Germany and the Europeans are in a difficult position on this issue. Of course, when companies are sold to China, it makes sense to check whether national or EU interests stand in the way or whether there is no other solution. But is it really worse to be bought by the Chinese than by Anglo-Saxon locusts who are only after quick money? As a rule, no. The German government would do well to invest more energy in Germany's innovative strength instead of playing hostel father. After all, if you have enough to offer, it's not so bad if something gets sold.

The nervousness of the German government unintentionally shows how much Germany already has its back to the wall. After all, such decisions are a good bargaining chip with the Chinese. If Beijing moves, it is possible to give in again. After all, this power struggle is ultimately about one thing: "reciprocity." In this case, it means mutual equal treatment. The Germans want the same access opportunities to the Chinese market that the Chinese have in the German market. The Germans think it is unfair that the Chinese can buy a company like Kuka in Germany, but it is forbidden by the Chinese to buy a similar company in China. The Chinese can buy any amount of shares in Deutsche Bank. The Germans, however, cannot buy any amount of shares in one of the major Chinese banks. The Chinese argue the other way around. The Germans have already invested a lot in China and made big profits there, and now China must be allowed to invest just as much in Germany. This was also the topic at the EU–China summit in Beijing in July 2018.

And indeed, there is movement in this game. BMW will be the first Western automaker to increase its share from 50 to 75 percent in the joint venture with its Chinese partner. And Martin Brudermüller, Chairman of BASF's Board of Executive Directors since the beginning of May 2018, should be particularly happy. He gets to build a new Verbund site in southern China, a 10-billion-dollar project. It is the third site in Asia and the first in China that BASF can build without a joint venture partner. A gift from the Chinese on the demonstrating equal treatment.

Brudermüller is leading a new generation of top German managers whose careers are closely linked to the rise of China. BASF was one of the first major DAX companies to have a board seat in Asia. Brudermüller has spent a large part of his professional career in China. For almost 10 years, the chemist with a doctorate in chemistry was responsible for Asia, among other things as the member of the Board of Executive Directors responsible for Asia and Deputy Chairman of the Board of Executive Directors, based in Hong Kong. For several years, Brudermüller was also the China spokesman for the Asia-Pacific Committee of German Business. "China shaped my view of leadership," he says in our interview. "That's where I first learned to acknowledge the opportunities above the risks, and I understood then how important it is to have a long-term plan." The fact that China has opened up its market further shows Brudermüller that there is a relationship of trust between China and Germany. I object that Donald Trump may have helped a little in this regard. "In terms of timing, possibly," Brudermüller counters but not in terms of China's long-term strategy. "One should not overestimate Trump's influence on China's development. It's taking place with or without him — and it's heading toward a new world order, which we now have to get used to." The greater China's economic power becomes, he said, the more Chinese values also take on greater weight around the world. "The U.S. has put its stamp on world trade or certain geopolitical developments. The Chinese will do the same." That is their right, he said, and China deserves respect for what it has achieved so far — "and also a portion of admiration."

I would like to know from Brudermüller if there is anything that would make him concerned about China. "People in Beijing sometimes interpret reality somewhat one-sidedly in their favor," he replies. "The Chinese like to go to the point where they feel resistance. That's when we have to talk turkey." The political dialog formats between China and Germany are not always easy, he says, but they are always worth developing further. It would also benefit China's own progress to put itself more in touch with the interests, concerns, and needs of its partners.

"Are we representing our position adequately?," I ask."The chancellor is doing a good job. I have been able to witness this every now and then in recent years," says Brudermüller. He believes that the Chinese are generally much more strategic and forward-looking than German and European politicians. The media and politics in Europe are primarily fighting for daily air supremacy over current topics, says Brudermüller. This makes it obvious "how important a long-term orientation is." How the Chinese pull something through, for example, building up individual industries or environmental protection, is impressive, says the manager and adds: "In Europe, we rely on creativity through controversial discourse — but we need to find ways to ensure that public discussions around new technologies do not overwhelmingly lead to their rejection. This is where we have glaring weaknesses," says the manager.

"Can Europe still catch up at all?" I want to know. "We must not belittle ourselves," Brudermüller replies. According to him, Europe has enormous capacities but needs to put them to better use. "I'm far from giving up on Europe, however, I am an optimist by nature. Our innovative power is definitely at stake. In this respect, we in the West have been a bit arrogant toward the Chinese. Always according to the motto: For creativity and innovation, you need Western-style freedom! But they don't have that in China, and I doubt that they are striving for it. We must now admit to ourselves that China may not be a democracy, but they still have the freedom to be innovative, creative, and unconventional."

For us, this will mean that the world's prosperity will be distributed differently. The Chinese and other emerging countries will increase their share or at least demand it. "We are used to the fact that the rules of international relations of past decades have always been Western-dominated. Now, we are moving in a world that is multipolar. We have to take a step back," Brudermüller says. "But that is difficult for us. On the other hand, we could solve problems better if we had international institutions in which the Chinese felt more adequately considered. That in itself would be a big step forward. In any case, to oppose the rise of China is short-sighted."

I ask Brudermüller how we can at least remain on an equal footing. The fact that the Chinese are now also part of the international networks, he says, makes it easier for us to succeed in China. "But that's just the way it works if we are interesting for the Chinese," I say, "And that used to be easier. Innovation used to travel on a one-way street from west to east, now it gets two-way traffic." Brudermüller laughs, "That's true. But ideas can also get much better when they are shared! Which means, however, that we ourselves have to do our part, to return to our competencies." The other day, he was sitting next to the CEO of Huawei, the largest Chinese smartphone manufacturer, Brudermüller says. The CEO pulled the prototype of a new model out of his pocket and proudly showed Brudermüller that you could watch a 3-D movie on the screen without putting on virtual reality glasses. "That's going to happen to us more often in the future. It's called competition. And competition I think is good, as long as everyone has an equal chance." That's not the case everywhere in the case of China, he said, but it's getting better step by step. "The fact that we are allowed to build a BASF plant without a joint venture partner is a sign of that. The Chinese have to give us the same access to the their market that they have to our market."

"Do we need an industrial policy?," I want to know. "We in Germany and Europe have always shied away from industrial policy. But the world around us is setting clear industrial policy accents, so we have to rethink as well," says Brudermüller. "We can no longer be a player at every stage of the value chain. Once we have agreed on the focal points, the state must steer development with the right regulatory and incentive system and then implement the decided path in the face of resistance. We cannot always argue everything out to the end, but must learn again to find viable compromises quickly and then implement them promptly. We have to rebalance our Western political system accordingly. If we don't do that, we have a real problem." That does not mean giving up our pluralism as valuable, he said. At the same time however, this should not lead to a situation in which no decisions can be made at all.

One thing is clear: "If the chances of making money in Europe become smaller, then we will have to go to other regions. And then it will depend on who has what to offer. The China–Germany relationship in particular will be determined by how powerful the other is at any given time."

The harsh reality already looks like this today: Europe needs the Chinese market more than China needs European technology. And every day, this relationship shifts a little bit in China's favor if we believe we don't have to make an effort. Incidentally, the fact that the Chinese are pulling away from us can also be a reason for a German entrepreneur to sell quickly. Germany and Europe need to get their priorities right. But the most important thing is that we have to join forces with Russia to be in a stronger position. We must integrate the dissatisfied EU countries in the east in such a way that they no longer have any interest in being unruly. We must not let EU candidates wait too long. And finally we must start focusing on innovation again. If we don't do that, we will continue to lose power and then be treated accordingly. We can shout as loud as we want for equal treatment.

# Chapter 2

# Artificial Intelligence and Other Future Technologies: Dramatic Digitalization

## How China Is Becoming the New Tech World Power and Setting Our Standards in the Process

*The greatest strength of democracy is its ability to recognize and correct its own weaknesses.*

Federal President Frank-Walter Steinmeier

He looks a bit like a reptile in the sun. The lanky man in a too-large light blue shirt and dark jacket hardly moves. Slightly bent forward, he sits in the spotlight, his face resting on his left hand. Only his right thumb and forefinger touch each other, at a high frequency, as if he were speaking in Morse code. Slowly he takes a black stone from a small wooden bowl and places it on a plain wooden board with 19 vertical and 19 horizontal lines. Lee Sedol plays Go. It was invented in China 2,500 years ago and has been the only board game in the world that has been played continuously ever since. No other is more complex and no one masters the game as well as the 33-year-old South Korean.

Across from Lee sits a man no one knows. It is the Taiwanese Aja Huang, one of Alpha's chief programmers. He executes the moves given to him by Google's AlphaGo program. Lee thinks about it and places one last stone. Then, he gives up. He has lost four out of five games, winning

27

one by a narrow margin. "Oh," the commentator says into the silence. Also, the several hundred spectators in the room are disappointed. And even the Google programmers don't break out in jubilation. Reverence for their own invention prevails because March 19th 2016 marked the end of the first official Go competition between a machine and a human. At the same time, a new chapter in the history of science was opened.

Sure, computers were already beating chess masters 20 years ago. They followed so-called brute-force algorithms, in which they basically went through all possible moves every time. In Go, however, this is not possible. Too many moves are possible. Researchers were only able to find out the exact number in 2016. It states: 20816819938197998469947 86333448627702865 22453884530548425639456820927419612738015 37852564845169851964390725991601562812854608988883144271297 15319317557736620397247064840935 — that's more moves than there are atoms in the universe. That's why "Go is something like the holy grail," says Boston-based magazine *The Atlantic*.

AI researchers had long assumed that it would take a good decade before this holy grail could be cracked. But then, in February 2016, the British science magazine *Nature* reported that a computer was now able to beat the Go world champion 5:0 in five games. The article hit like a bomb. And of course, the researchers wanted to prove it as soon as possible. Even if they were not sure whether AlphaGo would really stand up to Lee Sedol.

That the competition took place in Asia and not in San Francisco, where Google is based, or London, where the AlphaGo researchers have their headquarters, was no coincidence. Interest in Go is much greater in Asia than in the West. In China alone, 60 million people watched live via television and the Internet as the machine defeated the human. A key moment for many researchers and developers. In the European media, however, the event went largely unnoticed. Hardly anyone here knows Go, and very few people can appreciate what the computer program has achieved. The savvy viewers in Asia, on the other hand, sensed that something very unusual had happened at the moment Lee threw in the towel. And Lee himself will never forget how it felt to play an ingenious strategy that seemed to be succeeding until the computer anticipated his moves and beat him at his own game. AlphaGo, the machine, had not been unfocused for a second, he said. "No human can do that," Lee said, sobered.

It was a historic moment for many top Chinese politicians as well. Most of them play Go themselves and know how complex the strategy game is. In retrospect, the victory of the machine over the Go world champion in China is seen as the initial spark for the decision of the leadership in Beijing to become the world leader in artificial intelligence by 2030.

The fact that Beijing's politicians are so open to new trends also has to do with a historical trauma from which the nation still suffers today. Since the Chinese emperors at the end of the 18th and beginning of the 19th century were too arrogant and did not take the West seriously, they missed out on the innovative thrust of the Industrial Revolution. With the words that there was "nothing that we do not possess," Emperor Qianlong had rejected a trade agreement with the English King George III in 1793. The duped English returned in 1839 as colonial masters with gunboats. The British forced the huge but weakened country to open its markets and made the Chinese dependent on opium. The emperor was forced to abdicate. A civil war broke out between nationalists and communists, threatening to break up the country. China, the world's leading economy at the time, crashed. Mao Zedong succeeded in reunifying the empire and rebuilding the country — an undertaking that came with with great sacrifice. However, he was still convinced that China could catch up with the leading nations on its own. Only the reformer Deng Xiaoping realized that China was too weak to do so. So, he opened up the country.

All Chinese politicians in power today have experienced the cultural revolution, and the suffering they saw keeps them focused. After China missed the first industrial revolution in 1800 with mass production, was at the bottom of the second in 1900 with electricity and cars, and was still weakened by the Cultural Revolution in the third starting in 1970 with computers, the Chinese now want to play a role in the fourth industrial revolution — and a leading one at that. Beijing's politicians have long since recognized that artificial intelligence will not only change the balance of power in the global economy but also rebalance international relations. For a long time, it was armies that changed the world and then trade agreements, banks, and stock exchanges became increasingly important in parallel. Now, artificial intelligence is developing, and China is convinced that countries that are leaders in this field have a decisive geo-strategic advantage that extends into all other areas.

There are three waves that are now crashing over us. The first is artificial intelligence that will turn our working world upside down. Many professions will disappear and new ones will emerge. Second, the economic power struggle with the help of artificial intelligence will replace the traditional war with large armies. And third, a non-Western superpower will play a central role for the first time. So, something is brewing: China wants to become the leader. The USA wants to remain the leader. Europe, which no longer plays on an equal footing in the field of AI, is in danger of being caught between the fronts. If we don't wake up, China will be in a much stronger position than we can imagine today to determine how the world is run. There is no question that Beijing will not always play fair and will change the rules during the game. No one should underestimate the absolute will of the Chinese to play at the top. The fact that Beijing is now doing everything in its power to bring highly educated Chinese back home and to offer young scientists such optimal research conditions that they will not even leave their country is one component of this strategy. At the same time, top foreign researchers are being offered attractive opportunities. A permanent visa is now no longer a problem.

In the West, on the other hand, we now seem to be almost at the point where the Chinese were in the 19th century before they crashed. We still behave as if we were the center of the world. We have been skeptical of new technologies for a long time, just as the Chinese were back then. We actually believe we don't need them, and we get sloppy. Our German telephone and Internet networks are full of holes, even by European standards. With its mobile network, Germany currently ranks 32nd in Europe — even behind Albania. Our public authorities still work largely analogously. This means cumbersome processes, telephone loops, crowded waiting rooms, and forms that are only valid in printed form. The national regulatory control council soberly summed up the situation at the end of 2017: "There is still no sign of effective e-government in this country." The German chancellor even speaks of an "obligation to act."

However, if we can't even withstand the competitive pressures of our European neighbors, how are we supposed to keep up with what is developing in China? Especially since we don't even notice much of what's going on there or don't take it seriously. We genuinely believe that it is enough to concern ourselves with which companies we sell to China and which we do not.

The Chinese also battened down the hatches back then. It didn't help. On the contrary, just like the British did back then, today the Chinese use our mixture of ignorance and arrogance to fly under the radar and then suddenly become visible. That's how most Germans still think chess is the measure of all things — without knowing how much more complex Go is. "We have landed on the moon," tweeted AI researcher Demis Hassabis after the game was won. Hassabis, the son of a Greek Cypriot and a

Singaporean residing in London, convinced Google to invest $500 million in his company DeepMind two years before the Go breakthrough. Elon Musk, the Tesla CEO, was also one of his early backers.

Only those who know the game can understand that the moon landing was not an exaggeration. Hassabis can sum up the problem that machines have had with Go so far in one sentence, "Chess is a logical game, Go an intuitive one." Together with his 700-member team from DeepMind, he tried to simulate intuition in the computer. Since intuition is also based on experience, they had the computer imitate 100,000 games played by good amateurs. Then, the machine had to win 13 million times against older AlphaGo versions and learn as it went. The programs that developed in the process already behave in such a way that we humans can no longer predict their actions and can hardly comprehend them. This is the big difference to machines we developed before. "The algorithms remain opaque," says Pedro Domingos, one of America's leading algorithm experts. "Even we don't understand exactly how they work. All we know is *that* they work." That's where European worriers come in, led by the Germans. Many consider artificial intelligence researchers to be sorcerer's apprentices and what they produce is the devil's stuff. What they don't mention is that they are and remain machines that have a plug that we can unplug. They are machines that we can tell at any time what to do and what not to do, just like a car that can drive 250 kilometers per hour within a city, but doesn't have to and isn't allowed to.

The best witnesses for the correctness of this assertion are the Beijing politicians. They are the last ones who have an interest in bringing something uncontrollable into the world. They are not bothered by the fact that it is not known exactly how the machine arrived at its result. After all, you don't have to accept its result. The new EU data protection regulation, on the other hand, not only wants users to be able to control their data but also requires that the decisions of artificial intelligence must be traceable.

The different attitudes toward new technologies are initially irreconcilable. The Chinese are the most carefree. The Americans are somewhere in between. The Europeans have the most objections, and in Europe, the Germans are the biggest worriers. Unfortunately, the question is not who has the better arguments but rather who is powerful enough to assert his interests. No one disputes that we need common rules, especially when it comes to artificial intelligence but the West will not automatically prevail, as it did in the past.

The advantages clearly lie with China, where the development of future technologies is virtually decreed by the state. In this respect, the question is no longer whether the Chinese will manage to catch up but only whether the Americans will manage to keep up. After all, they have long since lost their lead in many areas.

Unlike in the West, the Chinese government is able to quickly adapt its policies to new circumstances. Only about two months after the historic Go game, the Ministry of Industry and Information Technology (MIIT) approved a three-year action plan called "Internet Plus" for the implementation of artificial intelligence. Then, in August of the same year, Beijing laid out 15 megaprojects in the field of AI in the 13th Five-Year Plan. In May 2017, another one was added to the list: "AI 2.0" — until two months later, when the State Council finally approved the "New Generation Artificial Intelligence Development Plan." In total, an industry worth 150 billion US dollars is to be built up by 2030. That's industrial policy, Mr. Juncker! Mrs. Merkel!

Of course, it is one thing to provide enough money and create the ideal framework conditions. Unleashing the urge to research is another thing. "While there is a widespread belief that an authoritarian political system is per se hostile to innovation, the startup scene in China sees better conditions than elsewhere," says German Ambassador Michael Clauss, summing up the situation. Premier Li Keqiang did the groundwork back in 2015, creating incubators for inventors and entrepreneurs in the same way that biotechnology has incubators for cell and tissue cultures, that is, business incubators. In 2016, there were already 8,000 such centers, which helped nearly 90,000 startups get on their feet. This rapid success also has to do with the private sector putting pressure on the government; in this respect, Beijing is quite sensitive to pain. That pressure came, for example, from Li Yanhong, the CEO of search engine Baidu. He founded the Institute of Deep Learning back in 2013 and the Silicon Valley AI Lab a year later. Deep Learning is, in a sense, the turbocharger of artificial intelligence. As a member of the Political Consultative Conference, the highest advisory body of the Chinese government, Li demanded, in as early as 2015, that the state set up a "brain plan" to promote artificial intelligence. But the platform didn't take off until a year later. Since then, however, there has been no stopping it.

In August 2017, the National Natural Science Foundation of China issued guidelines for basic research in the field of AI and identified research projects that it has since been funding with large sums of money.

And in October, the State Development and Reform Commission defined a series of new projects. No fewer than 15 government units now deal with the subject, and they are also competing with each other to make sure no one lags behind. It's one blow after the other. Corporate representatives from Baidu, China's Google; Alibaba, China's Amazon; Tencent, China's Facebook; iFlytek, China's Siri; and Horizon Robotics, Intel's competitor, sit together on a commission with the flowery name of the New AI Generation Strategic Advisory Commission. In Spring 2018, the People's Congress' handpicked but thoroughly influential policy consultative conference was filled with IT entrepreneurs and venture capital investors. The number of members is limited. 20 construction entrepreneurs had to leave the panel — construction was yesterday.

In 2014, China already invested 129 million US dollars in artificial intelligence; three years later, it was over 50 billion U.S. dollars. And what is Germany doing? With the grand coalition finally in place in Spring 2018, Angela Merkel, who after all heads one of the most technologically advanced countries in the world, seems to be finally tackling the issue. She is establishing a new department in the Chancellor's Office for "Policy Planning, Innovation, and Digital Policy," which will, after all, be headed by one of her closest confidants: Eva Christiansen. And she appointed Dorothee Bär as Minister of State for Digitization; however, Bär does not have the budget and staff of other ministries. Federal Transport Minister Andreas Scheuer sets up an app that can be used to report dead spots. No one in China needs such an app. There people are already discussing introductory courses for artificial intelligence in elementary schools. "Children should have fun learning about artificial intelligence technologies, instead of fearing them," says Liu Qingfeng, the founder of iFlytek, which advises the government on these matters. In the Spring of 2018, he presented a corresponding draft.

Germany's digitization plans — and we're not even talking about artificial intelligence yet — are more or less the same as in the 2013 coalition agreement. These plans are all about networking the republic. But at least this time they will actually be implemented. In July 2018, there was at least one small ray of hope; the federal cabinet presented the key points for a national AI strategy. "The strategy states that Germany should become the world's leading location for AI." Third place would be enough.

"We have to manage this because it depends on whether Germany will continue to be economically successful in the future," Chancellor's Office Minister Helge Braun later explained. That had "become clear in the past twelve months" — four years after Beijing understood it. However, the state budgets have not yet been set, even in the summer of 2018. Yet Germany would be in a much better position to invest than any other European country. Not since reunification has the debt of the German state fallen as sharply as it did in 2017. At least Braun now asked one of the right questions: "How can companies that don't have the scale of Google and Alibaba continue to be successful in the digital competition — and how can we as the state properly support them?"

Christian Bauckhage, Professor of Computer Science at the University of Bonn and Lead Scientist for Machine Learning at the Fraunhofer Institute for Intelligent Analysis and Information Systems, has long complained that the topic of AI is "not a top priority for us." But the fact that the chancellor herself is not leaning further out of the window on this topic also has to do with Europe. Merkel sees how difficult it is to find a consensus at the European level. She admits that the Europeans "have not yet made up their minds" and warns that Europe could be "influenced by Chinese or American interests" left behind by Chinese or American companies that have long since made data the core of their business model. At the end of April 2018, the EU announced its intention to invest 20 billion euros in artificial intelligence by 2020, starting with 1.5 billion euros from the EU's Horizon 2020 research program. With this, it wants to trigger an additional 2.5 billion euros through public–private partnerships. Another 500 million euros are to be raised via the Juncker Fund. But then immediately follows a suspicious sentence from the EU Commission: "Legal issues need to be clarified." The Commission wants to present ethics guidelines for the development of AI by the end of 2018, which should reflect the principles of data protection and transparency. There it is again, the old problem — first the rules, then the game. It's decided differently in most other regions of the world.

Meanwhile, the Chinese are not only investing a lot of money, they are now also considered movers and shakers. In some high-tech sectors, they have already proven that things can move fast when they need to move fast. These include high-speed trains as well as new aircraft, e-cars, and e-buses. Artificial intelligence will further increase their lead in these areas. Today, they are the most advanced in high-speed trains. As early as 2010, Beijing announced its intention to take the lead in this field. Just six years later, 60 percent of the world's high-speed trains were already manufactured by China. The trains are so competitive internationally that French train manufacturer Alstom (TGV) and Siemens (ICE) were forced to merge in 2017. Probably too late.

China has now also achieved astonishing feats in the field of electro buses. Not Berlin, London, or San Francisco, but the southern Chinese city of Shenzhen with its 12 million inhabitants is now the world capital of e-buses. No other major city has so far so radically converted its public transport to electricity. The tech metropolis maintains an electric bus fleet with a total of more than 16,300 vehicles — quieter and more environmentally friendly than conventional diesel buses. The Chinese metropolis is thus reducing $CO_2$ emissions by 1.35 million tons a year. The first buses started rolling in 2011. At that time, we in Europe were still convinced that these were just figments of our imagination. We were as skeptical as we are today about artificial intelligence.

When BYD presented its model of an e-bus at an industry conference in Belgium, the reactions were clear, "Everyone laughed at us because they thought we had built a toy," says Isbrand Ho, BYD's European head. Seven years later, 183 all-electric buses were registered in Germany. In July 2018, another year later, Daimler followed suit, becoming the first German manufacturer to introduce the E-Citaro. In 2019, it will first be tested in Berlin, Hamburg, and Mannheim. The range is 150 kilometers. "Quality comes before speed," says Daimler commercial vehicle boss Martin Daum. "It's not the fastest that wins out in the end, but the best." Some consider that self-confident, others arrogant.

The city of Hamburg, considered Germany's most progressive in this area, has announced that it will purchase only zero-emission buses from 2020 onward. By the beginning of the 2030s, all public bus transport is to be converted to e-mobility. Why is this taking so long? Good question. Especially since we are only talking about 1,500 e-buses, i.e., one tenth of the vehicles that are already running reliably in Shenzhen's tropical heat.

Most of the e-buses in the southern Chinese city come from the Chinese company BYD, which also has its headquarters there. The abbreviation stands for "Build Your Dreams." In fact, the car manufacturer has done much to make a dream come true — that is still a pipe dream in the established industrial nations. The company was founded in 1995 by the chemist Wang Chuanfu as a small factory for rechargeable batteries. It was not until 2003 that he entered the automotive business. Just six years later, the company launched the world's first mass-produced plug-in hybrid car. Today, BYD is one of China's largest automotive producers and one of the world's biggest pioneers and innovators in e-mobility. Wang has risen to become one of China's richest men. His success in Shenzhen, however, is not only related to the quality of his cars but also to Wang's good contacts with the central and local governments. The latter contributed around 60,000 euros to each of his buses in Shenzhen. This also benefits the state; although the purchase costs are higher, the significantly lower operating costs make up for the subsidy, so to speak. Added to this is the positive environmental impact. After eight years of operation, the additional purchase costs compared to a conventional diesel bus will have paid for themselves.

Meanwhile, Berlin's BVG spent 15 months testing four (!) buses from the Polish manufacturer Solaris between Südkreuz Station and Zoo Station. The trial period went anything but smoothly. On average, only three of the four test buses were permanently available; the failure rate was 25 percent. The reasons were "unplannable damage," according to the Berlin Senate. Mostly the control, drive, and charging technology had repeatedly failed. Meanwhile, the Chinese buses are running in England, Spain, Italy, and Norway and, in July 2018, Chile also ordered 100 BYD buses. They are now also being used in Germany for the Munich-based company FlixBus. Since Summer 2018, three Chinese e-buses have been operating on the Mannheim–Frankfurt route.

In August 2018, Minister of Transport Andreas Scheuer was outraged that German manufacturers were not yet able to offer any models that year. This is despite the fact that the German government's "Clean Air Immediate Action Program" has promoted the purchase of and wants to provide financial support for e-buses. "I don't want to set up a support program for the Asian economic area here," he said. Well. What can one say to that? How are we supposed to master the challenges of artificial intelligence if we can't even get electric buses on the road?

Perhaps the biggest difference between China and Germany is that in China, the state exerts pressure to promote innovation and supports companies where it can. In Germany, it still seems to be more important not to incur new debt than to promote German innovation. E-buses are just one niche example of this. In the automotive industry, developments in China are so dramatic that I am devoting an entire chapter to this topic (see Chapter 3).

Anyone who can't imagine how quickly a once leading industry can miss the boat need only look at what happened to the textile, coal, or, most recently, steel industries in Germany. These were all industries that were influential in their time and even set international standards. In the textile industry, for a long time, German manufacturers did not want to believe that customers would buy the cheap "Made in Hong Kong" goods. For this arrogance, the decline was comparatively slow; between 1955 and 1980, more than 400,000 jobs were lost. In the meantime, production has migrated from Hong Kong and Taiwan to Mainland China, Bangladesh, and Ethiopia. So far, Germany has always come up with something new after such upheavals. However, this is not a matter of course, as can be seen at the European level with Nokia. First, the Europeans led with Nokia, then the Americans with the iPhone, and now the South Koreans and the Chinese have taken over. The collapse of a single company like Nokia, which had a 40 percent share of the global market around 2008 in its heyday cost around 25,000 people their jobs. The decline took place within just five years. It is not improbable that the German auto industry will be faced with something like this, unless we finally wake up.

In aircraft construction, the Chinese are also catching up at a breathtaking pace. A for Airbus and B for Boeing are now followed by C for Comac. The Chinese aircraft market is the fastest growing in the world. One in three Airbuses currently goes to China, a European company, by the way, that would not exist without a smart industrial policy. Airbus has operated a final assembly plant for its A320 medium-haul jets in the northern Chinese port city of Tianjin since 2008 and a completion plant for the A330 widebody jets since 2017. The Aviation Industry Corporation of China (AVIC) has a stake in both plants. Competitor Boeing is currently building a delivery plant for the 737 in China. The partner is, of all things, the Chinese competitor Comac. In Spring 2018, President Xi Jinping decided to drop the limit on foreign involvement in building aircraft in China. What looks like an opening is a smart move. By doing so, Beijing is luring American and European manufacturers deeper into its market and only making them more dependent. Airbus and Boeing see the market opening with one eye smiling and one eye crying. Of course, they would prefer to continue producing at home and exporting the aircraft to China. The option of manufacturing in China without a local partner is still the second-best solution. Theoretically, at least. Beijing will most likely come up with new rules of the game so that Boeing and Airbus don't get cocky. The Chinese government could, for example, raise the so-called localization requirements. More and more parts would then have to come from Chinese suppliers.

The situation will become dramatic in four years at the latest when China's first own aircraft will enter daily service. The C919 is a direct competitor to the Boeing 737 and the Airbus 320. Around 800 orders have already been placed, although almost exclusively from Chinese companies. Some of them have certainly been encouraged to get involved in this direction. Comac can rely on the fact that Beijing is already pulling out all the stops to push the domestic company into the market. Boeing and Airbus say the market is big enough for all of them. After all, the world's soon-to-be largest aviation market is estimated to need 5,000 new aircraft in the next 20 years. But that sounds like whistling in the wind. Beijing also wants to sell the C919 internationally; until the end of April 2018, Beijing blocked the approval of the Airbus A320neo, which was supposed to fly in China the year before. Beijing wanted to push through to finally be recognized as an international certification body by international regulators EASA and FAA. In the course of the trade dispute with Washington, Beijing has now apparently given in, for the time being. At the end of May, Airbus was able to deliver the first aircraft to Chinese airlines.

Thus, a battle is lost, but not the war. The outcome of this is foreseeable. The day Beijing is able to replace Boeing and Airbus aircraft in China with the C919 in large numbers, the game will turn. Then, Boeing and Airbus managers will have a choice between plague and cholera. "Either you help us become an international certifier or the Chinese market closes for you," will be Beijing's negotiating posture. Even if it takes a little longer, a Chinese aircraft on a par with Boeing and Airbus will come and establish itself. This is a matter of national pride. Perhaps Boeing and Airbus will still have record sales for a while because the Chinese market is growing so fast. But their market shares will certainly decline. And what's worse, their margins will shrink, too. This will then also affect employees in Hamburg, the most important Airbus site in Europe alongside Toulouse. Beijing has already demonstrated that they are capable of catching up and setting standards in buses, trains, and cars. Artificial intelligence, however, will be their masterpiece. It will be tight for Europe.

"The greatest strength of democracy, in my view, is its ability to recognize and correct its own weaknesses," German President Frank-Walter Steinmeier recently told students at Delhi University in India. If only

Steinmeier were right. Do Western politics and the Western economy really recognize the signs of the times? Does democracy really still have this strength? Or do the many elections not obscure the detail of its own weaknesses?

After all, every now and then one or two German politicians say, "We have a problem. A big problem. A problem that affects the statics of our country." Or, as the politicians usually like to put it as follows: our future is at stake. But the rise of China and the triumph of artificial intelligence do not dominate our political debate. If at all, these topics are touched on quietly and casually. After all, they do not have the drama of the refugee crisis, which penetratingly overlays the discourse. Perhaps, it would be better to say that the drama that is about to unfold has not yet reached us. After all, there is hardly a topic that is as important for our future as AI and the closely interwoven Chinese dominance of many key technologies.

For a long time, the economic balance of power between China and Germany offset each other. Germany provided the technology and China had the market and the production facilities. Now, the game is turning. China is developing its own technologies at a speed that we would not have deemed possible just five years ago. Stealing was yesterday. Inventing is today. Our problem is that if we no longer lead the way technologically, the Chinese will no longer be interested in giving us market share. But we urgently need them to keep our economy going. Our 1,000 or so medium-sized world market leaders, the hidden champions, live on this. They know that any technology, no matter how advanced, is worthless without a large market. Our domestic market is too small and is slow to absorb new developments. Even the European market is not enough in the long run, especially since the British will soon be leaving and it is not foreseeable how solidly the European confederation will stand together in the future. Volkswagen already sells over 50 percent of its cars in China. The average for the DAX companies is around 20 percent, and the trend is rising.

China will do its utmost in the high-tech sector to first catch up and then become better than German and European companies. They will succeed in this in more and more areas. Then, the tide will turn; the profits that our large and small players are still raking in will melt away because China is no longer interested in our products. And, because the Chinese manufacture so many of these products, they will be able to offer them internationally at lower prices and will also be able to determine the rules of the game in these markets. They will set standards that favor their companies. That's what we've been doing for a long time.

Beijing knows what it wants — China should develop as quickly as possible from the workbench of the world to an innovation-driven economy that determines international trends. Wherever possible, it does not develop itself but buys-in internationally. In 2016, for example, the tech group Tencent acquired the Finnish game developer Supercell, which became famous with the smartphone hit "Clash." A year later, the company secured a 5 percent stake in the American electric car manufacturer Tesla for 1.8 billion US dollars.

Already the West is losing technological influence every day. Apple may be the world's most expensive company at $1,000 billion. But Tencent's market capitalization, for example, has overtaken that of its rival, Facebook. Tencent was only founded in 1998 and invented WeChat, for example, which is technologically much better than WhatsApp and is in the process of taking over the world. The volume of venture capital activity in China has already overtaken that of the US, breaking the $50 billion mark in 2017. Clearly, money alone does not make innovation. And innovation must be coordinated in order to succeed. That's exactly what Beijing is doing. And what's more, 40 years after the start of the reforms, the party cadres seem to have actually achieved the unbelievable. They have unleashed the creativity of the younger generation and sent entire cities and regions into a start-up fever. The drive for innovation is enormous and the many competing companies are firing each other up.

Innovation comes about when you can no longer deal with the old; it is no longer useful enough. Innovation arises in the tension between the old and the desire for the new, without already knowing what it might be. Meanwhile, the state wants creative minds to think outside the box. Beijing has first made sure that people are networked. This shapes the attitude toward life of this young reform generation, which does not perceive the lack of political freedom as being as restrictive as we in the West believe. Other freedoms have emerged that make up for these deficits. One no longer has to be the ingenious inventor who is in the right place at the right time. You no longer have to travel to a foreign country to be ahead. Even from the Chinese hinterland, young people can now develop innovative ideas together in a virtual group. China has become a networked start-up center. This is overwhelming, especially in such a large country.

Young techies are currently experiencing freedom they have never felt before. This makes the desire for traditional political freedoms pale into insignificance — at least for now. Who longs to vote when they can invent? Having the opportunity to take risks and also to be allowed to fail sometimes, to take paths that no one has taken before, to give the world a technology that it can no longer do without, is also a form of freedom.

To move even faster, Beijing is now making it easier than ever for international talent to work in China. Silicon Valley Chinese can now bring Indian or American colleagues from their team to China. They are allowed to enter and leave as they wish, and they are also allowed to bring their families. In the U.S., President Donald Trump is making policy in the opposite direction. It's getting harder and harder to get a Green Card. Eric Schmidt, former Google chief and now chairman of the umbrella company Alphabet, laments the U.S.'s more restrictive immigration policies, saying Iran, for example, is currently producing some of the world's top computer scientists. "I want them here. I want them to work for Alphabet and Google." Now, they are more likely to go to China.

Another advantage of China is that the money for start-ups is more available than anywhere else. "The way the government invests its money is getting smarter," says Ming Lei, one of the co-founders of Baidu and now co-director of the Innovation Center for Artificial Intelligence at Peking University. In the past, financial injections went to research institutions and state-owned enterprises, but now money is flowing to private companies, which turn investments into products and services more quickly. For example, the Singaporean sovereign wealth fund Temasek has equally large teams in Silicon Valley and in China to identify new investment opportunities.

Another argument in favor of China is that the huge market absorbs ideas very quickly. That is an advantage that should not be underestimated. China is not yet as developed and therefore the hunger for new things is much greater. It can also be an advantage if a country has some catching up to do. If you skip a step, you often end up being faster. Many Chinese have never owned a computer, but most now have a smartphone. And instead of using a credit card, most have switched directly from the old cash system to mobile payment services. Even street vendors now collect payments via Alipay or WeChatPay, which account for 90 percent of the mobile payment market in China.

One of the most important issues, however, is access to data; "You need a mass of data for artificial intelligence," explains Professor

Dr. Reimund Neugebauer, president of the Fraunhofer Society. Neugebauer called for "a national show of force in a European context" back in 2017. Although we are involved in collecting and storing data, "there is a need to catch up when it comes to evaluating data — generating algorithms for algorithms. One of the reasons for this is that we are very cautious when it comes to data analysis — and for good reason. Germany also owes its prosperity to the protection of intellectual property," Neugebauer said in an interview with *Handelsblatt*. "We have a lot to lose there. But there is legislation in the EU, for example, that also hinders us from developing here." He believes that the Americans and especially the Chinese have a treasure trove of data that Europeans simply cannot get their hands on.

When it comes to the question of how to turn an idea into a marketable product, China is now ahead. In contrast to Silicon Valley, production facilities are located around the corner, especially in southern China. Developers can discuss their software or product with a production manager who can tell them immediately what they need to change. This means that the period between the idea to a product suitable for everyday use is much shorter. "Chinese start-ups are faster," is how Constance-born Cyriac Roeding, an investor from the Valley, sums up his impressions from a trip to China. The industrial engineer and tech pioneer says, "Large start-ups are ramped up in China in three to five years; in the U.S., it's five to eight years." And they also make money much faster than in the U.S.

Due to all these reasons, Silicon Valley is suffering from a reverse brain drain. The majority of the Chinese elite who were educated and worked abroad are now returning to China. Among students, that was only one in two in 2011. Now, it's over 80 percent. And German techies now also prefer to go to China rather than the United States. For example, Sören Schwertfeger: "The conditions in Shanghai are much better than in Germany, but also better than in the U.S.," says the 38-year-old. Schwertfeger has access to one of the most modern AI labs at ShanghaiTech University. Whatever he needs in terms of hardware and robots is delivered to him immediately. "The state pays a lot of money for good ideas," says Schwertfeger, an assistant professor in robotics and AI since 2014.

Beijing has succeeded, through clever promotion, in creating a new Chinese sense of life and self-worth, which can neither be planned nor commanded, but which has nevertheless been created by a long-term plan. A plan that inspires experimentation and creativity. And some may indeed feel like sorcerer's apprentices in the process. In Germany, on the other hand, and indeed throughout Europe, we are experiencing the opposite trend. Those who cater to the fear of new technologies get more attention than those who develop something. Which start-up entrepreneur in Germany is as well-known as German philosopher Richard David Precht, a torchbearer of German despondency? Precht claims that the founders in Silicon Valley see the human being as something that does not "function any differently than a rat in a laboratory. Man is to become a 'man-machine'." For him, the "central insight of cybernetics is that everything or being can be predicted and controlled." Silicon Valley is "in the totalitarian tradition" of Mao and Stalin. They wanted to "influence people artificially and by force." That seems a bit exaggerated to most Americans and the Chinese. Not to mention sentences like this one: "Technicians have never understood what people want." Precht, however, can claim to have hit the nerve of the Germans exactly. A great achievement. The fact that he made it to number one on *Spiegel Magazine's* bestseller list says a lot about skeptical Germany and is also an important reason why German politicians are so cautious when it comes to pushing through to the next technology. After all, they want to be re-elected.

"How do we want to live?" asks Precht. That is indeed an important question. What he doesn't tell people is that we are no longer the ones who decide what the world needs. Granted, we could opt out, but that will be difficult. See Brexit. Even today, ordinary people in England don't want to have to go to the doctor; there is no money for decent health care.

What Precht is doing is by no means new. However, people have always managed to be open-minded about inventions, if they have made their lives easier. And critics have always made sure to define the disadvantages of an invention and tame it with rules or new technologies. Let's take the Germans' favorite thing, the car. Today, hardly anyone doubts that its invention made sense. Nevertheless, there were contemporaries of Carl Benz who made a good living from stirring up fear of these newfangled infernal machines. How much safer and more comfortable is the good horse-drawn carriage. Today, their names are just smoke and mirrors. The car is still around. No question, many people have died in car accidents. Nevertheless, the advantages still outweigh the disadvantages. And the risks of the car have been minimized step by step. The seat belt was followed by the airbag and all kinds of assistance systems. Now, we are on the verge of another giant step: e-mobility and autonomous driving. Artificial intelligence makes it possible.

The progressiveness of a society can therefore be measured on the one hand by how open it is to new ideas and, on the other hand, by how quickly it is able to correct the weaknesses of a new technology. In Europe in particular, the fear that it may not be able to control its weaknesses is stifling curiosity. This is how societies that have passed their zenith behave.

Instead of badmouthing the successes of the Chinese or panicking about future technologies that have long been present, we should admit to ourselves that Europe will no longer play a significant role if we do not quickly turn things around now. It is high time because we are receiving weekly updates about groundbreaking innovations from China. Silicon Valley may not have passed its zenith yet, but it has become more saturated and inflexible. For the first time since the statistics have been recorded, five Chinese and five American start-ups were counted among the world's top 10 "unicorns" in 2017. So, when it comes to start-ups that achieve a market valuation of more than one billion U.S. dollars even before going public, China and the U.S. are tied. In total, the Chinese Ministry of Research and Development counted 164 Chinese unicorns that year. The most valuable is Ant Financial, the financial services subsidiary of Alibaba Group, valued at $75 billion, followed by Didi Chuxing, China's Uber, at $56 billion, and smartphone maker Xiaomi, valued at $46 billion. In 2013, the balance of power was still different in that China was not yet on the list. Two-thirds of the unicorns came from the USA and one-third from Europe.

Adam Segal, director of the Digital and Cyberspace Program at the U.S. Council on Foreign Relations, sees the following as the reason why not only the Europeans but increasingly also the Americans are coming under pressure, "The Chinese have a strategy and an industrial policy regarding artificial intelligence. The Americans don't." One would like to add, neither do the Germans!

This strategy is also reflected in other areas. In 2017, for the first time, China published more scientific papers in one year than any other country in the world, according to the US National Science Foundation. One can argue about the quality, however it is still a milestone. China now spends more than 2 percent of its economic output on research and development. In the United States, the share is even higher at almost 2.8 percent — but it has hardly changed over the past 20 years, while in China, it has almost quadrupled and continues to rise.

And a few more statistics documenting the historical shift: the Chinese invest more per capita in startups than Americans. China accounts for about 18 percent of the world's population but already derives 25 percent of global revenues from online app businesses. Furthermore, the Chinese spend 4.5 times as much time on apps as the Indians, who in turn are far ahead of the Americans.

But because numbers alone are not enough, I meet with a "Crown Witness." He is not one of these booming young Chinese and is old enough not to be impressed by every new trick. We talked to a conservative who holds Germany dear and who knows his way around innovations: Peter Jungen. He is 79 years old. Ex-president of the European Association of Small and Medium-Sized Enterprises and co-founder of the European Business Angels Network (EBAN); these are investors who help start-ups with financial injections, know-how, and contacts. Jungen even has his own holding company for this purpose, which, among other things, is the only investor to have co-founded the online price comparison portal Idealo and invested in the medical technology company Smart Therapeutics and Penumbra, respectively. In 2017, Jungen was invited by the Chancellor's Office to address the Hamburg G20 Summit on the topic of start-ups.

One sentence from our conversation has stuck in my mind: "Perhaps Europe has already given the world everything that Europe could give the world," Jungen said. But first things first: Jungen, who lives in Cologne, is not easily irritated. But his trips to China — at least two or three per year — always leave him worried. The speed with which China is catching up concerns him. In Germany, he says, there is still the idea "that a society is only innovative and creative if it is democratically legitimized. But a society is innovative first and foremost when people have the freedom to implement ideas," says Jungen. In a democratic Europe, he sees a great danger that innovative strengths will be equaled out. "If Germany is less competitive, that's an advantage for Europe — that's ultimately the logic behind it among our European neighbors." He says this means Germany does not necessarily immediately lose its ability to innovate, but it does lose innovation momentum in any case. "Many of our companies are innovating abroad, but investing less in Germany," Jungen says. "That's worrying." Germans have become rather risk-averse anyway, he adds. "The better off Germany is, the less willing they are to venture a new start," he says. These are the lyrics that one should actually hear from politicians. In fact, the proportion of founders from Germany has been falling since 1995 and has more than halved since 2003. This is not the conclusion of gloating competitors from Silicon Valley or China's propaganda but of the Kreditanstalt für Wiederaufbau (KfW), the world's largest national promotional bank: "This should make us lie awake at night."

I would argue against that. Among the SMEs in particular, we still have plenty of hidden champions, in-house founders, so to speak, who set standards in their industries, some of which are highly specialized. These hidden champions, Jungen immediately counters, are really good at mastering step-by-step improvement. "That is a great strength of German engineers. Think of the continuous perfection of cars or machines. But that perfectionism can also turn out to be an obstacle, particularly when it prevents you from daring to do something completely new." The Germans would never launch a product on the market that was not altogether 100 percent perfect, says Jungen. In China, he says, the basic attitude is different, with more daring and experimentation. "The Chinese are not always looking for the big bang solution like we are. They also invest in low-hanging fruits, and that's what sets them apart." He says it's hard for him to admit but, "The Chinese are more willing to experiment today than we are."

A look at the statistics confirms this. In 2016, China, for the first time spent more on start-ups than the Europeans — not just in absolute terms or as a percentage of GDP but per capita. In China, the figure was 24 U.S. dollars, and in the EU, only 22. In the U.S., the figure was still 200 U.S. dollars, although the previous year's total was 20 percent higher. Measured in terms of GDP, the figures are no better. In Germany, the figure is currently only 0.086 percent of GDP. And one thing is certain for Jungen: "The broader the innovations are spread, the higher the probability that some will get through."

The fact that the Chinese have leaped at this opportunity did not surprise anyone. The departure from low-cost manufacturing and the push into the high-tech sector have long been promoted by China's politicians. "We just didn't want to admit it." He takes autonomous driving as an example of how much we underestimate reality. Actually, this should be a huge topic in Germany, the country of carmakers, "but we're playing coy." Yet autonomous driving would increase productivity enormously, "if you're no longer stuck in a traffic jam every morning with your hands on the steering wheel." In Germany, that's an average of 25 hours a month. In other words, three working days. "Not to mention all the traffic deaths. In China, people understand that right away."

Jungen believes that one reason we have underestimated China's innovative power for so long is that we have always overestimated the export share of China's economy. The share of China's exports is not even half as large as the share of Germany's exports in its gross domestic product. This means "Germany is far more dependent on the development of the global economy than China. We are very vulnerable. I'm not sure that the consequences and risks arising from this are properly perceived in Germany."

From Jungen's point of view, China has embraced a remarkable strategy that previously took place in Europe: competition instead of centralism. "Think back to the 16th century. If someone in China had a good idea and it didn't make it to the top, it was dead. In Europe, on the other hand, you could just move a few hundred kilometers away, to where another ruler ruled. In this way, Columbus, who came from near Genoa, won Isabella and Ferdinand II as sponsors for his famous ship voyage in Spain. Similarly, this is now possible in China." An accurate observation, I must concede. The provinces are run like self-permanent subsidiaries; if the numbers or policies don't add up, the CEO is replaced. Otherwise, they compete fiercely with each other. "It seems to me," says Jungen, "Europe, on the other hand, is becoming more and more centralized when it comes to innovation. We talk about more harmonization and the Chinese talk about more competition — even within their own country. It's curious."

The Chinese took their cue from methods of European intellectual history, perhaps without being aware of it. "And we, like Confucius, talk about harmonization, but basically mean leveling." A long silence follows. And then comes the sentence that I still can't get out of my head, "Perhaps Europe has already given the world everything that Europe could give the world: The Renaissance. The Enlightenment. The scientific revolution. The Industrial Revolution. Capitalism. Great developments. All of that changed the world dramatically, and the world today is European. In the end, the Chinese pay us the greatest compliment when they admit why they were unable to hold their own against Europe and the West for so long. They admit that they closed themselves off, misinterpreted the signs of the times, and slept through the future. Something like that will not happen to them again."

Nevertheless, he said he was surprised by the speed at which China has not only caught up but is now leading the way. Germany must act now, he said. "If we always just want to preserve everything, we will become like the French. Perhaps, we need a Minister of State for Digitales. However, what we need most urgently is a Ministry of Economic Affairs that has the foresight to improve framework conditions, remove obstacles, and create incentives for innovation and for new entrepreneurship. Germany lives on its substance, and if you take a closer look at individual countries in the EU, you can't exactly say that things are going well. We need to get out of our comfort zone, wake up, and finally be willing to take risks again. In our country, if possible, you always walk the middle of the road between success and failure, nothing can happen to you there."

A willingness to take risks is an important prerequisite for innovation. According to the statistics of the European Patent Office, Siemens is Germany's most innovative company. With an increase of almost 19 percent in patent applications in Europe, the electrical engineering group moved up from sixth to second place in the patent watchdog's ranking. However, it was not a European company that topped the list in 2017 but the Chinese technology group Huawei, which filed 2,398 patents in twelve months. This was the first time in the history of the European Patent Office that a Chinese company had the lead among the most important applicants. Huawei not only beat Siemens but also the South Korean suppliers LG and Samsung, as well as the US mobile phone and semiconductor manufacturer Qualcomm.

The Chinese have been setting the pace worldwide for some time now. Already three times, telecommunications equipment supplier Huawei secured first place by a wide margin in the global ranking of the World Intellectual Property Organization (WIPO). In addition to Siemens, there is only one other German company in the top 10 of the world's most important patent applicants: Bosch in ninth place. In as early as 2016, a U.S. government report warned that Chinese scientists were publishing more research results on deep learning than American scientists. The computing method is based on the way the human brain works, simulating a densely interwoven network of nerve cells.

Of course, China is not already at the top everywhere. If you look at the different areas of application of artificial intelligence separately, the picture is mixed. China is ahead in Internet AI because the country has no resistance in analyzing the data of its citizens. In business AI, the West is — still — ahead because we are better at optimizing factories. When it comes to perception AI, i.e., sensors that collect new data, China is further ahead, and while it has no problem with autonomous AI, the self-driving cars and autonomous robots still lag a little behind.

"A lot of people take it for granted that the U.S. makes the best technology in the world when it comes to AI," says U.S. security expert Paul Scharre of the Washington-based think tank Center for a New American Security. "That's a very dangerous assumption." Americans are still ahead when it comes to the best AI researchers in the world. Google alone employs about 50 percent of them. China has only a fraction of that. While one-third of Silicon Valley techies are foreigners, only 10,000 foreigners work in Beijing's Zhongguancun Science Park. But that is about to change. The Science and Technology Center maintains scouting offices to recruit talent from the U.S., Canada, England, Australia, and Finland. They don't have an office in Germany, by the way. Obviously, it's not worth it. The USA's previous advantage of being able to retain researchers comparatively easily due to its excellent working conditions is dwindling by the day. In particular, more and more Chinese who have learned and worked in Silicon Valley are going back to their home country. They are well educated and find opportunities in China that are not available anywhere else. The huge amounts of data collected in China are a deciding factor. "I'm not saying that Chinese companies are better than American companies. I'm not saying Chinese engineers are better than American engineers. What will make China great in artificial intelligence and Big Data is, first of all, there is no serious law in China that protects data," explains Dong Tao, responsible for the Asia-Pacific region at Credit Suisse. You can regret that. You can criticize it. But only the Chinese can change it. And they don't seem to be interested at the moment. That is their right and does not mean that they are controlled by others. We are creeped out by the fact that most Chinese have nothing against the fact that Beijing capital's video surveillance cameras produce 5,000 years of footage everyday. That's what companies like Facebook thrive on. The Chinese facial recognition start-up from Megvii Research won three competitions at their first attempt against teams from Microsoft, Facebook, Google, and CMU at the International Conference on Machine Vision in Venice in the fall of 2017 and came second in a fourth.

The Chinese tech company Tencent processes five billion photos everyday. The US bank Citigroup raised its share price target for Tencent shares by 12 percent in 2018. The reason is the company's strength in the field of artificial intelligence. Of the 1.4 billion Chinese, 800 million are regular internet users.

Nowhere in the world is smartphone density higher than in the Middle Kingdom. And in no other major economy is the sense of data protection lower. Through websites and apps, Jack Ma's company Alibaba collects data on its users' shopping behavior, media consumption, logistics needs, payment and credit history, search preferences, use of social networks, and keyword searches in search engines. Computers calculate more than 8,000 parameters per month from the data of more than half a billion active users. Instead of making suggestions based on past orders, as Amazon does, Alibaba also guides its customers to brands and products that they may not even know about.

That may scare us, but Chinese customers like it. For them, the main question is as follows: Does the new technology make our lives easier? Will facial recognition, for example, mean that we no longer have to wait in line at the train station or airport? Will it make it possible to shop or go to a restaurant without a credit card or even a smartphone? That you can no longer be mugged and robbed? The Chinese see it as reassuring that the many cameras make life in the cities safer; the fact that these cameras also screen their private lives hardly upsets them. Nor does the fact that dissidents or innocent people can be targeted in this way. According to an international survey, not even half of the Chinese are concerned about how their data are handled. In Germany, the figure is around 80 percent. Other countries, other situations, it used to be said.

So, it is not the case that the data privacy debate would have to be suppressed by censorship at great expense. Ultimately, that wouldn't work either if the majority of the population were really concerned. You can see this with other issues, such as environmental pollution or food safety. If a large portion of the population are convinced, in an authoritarian regime, the government has to act. In Europe, we are faced with a dilemma. While we, as usual and for good reasons, are still thoroughly examining the pros and cons of a technology, the Chinese have long since developed it further and thus also exercised their power to set the rules of the game again. There is little point in accusing them of blind faith in progress and us of critical distance. They simply do what they think is right. And they reject our accusations out of hand. They are not interested. That's how the new global co-determination works.

Our desire for regulation is driven by fear; the fear that we will lose our jobs through digitalization and artificial intelligence. 65 percent of the Chinese are convinced that AI and robotics will bring them new jobs and new opportunities. Only 19 percent of the Germans and the French believe this; they are the most skeptical. In the USA, the figure is 23 percent. Pedro Domingos, one of the leading computer scientists in the United States, has also experienced this skeptical attitude. He wrote the bestseller *The Master Algorithm.* A book that even President Xi Jinping had behind him during his New Year's speech. "My agent told me from the beginning, 'You will sell this book all over the world, but not in France and Germany.' The Germans and the French don't like these things. That's exactly how it turned out." Domingos has no illusions about the role China will play in the future. "We could soon be living in a world that is not literally controlled by China, but factually, because China controls the cyber world."

And yet another episode that reflects us Germans: At the end of May 2018, German Chancellor Angela Merkel travels to Shenzhen, the Mecca of Chinese innovation. Forty years ago, it was still a small fishing village with 30,000 inhabitants; today, 21 million people live in the metropolitan region. Will Merkel try to shake up the Germans when it comes to innovation? The day of her visit is disappointing in this respect. She arrives from Beijing at the Shangri-La Hotel at 12:30 p.m. She knows there is little time. So, she walks with long strides across the red carpet, 70 important delegation members in tow. These include Dax board members, academics, and medium-sized companies. On the third floor, the party secretary of Guangdong province is waiting for her to have lunch together. Immediately before that, she meets the managers of the Innovation Hub of the German Chamber of Foreign Trade. The duration of the conversation is three minutes and thirty seconds.

After dinner, she doesn't visit one of the major players of the city, like Tencent or Huawei, but goes to Siemens — the company manufactures medical technology products in Shenzhen. In terms of protocol, there is no other way. No time for anything. At Siemens, she briefly said a few sentences for television, in front of a gray wall with three flags, "You can see that there are good opportunities for cooperation here. But you can also see that we are called upon to deal with digitization and the resulting changes in the labor market. We are not ahead of the game in all cases. In some areas, however, we are a world market leader. But that has to be worked out again day by day." And she hurries back to the car. In a way, she has already said everything. Merkel clearly sees the dilemma of Western politics. Far-sightedness is not in demand in the media but quick reactions to every little thing, at home or in the world. Even she, probably the most powerful politician in the world, cannot change that.

Finally, the car takes us to a start-up. iCarbonX, which deals with health care, is located in an inconspicuous prefabricated building in the middle of the city. Right next to it, laundry is still blowing on the balconies in one of those workers' dormitories that used to be everywhere. Merkel is met by company founder Wang Jun, in a black T-shirt and a gray suit. He speaks English fluently and gives the chancellor a tour of his company. "Merkel told me that she has never seen software like this," he says afterwards. Software that knows exactly what's going on in our bodies at any given moment. With the help of DNA, saliva, blood, and urine samples, the 41-year-old wants to create an individual digital map of his customers' bodies that provides information about their current state of health and sounds the alarm in the event of impending illnesses. To collect the necessary data, iCarbonX has set up "collection points" in four major Chinese cities and is cooperating with fitness clubs and clinics. In the long term, however, the information is to be collected via smart devices in the home. The toilet will then analyze urine, the toothbrush saliva, and the bathroom mirror will scan the condition of the skin with the help of a 3-D camera. Environmental measurements such as air quality and factors such as exercise and diet will add to the overall picture. "I'm trying to build a crystal ball," says Wang, a biologist and computer specialist. The crystal ball, a vast treasure trove of data from potentially millions of users, is valuable not only to the users themselves to provide early warning but also to iCarbonX who is considering partnerships with insurers and government agencies, which puts Wang's ideas in a different light. Software that makes people less likely to get sick and at the same time realizes his dream. What do you do with all this information? And am I also taking part in this? That's a big moral question, and there's a lot of money behind it.

Investors have already given the company a thumbs-up. Internet giant Tencent is one of the most prominent backers of the biotech company, which is now one of three Chinese health unicorns with a valuation of over one billion US dollars. No other start-up in China has been valued at such a high sum so quickly — just six months after its founding.

Wang first made headlines when he ordered 128 DNA sequencing machines for his BGI research center in 2010, at a cost of $1.58 billion, giving him more sequencing capacity than all U.S. universities, research institutions, and companies combined. Wang wanted China to make its contribution to deciphering the genome. The fact that he was supported by the Bill & Melinda Gates Foundation, among others, did not meet with universal approval in the U.S. When BGI bought the American equipment and software manufacturer Genomics two years later, the most important American competitor Illumina tried to prevent this with a counteroffer. When this failed, Illumina filed a complaint with the Committee on Foreign Investment in the United States (CFIUS). The complaint was rejected. The foreign investment control authority in the United States simply could not imagine that China would be competitive in the foreseeable future. However, this happened faster than expected.

Wang's team was instrumental in the genome development of the first Asian, the rice plant, the giant panda, SARS disease, and also the silkworm, the pig, and the chicken. It's all there somewhere in the documents preparing for her visit. Wang would certainly be someone with whom Merkel could easily spend two hours discussing the risks and benefits and how the different attitudes of Germany and China could converge. But there is no time for that.

Merkel's short visit to Shenzhen also tells us about the constraints she is under. With Brexit, Trump, French President Emmanuel Macron, and even the new old coalition, Merkel's world has become more complicated and her own position weaker. Instead of being able to talk in detail with Wang about future technologies, which would also have been good for Germany as a business location, she had to rebalance the Sino-German relationship in Beijing beforehand — without being allowed to let domestic politics out of her sight for even a moment. She talked turkey in Beijing but also found conciliatory words. She recognized China as a new partner with whom she now has a greater political overlap on climate change, Iran, and free trade than with the United States. But all of it without snubbing Washington and its partners in the EU too much. She has lobbied for the departure from China of the widow of dissident Liu Xiaobo, who died in prison in July, but also for relief for German industry. It must carefully balance the complex international situation and always ensure that it remains socially acceptable in domestic politics. What moves her is none of the public's business. "They were shocked at the speed of development and how much data we were collecting in large quantities," Wang recalls.

We must not allow ourselves to be forced to set the pace but must stick to sustainable, ethically based technological development. But the further behind we are in artificial intelligence, the less we can have a say in matters of ethics. I remember a quote from Professor Peter Bofinger, one of the five economic experts in Germany, "I'm not so much afraid of the artificial intelligence machines but of the Chinese. We have to be careful that they don't take the butter off our bread." He uttered this sentence at an event marking the 75th birthday of the great Hamburg entrepreneur Michael Otto, which was about future values.

I also remember Lee Kai-Fu saying, "The countries that lead in AI have the strategic advantage of being able to write the rules of the game for the next world order." Lee knows what he's talking about. The Taiwanese Columbia graduate worked for Apple, Microsoft, and Google before starting his own business, Sinovation Ventures, and the Sinovation Ventures Artificial Intelligence Institute in Beijing. The U.S. is still the technological leader, he said. But the chances of China taking over are already "50-50," Lee says. For him, it is clear that the West will only be heard in the future if it still plays a role in global competition technologically.

Many politicians — Merkel is not one of them — and also many voters still seem to believe that the West is a moral authority *per se* that would be listened to in any case. More than a decade ago, the Singaporean philosopher and ex-diplomat Kishore Mahbubani summed up this arrogance in a catchy book titled *The West and the Rest*.

In fact, our overconfidence leads us to envision the new world only in the parts we want to see. If we now pillory Facebook and Google & Co. in Europe, we are convinced that we are opposing the Americans' impositions out of a moral sensibility. When Beijing did exactly this years ago, we were happy to assume that Chinese politicians were only interested in protecting their own market by shouting "Censorship!". We make it a little easy for ourselves if we think we are morally right per se and the others are cynical. We, too, want to protect our market, and the Chinese don't want to be infiltrated by the Americans. Basically, Europeans and Chinese both think it is not wise to reveal the innermost to the Americans. It just took the Europeans much longer to understand this.

The American Internet giants have been locked out of China for over 15 years. But they can always be reached via a VPN channel that can be installed at little cost. While we criticize censorship, the Chinese, and not the Europeans, have managed to establish serious competitors to Facebook, WhatsApp and Co. It is thanks to them that we now have duopolies instead of monopolies. Why haven't the Europeans managed anything comparable? Why haven't we developed platforms that correspond to our values? Why did we allow ourselves to be overrun by the Americans out of a misconceived liberalism? I don't even want to think about it anymore.

How powerful China has become is convincingly obvious. The supposedly omnipotent Apple, Facebook, and Google CEOs' behavior toward China is a reminder of this. For example, in July 2017, Apple was told by Beijing to remove VPN providers from the Apple app stores. CEO Tim Cook complied with that request. China is the largest market for Apple's iPhones after the United States. Apple makes around 20 percent of its profits here and most iPhones are also manufactured cheaply in China. Did Cook show disgruntlement at this intervention by Beijing? Was he complaining about censorship? On the contrary, in December 2017, he traveled for the first time to China's fourth World Internet Conference in Wuzhen, near Shanghai. In previous years, the state-dominated conference had made do without Western Internet celebrities. The powerful Cook also held the Keynote Speech. He spoke fourth, after Wang Huning, the Communist Party's ideology chief; Huang Kunming, the party's propaganda chief; and Che Jun, the party secretary of Zhejiang province, where the event was held. "The theme of the conference — developing a digital economy of openness and shared benefits — is a vision that Apple supports," Cook began his remarks. "We're proud to have worked with many of our partners in China to build a community that participates in a shared future in cyberspace."

These first two stilted sentences alone testify to his difficulty in finding the right tone. After all, the state also called for increased censorship at the conference. Did Tim Cook make himself a willing helper of the Chinese communists? Many in the West see it that way. "Cook has crossed a red line," wrote *The New York Times*. And this red line shows how powerful China already is technologically, otherwise Cook's business pragmatism would not have forced him to relent. Ignoring it no longer works nor does flexing ones' muscles. Cook must take the difficult path: Change through rapprochement.

"I've never been one for talking only to people with whom I agree 100 percent," Cook said flatly on the sidelines of the conference. "I don't see the world that way." His chain of reasoning works like this, "I try to find areas where you can collaborate. In the areas where there is no agreement, I try to understand why they disagree. And if I get criticized for it, so be it," he elaborated elsewhere. "When you go to a country, you have to follow the laws there. Those are not always the laws you would want. As an American, freedom is very important to me. You have a choice. Do you participate or do you stand on the sidelines and yell at how things are supposed to be. My belief is that you have to get involved, you have to get in the arena because you don't get anything changed from the sidelines."

The constraints under which one of the most powerful American companies now finds itself cannot be made any clearer. China and Apple are already too intertwined. "China has about two million developers working for the iOS app store. They are among the most advanced in the world. But what's the biggest attraction for us is the commitment of the people and the way they produce the iPhone." Not to mention the price.

Facebook CEO Mark Zuckerberg is also feeling the pressure and reacting accordingly. Despite high smog levels, Zuckerberg jogged past Mao's giant portrait across Beijing's Tiananmen Square in good spirits in May 2016. Photos of it were shared millions of times among Chinese Internet users. He later met Beijing's then propaganda chief Liu Yunshan as well as Alibaba chief Jack Ma, the pop star of the Chinese IT world. State media reported favorably on Zuckerberg, who is married to a Chinese-born woman. He is learning Chinese and has given his daughter the Chinese name Mingyu. And he has already become the most popular and well-known foreign corporate leader in China. Almost a quarter of the world's population — 2.02 billion people — has a Facebook account. Yet he can no longer ignore the 1.4 billion Chinese people and their technological developments. He knows full well that Chinese competitors like WeChat are more likely to conquer the world than Facebook being allowed in China. The fact that this will not happen under fair market conditions is secondary. We are already allowing the Chinese versions of social media in the West because they are being used by people who have a lot of money and are our customers.

The only choice Zuckerberg has now is to think about how it can be useful to the Chinese. Facebook is no longer just the world's largest social network; like Google, the Internet company has long been active in dozens of other business fields. Many Chinese Internet companies, above all Jack Ma's online retailer Alibaba, want to grow abroad in the future. Facebook could be their cooperation partner. That would help China's companies and at the same time make Facebook even more powerful. At least temporarily.

Google initially took a different route. The search engine stopped all further activities in China after it was officially banned there in 2010. Even under censorship, Google "would have been able to offer many valuable services to Chinese users," according to the renowned American monthly magazine *FastCompany*. "Leaving the market was a double loss, both for Internet users as well as for Google."

In the meantime, Google CEO Sundar Pichai has bowed to the power relations and has also decided to approach China. Pichai was also present for the first time at the Internet conference in Wuzhen. While Cook was still speaking to packed crowds, Pichai ended up giving his speech to an almost empty room. It will probably be a while before he is welcomed with open arms. Pichai is not deterred by this. After Beijing and Shanghai, Google has now opened an office in Shenzhen, the hometown of Tencent and Huawei. And in 2017, Google bought a large stake in Taiwanese smartphone manufacturer HTC, which is also very successful in China, for $1.1 billion.

Then, in August 2018, *The New York Times* reported that Google would launch a search engine in China that would do the work of Chinese censors. Activists and human rights activists reacted indignantly and spoke of a "black day for internet freedom." The search engine, named Dragonfly, will be able to access blocked websites in China and respond to search queries for content related to human rights, democracy, religion, or peaceful protests. If such pages became available, that would be a fundamental intervention on the one hand, but on the other hand, it would undermine China's strict censorship regulations. Google began the Dragonfly project in spring 2017 and has accelerated it since a meeting between the company's CEO Sundar Pichai and a senior Chinese official in December, writes the US portal *The Intercept,* citing internal company documents and informants. The search engine has already been demonstrated to Chinese government officials. If Beijing gives the go-ahead, Google could launch the app for Chinese users within the next six to nine months. Nevertheless, *The New York Times* also reported that there is internal resistance to the project at Google. Who will prevail in the end is unclear. "Google wanted to change China, and now China has changed Google," writes the *Financial Times*.

Will Google, Facebook, and Apple be able to maintain their position? Probably not. At best, they can delay their decline in power. At least they are trying to get out what is still possible. Now, we Europeans are fighting with Google and Facebook. We may yet long for the times when our data were in the hands of a few powerful private companies and not in the hands of a powerful state. There is one thing we should have no illusions about and that is that in China, there is a lot of new stuff being invented at the moment. The Chinese state is creating a particularly large amount of freedom for innovations that can be used to control people better. One of these companies is Face++, which I mentioned earlier.

Face++ is allowed to work with the facial scans that the Department of Public Safety stores to identify its nearly 1.4 million citizens. Already there are special glasses for police officers that are being tested for everyday use. A program, with a list of people wanted by the police, automatically runs people in the police officer's field of vision and alerts when there is a match.

Just how far control can go is shown by the government's plans to introduce a "social credit point system" for China. It is intended to monitor the "law-abidingness, moral conduct, social commitment, activities in the public interest, and environmental protection behavior" of each individual citizen. It will be controlled by data filtered with the help of artificial intelligence. Orwell sends his regards.

However, a closer look shows that there are positive and negative controls in China, even from our point of view. This makes the evaluation of the advantages and disadvantages of this technology much more complex than it appears at first glance, as the following examples show: The fact that the state uses cameras to ensure, as completely as possible, that road users obey the rules is reasonable. It is annoying, but understandable, that you have to hand in your driver's license if you exceed a certain number of points. This is also the case in Germany with the Flensburg traffic offender register. The difference is that our checks are carried out on a selective basis and do not cover the whole country. In China, cameras are already used to record the average speed between two points on the most important roads — for every car. If the speed is too high, penalty points are awarded. The positive consequence is that no one speeds any more. More about the negative consequences in a moment.

When you borrow money via cell phone in China, a check computer can check a person's creditworthiness in a matter of seconds. This is a further development of our Schufa (Germany's credit investigation company), which helps us to avoid excesses, such as the real estate crisis in the USA in 2008, when a series of loans collapsed.

An app called "Honest Shanghai" is being tested in Shanghai. It calls up around 5,000 individual details from 100 offices and authorities and then creates a profile that is evaluated with categories. These range from "socially exemplary" to "asocial." The app, which is currently only being tested with volunteers, also scans the user's face.

The fact that the Chinese state can use facial recognition to check whether someone is polluting the environment or simply leaving living space empty may still seem sensible. But how far will this control go? And what penalties are to be feared in the event of a violation? Today, it is already possible to monitor what people order to eat in a restaurant or via a delivery service. Would people who eat unhealthily have their points deducted and possibly have to pay more for their health insurance? Would that make sense because a vegan doesn't want to pay for the glutton's illnesses? Or would this be too great an invasion of privacy?

Does it make sense to punish sons and daughters who do not take care of their parents? Does that then fall into the category of " asocial"? Or is it part of our freedom of choice not to take care of our parents and have the state pay for it?

What about political opinions? Are they also sanctioned if they are not liked? Allegedly, critical — or as it is called in Beijing: "inappropriate" — statements on Tencent's short message app WeChat, which has around 800 million users, are to be punished in the credit rating system with a point deduction. Even political statements by Western NGO employees are to be rated according to a point system.

Chinese media also reported, for example, about a man who worked as a tour guide without a valid certificate and was therefore not allowed to register his child at the nearest elementary school. This is also not okay. Many Chinese would agree with us on this issue. This happened in Zhejiang province, where Alibaba is based in Hangzhou, the capital. There, every citizen's score is open to every Internet user on state websites.

And then there was a restaurant owner named Ye, who had no license and was therefore no longer allowed to get bank loans or credit cards, buy an apartment, a car or airline tickets, or travel abroad. We don't know whether this will become the rule or whether these are just isolated cases where the local government has gone overboard.

Cases like these are commented on in detail and in a very differentiated way on the Chinese network, without the censors intervening. There is no trace of naive belief in progress in these contributions. In China, too, no one wants such cases to be decided by the artificial intelligence of a machine. And in China, too, the state will have to respond to public pressure. The state cannot get away with everything, and this is precisely where the people's negotiating leeway begins, where the Chinese have the chance to push through their ideas.

The Chinese must decide for themselves what they find moral and what they find immoral. They also have to decide for themselves what they will and will not let their state get away with. The fact that the "Honest Shanghai" app is not yet in everyday use shows that Beijing has to show a sure instinct. Even if the thrust is clear, the Chinese state wants to evaluate the data traces of its citizens and, if necessary, force them to behave better in the future. The state wants to determine what is good and what is bad behavior. And it will go further than seems acceptable to us in the West.

The fact that Beijing can do this is the new freedom China has as a technology leader. Its influence on the rules of the world game is growing every year. An influence that the West has had for centuries, which we have enjoyed to the hilt and which we are now recklessly squandering.

# Chapter 3

# The New Car: Autonomous Dissenters

## How China Is Revolutionizing the Auto Industry and Threatening the Mighty German Manufacturers

*The robot car will come, but it doesn't fit into the German car culture.*

Karl-Thomas Neumann, CEO of the start-up
Evelozcity and ex-Opel boss

If only Nicolas Hayek was still alive to see this, this bearded little enigma with sparkling eyes, Swiss of Lebanese origin. But the legendary inventor of the Smart car has been dead for a decade. He wanted to build a car like a Swatch watch. Cheap, reliable, and chic. An electric car with few parts. A new Volkswagen, so to speak. That was at the end of the 1980s. At that time, he was 60 years old and had already saved the Swiss watch industry. Hayek knew that he needed a partner for his project. He was a watch man, not a car man. So, he went to Volkswagen in Wolfsburg and convinced brand manager Daniel Goeudevert of his idea. Goeudevert, too, is a lateral thinker and ahead of his time. Like Hayek, he enjoys trying out new things. He wrote books with titles such as *Like a Bird in an Aquarium* or *The Horizon Has Wings*.

But none of this fit in with Ferdinand Piëch, then Chairman of the Board of Management of Volkswagen AG. He is also incredibly innovative, but only in the context of the classic car; he wants ever more sophisticated technology in ever larger cars. In this concept, he is one of the best in the world. Piëch has little use for the disruptive ideas of Hayek and Goeudevert. He dreams of the Phaeton, not the Smart. Even the name Phaeton suits him better. Phaeton is the name of the son of the sun god Helios. And that's what they used to call open, stately horse-drawn carriages in which the ruler himself drove. Piëch doesn't just think he's smart. He thinks he's brilliant, and in a way he is. But anyone who wants to think "out of the box" is welcome to do so — outside his company. In 1993, Goeudevert had to leave. His thinking was too lateral for Piëch. And with him went the ideas of the irrepressible Hayek.

That was a quarter of a century ago and will perhaps go down in the history of the automotive industry as the year when Volkswagen made a crucial mistake. Historians will say that the Wolfsburg company should have taken a two-pronged approach to remain competitive in the first half of the 21st century. An inexpensive e-car on the one hand and the classic and technically sophisticated Polo on the other.

Hayek, however, is not one to give up. He moved on with his idea, moving to Daimler in 1994. The Stuttgart company turned it into a very small, yet very traditional car with a gasoline engine and a strangely jerky automatic transmission. In 1997, the Smart Car was presented. Hayek was bitterly disappointed. He got out of the car and said, "The gasoline-powered Smart Car is a product of Daimler-Benz and has nothing in common with the plans of the Swatch team."

A good 20 years later, the car Hayek dreamed of is finally on the market. It was largely developed by the Chinese. It is being built in Liuzhou, deep in the Guangxi province in southwestern China. It's only 300 kilometers from the Vietnamese border. Not exactly the navel of the world, not even in China. The two-seater is called the Baojun E100. In Spring 2018, it will be one of the hidden champions at the Beijing Auto Show, one of the most important car shows in the world. It is more colorful and cheekier than Daimler's Smart Car. What's more, you insert a tablet computer into a slot on the dashboard and off you go. The car is as short as the first Smart Car and has an extremely tight turning circle. That's important in the city. The cockpit is functional but not lacking, and it's fun. Unusual, but useful in China, is the labeling of the brake and gas pedal pedals with a big plus and minus so that even novice drivers know where to step.

Digital displays for the air conditioning have been dispensed with. No problem for the Chinese. The range is a good 150 kilometers. That is also enough for the city. The battery can be recharged overnight at any power outlet. The car has a speed of 100 kilometers per hour. The most attractive aspect, however, is the price: 4,800 euros, including government subsidies. For that you get an automatic transmission, antilock brakes, power steering, parking sensors, and a pedestrian warning system.

Daimler's E-Smart, on the other hand, costs 23,000 euros with the same range, but not with the same features. Even without government subsidies, the Chinese E100 would cost only half that. Daimler has another problem. Customers in Germany have to wait over a year for their E-Smart because Korean batteries are in short supply — Daimler was only able to deliver 3,000 Smarts in 2017. This is more than annoying, especially since customer demand in e-mobiles has increased domestically. In China, 5,500 units of the E100 were sold in December 2017 alone despite the fact that the car had only been launched on the market in August. Daimler can consider itself lucky that the Chinese are not interested in offering the E100 in the West, for the time being. The only question is for how long. Particularly bitter for the Germans, Shanghai-based automaker SAIC, Volkswagen's partner, developed the vehicle together with U.S. manufacturer General Motors. Volkswagen, on the other hand, did not have a single e-car on the market by the fall of 2018. And of the German competitors, not even *one* e-model makes it into the top 20 best-selling e-cars in China.

Of course, Daimler managers say that the two cars cannot be compared. They are talking about apples and pears. The workmanship, the attention to detail, the wiring harnesses of the air conditioning system, the gap dimensions ... in short the German thoroughness is still the yardstick of all things. Hayek would have smiled ironically at this opinion. The traditional Swiss watchmakers had come to him with similar arguments when he invented the Swatch. They too had turned up their noses when he only wanted to assist them. He was looking for a way to preserve their fascinating, unique capabilities, however, they resisted saying that electric quartz watches with displays instead of hands are beneath us. Nevertheless, Hayek developed the e-watch with the small battery further. Instead of 151 parts, it was to have only 51, shrink-wrapped in a molded plastic body that could be easily printed with the most colorful designs. The watch was to cost less than 80 Swiss Francs. No more. And it had to be so highly automated that it could be produced in Switzerland, where labor is expensive.

That was in 1983. A year later, Hayek had sold 800,000 watches. A decade later, it was more than 100 million. At the same time, however, he continued to develop luxury watches in the style of the art of Swiss watchmaking. Brands like Omega and Longines flourished under him. When Hayek died in 2010, he left behind the largest watch company in the world. Listed on the stock exchange with a turnover of over four billion euros and a return on sales of 15 percent.

There are astonishing parallels between the watchmakers back then and the carmakers today. The carmakers are determined not to launch any Swatch cars on the market, only Omega cars. The Swatch cars are now being built by the Chinese, according to their own rules. Regardless of whether the E100 prevails or, as is likely, is surpassed by another, even more sophisticated Chinese manufacturer, the Baojun and its siblings demonstrate how far the journey can go.

The German automotive industry is facing the greatest challenge since the founding of the Federal Republic of Germany. This is an economic sector that defines Germany's reputation in the world. Millions of German jobs depend directly or indirectly on it. Unfortunately, they depend almost exclusively on the traditional automotive industry. An industry that provides its customers with one of the best dealer and repair networks in the world but is attached to the combustion engine like a toddler to a pacifier. Nevertheless, this engine needs 10 times as many components as the electric motor. Comparing advantages to disadvantages, there are 10 times as many parts to be repaired.

It is an industry that not only builds the best cars in the world but also tends to overengineer, especially in the mid-range and small cars. It is an industry whose products are appreciated around the world, but for which fewer and fewer people are prepared to pay the price — especially in China, where there has long been a lack of viable alternatives. The German auto industry sells "Vorsprung durch Technik," which translates to "advance through technology," while more and more customers in Asia want advance through "interconnectivity and entertainment."

Germans do not yet have to worry about luxury class vehicles; these they will always be able to sell — Porsche, S-Class, A8, or BMW 7 Series. However, Chinese discernment is also becoming increasingly important in this segment, today, for example, every third S-Class goes to China.

Nevertheless, no one can hold a candle to the Germans in this class, not even the Japanese Lexus. The cars are not only technical masterpieces but also an expression of German passion. However, in the mid and lower segments, demand is getting tight. That's where the Chinese are now countering. "As a German engineer who worked for BMW for 20 years," says Carsten Breitfeld, now the head of Chinese e-car start-up Byton, "it pains me a tiny bit to say this — but the future of the automotive industry and mobility is being developed and shaped in China." The start-up is funded by Chinese companies such as Foxconn and Tencent. Foxconn makes the world's iPhones, and Tencent is a leading telecom equipment maker. Byton's trademark is a touchscreen on the dashboard that practically stretches from door to door — 1.25 meters wide.

Has Volkswagen recognized the signs of the times? At least the new VW CEO Herbert Diess has. In a *Handelsblatt* interview at the end of August 2018, he exposed himself as the first CEO of the major automakers saying he considers it quite realistic that German manufacturers will only win the race for new mobility with a probability of 50 percent. "We have to master the digital transformation if we want to survive." As for Germany not having its own batteries, Diess says, "I find it appalling that we have become so dependent." Germany has lost touch, he says.

If anyone can turn VW around, it's Diess. He is one of the good guys, the reformers in the auto industry. He already was at BMW, his former employer. But even for him, it's going to be damn hard.

It is little consolation that its German competitors are in no less serious trouble. The first fallacy — and here we are still a long way from autonomous driving: Diess and his colleagues believed that the Chinese would continue to drive German cars if only they were innovative enough. A look beyond Germany's borders would have proved them wrong. Most Americans drive American cars that can't hold a candle to most German vehicles. The majority of Japanese drive Japanese cars and the French drive French vehicles. Why should this be any different in China, of all places? Even though German premium brands are selling well, the market share of Chinese vehicles has grown steadily: 10 years ago, it was 30 percent; today, it is already 43 percent. This trend will continue to grow.

The Germans have lost sight of this because they are so successful in China. Volkswagen, for example, now generates almost 60 percent of its global profits in the Middle Kingdom. The Wolfsburg-based company is going from record to record. They were the most successful brand in China in 2017, selling 3.2 million vehicles. No other automotive market is more important. The downside of this success story is that the more successful they are, the more dependent they are on the Chinese market.

The incredible pressure on Volkswagen and others to be successful in the U.S. with "worse" diesel models has mainly to do with their dependence on the Chinese market. Managers were desperate to build up a counterweight to China in the USA. Their strategy was to offer particularly environmentally friendly vehicles. When this became technically more difficult than expected, they began to cheat with emissions — and were caught. The consequence for VW and the others is that they are now more dependent than ever on the Chinese market.

For BMW, with Mini and Rolls-Royce, Audi and Daimler with the Smart, China is the largest single market. The premium manufacturers each sell around 600,000 cars, with Audi still just ahead of BMW and Daimler in 2017, which achieved impressive growth of 26 percent in 2017. For lack of alternatives, the Germans had no choice but to focus on the Chinese market. Over the past 12 years, car sales in China have increased by more than 650 percent. In the EU, on the other hand, they fell by just under one percent. In the USA, they fell even further by 10 percent. India is not yet playing a role. Africa is just now taking off.

The problem is that despite the incredible success the Germans have had in the market in China, in 2013, it was 25 percent; now it is only 22 percent. In Wolfsburg, Munich, and Stuttgart, the hope is that it will still be possible to sell more cars every year despite the declining market share because the market as a whole is getting bigger. While only 80 cars are owned by 1000 Chinese, 553 vehicles are owned by 1000 Germans. That could actually give the Germans success for a while yet, however, relying on this is very risky. After all, the Chinese have no vested interest in the Germans playing a bigger role than necessary in the mass market.

Volkswagen is the first to feel the effects of this, the very company that was the first German automaker to venture into China more than 30 years ago. An extremely farsighted decision without guarantee of success. It is true that the two joint ventures with the Chinese manufacturers FAW and SAIC are Wolfsburg's most important revenue generators. They now sell every second car in China. In the meantime, however, the Chinese apprentices have become self-confident corporate managers who generate billions in sales with their own brands. Just a few years ago, all Chinese brands had a market share of less than 20 percent in their home country. In 2017, they already accounted for 43.9 percent. In the growth segment of particularly popular SUVs, they even achieved a market share of over 60 percent.

This is evident from SAIC's steep success curve. The Shanghai-based company, which also works closely with General Motors (GM), is China's largest automaker by volume. In May 2018, the group announced plans to build its fourth dedicated plant in the southeastern province of Fujian. The factory is expected to produce up to 240,000 cars a year under the GM and Roewe private brands — including for Southeast Asia. Incidentally, the two SAIC brands were formerly British and belonged to the MG Rover Group, in which SAIC acquired a stake in 2005 for just under 300 million euros.

SAIC took over 70 percent majority when the British were virtually broke. The English factory in Longbridge, which had been producing since 1905, was closed in 2016. Meanwhile, the new models produced in China have scored points with internationally competitive designs and unbeatable prices. If all goes according to plan, SAIC will sell more cars with its own brands in 2018 than Audi, Mercedes, and BMW each did on their own — a historic step for China's auto industry. It will be a while before it can match VW in terms of volume, but it will happen sooner than we think. The Group sold a proud 3.18 million cars in China in 2017. Volkswagen is still growing at 5.4 percent.

Apple experienced what it feels like to be top dog in China; for a long time, iPhones were the lonely leader in China's cell phone market. In the meantime, they have slipped to fourth place in terms of market share. Three Chinese manufacturers are ahead of the Americans, namely Huawei, Vivo, and Oppo. In 2018, the iPhone will probably also lose its fourth place in China. And in terms of global performance, Huawei overtook Apple in the quantity of smartphones sold for the first time in the second quarter of 2018.

Just as in the smartphone market, the same is very likely to happen in the automotive industry — with the difference that the Germans will not earn as much as Apple as their market share declines. This is because VW, for example, has long since ceased to be the international leader in terms of margins. The government will ensure that the Chinese become stronger and stronger in their own market and so will consumers. Beijing has the power to do this. China has been able to dictate the rules of the game in the Chinese market since the beginning of the 1980s, when the country was opened up. The foreign manufacturers were willing to go along with this because the new market was so large and important. Beijing forced foreigners to manufacture cars in China if they wanted to sell cars in China. Beijing determined that the cars could only be produced in Western Chinese countries. Joint ventures may be built, however these are with companies in which foreigners are not to have a majority, under any circumstance. Beijing forced foreign automakers to produce more and more parts locally and to use Chinese suppliers to do so. It also forced foreign groups to develop local brands with their Chinese partners. Some manufacturers, such as Volkswagen, even felt compelled to serve the entire Asian market out of China, even though they only earn 50 percent from it and not 100, as would be the case if they did it out of Germany. And they will invent rules of the game for the first foreign companies to be allowed to build cars in China without joint venture partners.

The Japanese, Korean, French, German, and American automakers have gone along with all of this. No one wanted to miss out on the opportunities in this huge growth market. No matter what the cost. And for most of them, it was worth it. But success is deceptive. For one thing, it was bought with time because it took the Chinese a long time to realize that they had no chance of competing against the Germans in traditional vehicle construction. The German engineers were simply too good, their production managers too experienced, and their foremen too smart.

Now, however, as the age of e-cars emerges, suddenly there are opportunities. In China, electricity is cheap. The air is polluted, the cities are congested, and, above all, people are much more open to new technologies than in the West. The state, and also the car managers, sees the opportunity to help with the next stage of development in the automotive industry. "Only if we develop vehicles with alternative energies will we manage to go from being a great car country to a powerful center of the auto industry," President Xi Jinping recognized back in 2014. It came as it inevitably had to. In 2017 there were already 777,000 new e-vehicles on China's roads, hardly any of which had been built by the old Western car giants. Their market share is less than 1 percent. Foreigners, especially the Germans, completely underestimated when and with what force the topic of electromobility would hit China. They had probably expected development to be as sluggish as in the USA, where only just under 200,000 e-cars were sold in 2107. In Germany, the figure was just 55,000. Even in Norway, there were more e-cars registered — and there are just under five million people living there.

The market has changed dramatically: in 2016, in China, sales of cars with internal combustion engines were still up by 15 percent. In 2017, the figure was only 1.4 percent. At the same time, however, 70 percent more e-cars were sold. China is already by far the largest e-car market in the world. BYD, the largest private manufacturer, already has nine e-models on offer. However, most e-cars are sold by a state-owned company that has also been smiled at for a long time: the Beijing manufacturer BAIC, a state-owned partner of Daimler. Since Western manufacturers refuse to become progressive, Beijing has tightened the thumbscrews. To the complete surprise of Western car managers, the government in Beijing announced a quota for pure electric cars and plug-in hybrids.

A quota that will increase in years to come. From 2019, carmakers in China are to convert at least 10 percent of their production to e-cars. One year later, this figure will rise to 12 percent. And by 2025, 25 percent of all vehicles sold in China are to be e-cars. That is a major challenge. If a company fails to meet its quota, it must buy points from more successful companies as part of a program. Conversely, those who exceed their target receive money from those who have not reached their target. This is a good solution that generates pressure and boosts competition.

Originally, the government wanted to introduce the quota system as early as 2018. The panicked foreign manufacturers were just able to prevent this. In the Summer of 2017, Chancellor Merkel had to put in a good word for the lagging German industry with President Xi: "I can only hope that, especially in view of the Asian markets, the German automotive industry will not lose touch," she said afterwards in unusually clear terms, long before the carmakers' executive boards put it that way.

The fact that it is losing out is not only due to the automotive industry itself but also due to the lack of a German industrial policy for electric cars. Now the Chinese are also making industrial policy for Germany. We have to let the Chinese set the pace for us. And to make sure that it is not too easy for foreigners to catch up, electric cars in China are subsidized by the state. For every e-car that can travel 150 kilometers, the state gives the equivalent of around 6500 euros. Unfortunately, only the Chinese brands benefit from the subsidies.

The chances of the Chinese taking the lead in an industry that is central to the global economy have never been greater. "The rule for electromobility is that whoever is the first to sell large numbers of units wins," said former Audi CEO Rupert Stadler soberly in early Summer 2018, disappearing into custody. The key drivers of this new technology push are electric motors, power electronics, and batteries. They account for a quarter of the cost of a car. Unfortunately the Germans specialize in combustion engines and transmissions. It's not that they haven't tried something now and then. Daimler tried Evonik in Germany. But the combustion engine faction in the company put the brakes on where it could. In 2015, Daimler CEO Dieter Zetsche dropped out. The automotive supplier Bosch tried Samsung. The Koreans knew batteries. The Stuttgart-based company knew power engineering and battery management. But Bosch was too late, and the Koreans were already too powerful. A win-win situation could no longer be created. The rest is history. The South Koreans are now the world leaders. Bosch is empty-handed in this segment. In the meantime, Bosch's boss Volkmar Denner feels that the gap between Bosch and the South Koreans and the Chinese is too big to risk it again.

This power struggle is over for Germany. The Germans have been eliminated in the intermediate round — South Korea and China are in the final. They are fighting fiercely for supremacy and the German automakers are in danger of being pulverized in the process. Because Volkswagen and Co. don't need to arrive in China with Korean batteries. Cars that run on Korean batteries will be at such a disadvantage that they will no longer be competitive. The 200 million euro new production of the Vizzion e-car cannot be started. Wolfsburg had signed with LG before Beijing closed the market to South Korean batteries. Now VW won't get permission to operate the factory. South Korean manufacturer LG Chem should soon control two-thirds of the market, and Beijing wants to prevent that with all its might — so it is unceremoniously changing the rules of the game as it goes. That's not fair, but so what?

Since July 1, 2018, vehicles with South Korean batteries are no longer on the list of vehicles sanctioned by the Chinese government. In retrospect, was it naïve to think that it would be possible to compete in China with the competitor's batteries? Not even that. However, this issue shows very precisely what power the Chinese have. Now the new rule is that you can't compete with the Chinese market leader Contemporary Amperex Technology Ltd (CATL). CATL has to work, even if its batteries are not yet quite as powerful.

The Germans are finally realizing that the race for the company's favor has long since begun. BMW is the fastest. In July 2018, they tie themselves closely to CATL. The German–Chinese joint venture BMW Brilliance buys a development department from CATL for around 100 million euros, which is to develop special batteries for the Munich-based company. BMW is paying almost 360 million euros up front for a long-term supply contract involving batteries worth a total of 4.7 billion euros. This opens up opportunities for BMW, while at the same time placing the Munich-based company in a position of enormous dependency.

After all, CATL is also investing in Germany. For the Chinese, this is a milestone in their industrial history. China is supplying us with a high-tech product that is central to a key German industry because we can't get it right. For 240 million euros, a plant is to be built in Thuringia by 2022 with around 600 jobs. It will be the first Chinese battery plant in Europe. BMW is already a committed customer, and Daimler is still considering. That's good for Thuringia, but it's actually a huge blow for Germany as a whole. "Can it work if we, as a continent that manufactures cars, have to buy battery cells from Asia?" asked Angela Merkel pointedly. And immediately gave the answer, "We must not give up such key industries." For once, the chancellor agrees with IG Metall head Jörg Hofmann, "The cell is the piston of tomorrow."

Precisely because we have long since lost this important key. It is no longer a question of whether we let the Chinese in or not. We have to let them in — or put our ambitions in terms of e-mobility on the back burner. Volkswagen and Audi are currently still relying on the Koreans, who have factories in Eastern Europe. In the long term, however, they will have to diversify.

BMW, at any rate, can be accused of not having developed anything themselves, but not that they didn't back the right horse early enough. In 2012, CATL, as a start-up, was already allowed to supply batteries for the Zinoro manufactured by BMW and Brilliance. CATL boss Robin Zeng made a great effort to adapt the quality to BMW's wishes. This went down well in Munich. "We learned a lot from BMW," says Zeng. "The high standards and requirements have helped us grow quickly." In Europe, BMW has also worked with Samsung, and that's not expected to change. Better safe than sorry.

The battery lapse should be a lesson to German industry; what is available and what is not is no longer decided in Germany or even in the West. Those times are over. And if CATL should ever fail to meet demand quickly enough, then everyone will know that it's "China first"; the rest of the world will be served only after all Chinese manufacturers are supplied with batteries.

The foreigners can now only hope for the next technological leap. This is probably the solid-state battery, an area in which at least the Americans are still relatively strong. The advantages of the solid-state battery are less weight and shorter charging times. This technology could dispense with cobalt and concentrate on lithium. That would already be an advantage over China. That's because Chinese companies refine about

77 percent of the world's cobalt deposits into battery-grade chemicals. China Molybdenum is the world's second-largest cobalt producer, after the British–Swiss conglomerate Glencore. It has a market value of $24 billion after buying a majority stake in the Tenke Fungurume mine in the Democratic Republic of Congo in 2016. 65 percent of the world's cobalt deposits are there. Here you get a small glimmer of how important it is to have a presence in Africa (more on this in Chapter 9).

Solid-state batteries could eliminate the need for cobalt and at the same time give China a run for its money. Unfortunately, Beijing has also long had its eye on the lithium market. In May 2018, China sought to buy a good third of Chile's SQM lithium mine. When the Chileans hesitated to approve the $4.3 billion U.S. dollar deal, Chinese Ambassador to Chile Xu Bu openly warned, "This could have a negative impact on the development of economic relations between the two countries." Chilean President Sebastián Piñera relented. China, itself the world's fourth-largest producer, has since controlled 70 percent of the global lithium market.

However, the switch to a technology in which the Chinese are leaders and have control over the corresponding mineral resources is not the only problem that the German auto industry has with China. After all, the idiosyncratic — one could also say self-confident — wishes of Chinese customers will completely change the traditional Western car — first in the lower and middle segments, i.e., where Volkswagen in particular must defend its position.

While we still grew up with the car quartet (and buy cars according to these criteria), where everything revolved around horsepower, displacement, cylinders, and top speed, Chinese customers are much less interested in this. Technology that they can't see and can't use in traffic jams isn't exciting: the two-liter engine with 4-wheel drive, a maximum of 400 Nm distributed variably to the front and rear wheels? They don't care. They also don't care if the diesel engine is powerful but not very vivacious. It also doesn't matter with whom the VW Polo shares the MQB-A0 platform.

For Chinese customers cars are like Swatch watches, it's all about "look & feel," as they say in the fashion industry. The cars have to look cool, be inexpensive, and work. Why they work and what happens under the hood, if there still is one, is irrelevant. Touchscreen is far more important than engine capacity and the music system connected to the mains is more important than the crumple zone in a traffic jam. A VW Polo or a

Mercedes A-Class fit less and less into this model. Too much technology for too much money. Too conservative. The Chinese want compact, agile cars for city traffic. German cars, however, are getting bigger and bigger. Even BMW's new Minis now look like they've been taking steroids. These Minis are little in common with the first generation that German designer Gert Hildebrand once created for BMW. Hildebrand now designs for Chinese manufacturers.

But the big break in the appearance and function of cars will only come with autonomous driving. In this respect, Hayek's smart dreams were only a prelude to the revolution of the old automobile. And it's no surprise that Beijing already has a plan for this. By 2022, the first cars that can drive partially or completely without human intervention are to be in everyday operation. Between 2026 and 2030, automated driving should already be widespread. The first cities in the world where autonomous driving will be commonplace will be Chinese cities; this much already seems certain. And it will bring a better quality of life for the people there. They will be transported inexpensively and individually in a vehicle directly to their destination without having to drive themselves.

At present, the technology still has teething problems, but the Chinese also deal with this differently than we do. This becomes clear when you look at their reaction to the first fatality. In Spring 2018, an autonomously driving Volvo from Uber ran over a woman named Elaine Herzberg in Arizona in the evening. Uber then stopped all of its test drives to investigate the case. In Europe, the first fatality is seen as confirmation that autonomous driving is the devil's work. Even before the first fatal accident, the vast majority in Germany rejected self-driving cars even when experts deemed them safe.

In China, it's a different story. Under the same circumstances, 81 percent of respondents would be enthusiastic about it. That was the result of a survey published a few months earlier by the consulting firm Deloitte. This accident was tragic, said the Chinese *Global Times*, but aren't thousands of people run over every day by cars driven by humans? Isn't it still very likely that the machine is more reliable than the human? In airplanes, where the risk of accidents with many fatalities is much greater, autonomous flying has long been relied on.

That doesn't mean Beijing is lax when it comes to risks. The rules of the game for test drives on open roads are strict. Only two companies will be allowed to test their vehicles on 30 roads totaling 100 kilometers in

Beijing and Shanghai in Spring 2018: only Shanghai state-owned SAIC and small start-up NIO. NIO's Autopilot is considered at least as good as Tesla's. The Shanghai-based manufacturer, which has large development offices in Silicon Valley and Munich, has developed the EP 9, the world's fastest e-car to date. In the Valley alone, 500 people work for NIO. Their boss is Yellepeddi Padmasree. She was born and raised in India and studied in her home country and at Cornell in the United States. *Fortune Magazine* has long ranked the former Cisco chief technology officer among the world's most influential women. "In the next few years, the car will change dramatically," says Padmasree, whom I met in her head office. "It will be more of an intelligent robot than a mechanical device. It will be more of a service device than a product. It will be a rolling battery, a node on the Internet." Getting the new cars on the road, "is easiest in China."

Karl-Thomas Neumann agrees. He was head of research at VW and then head of automotive supplier Continental. Back at Volkswagen, he was group representative for electric vehicles and then VW's head of China for three years before becoming CEO of Opel. After Opel was sold by General Motors to the French manufacturer PSA for 1.3 billion euros, Neumann got out. Now, he is where the lateral thinker has actually always belonged: He is a Board member at Evelozcity, a start-up in Los Angeles co-financed by the Chinese. "The traditional auto industry is facing insane challenges," Neumann says. There are four megatrends that can be summed up in the word CASE, he says: C for Connected, A for Autonomous Driving, S for Sharing, and E for Electric. Neumann sees the biggest problem in this regard, not surprisingly, in Europe: "What the German auto industry is trying to do is build an e-SUV that can drive 500 kilometers and the battery can be recharged very quickly." But that's very expensive, he says, and customers have no desire to pay more money for an e-car than for their gasoline car: "That's how this incredible pressure has come about."

"But don't the politicians also say that everything should remain just as it is, only electric," I ask.

"Of course, you can't do that," counters the manager "That's a huge mistake. If the German auto industry continues like this, the Internet companies will win the race." They could play up completely unencumbered. The battle is actually already lost, he says, "because Audi, Mercedes, and BMW drivers in China would rather use their Baidu navi in their smartphones than the navigation in their cars." They are simply better.

"And what if they team up with Baidu?" I ask.

"Then Baidu is still in the driver's seat because they control the most valuable thing, which is the data," Neumann responds. Building traditional e-cars is a simple task compared to connecting them, he says. "We have to reinvent the car," Neumann urges. The days of "owning a car, financing it, insuring it, keeping it in the garage, and washing it on Saturdays are coming to an end faster than you think." It makes much more sense, he said, to share your car with others. "A city car that I only drive relatively slowly needs much less fuel, technology, and a smaller battery than a car used to travel 500 kilometers over land. Alternatively, I then use the subway, the high-speed train, or the e-scooter. But the traditional car manufacturers hate the thought that this could happen," Neumann sums it up. "Because that means fewer and very different cars are needed."

"But isn't that reaching a little too far into the future?" I object, "especially with regard to Germans in rural areas?" — "Yes, it is," Neumann replies with a grin. "But new trends don't emerge in rural areas." For that, he says, you have to look to Berlin or even China. There, he says, are still comparatively few people who own a car, and yet the cities are totally congested. "Everyone realizes on their own that things can't go on like this," says Neumann. And the traditional bond with the car is not as strong in China as it is here.

"But isn't the car also a status symbol for the Chinese?" I want to know. "Is it so great if I can only move at walking speed with my status symbol?" Neumann asks and provides the answer right afterwards, "No. The new status symbol is that I can fall back on the right vehicle for any situation with the help of clever sharing concepts." The Chinese have become progressive out of necessity, says Neumann. "And the traditional car countries will be forced to follow suit." For us, it's time to say goodbye to the old car, which ultimately still functions just like the good old carriage-horsepower in front, the driver, the passengers behind and luggage in the very back.

In Neumann's start-up, the engineers have long been working on the "Carriage of the future." "We've developed a kind of e-skateboard, like the ones you see everywhere on the beach promenade, only in car size. We are completely free in our choice of bodywork and design, a metal frame, lots of plastic, and plenty of room for new ideas," he explains. The driver is to sit as far forward as possible, and then there will be space inside "like in a full-size SUV, and that's with a car the size of a Golf. A small truck could also be designed on the same platform.

"Where do you build these cars?" I ask.

"We have contract manufacturers in China and the USA who do that for us. We specialize in mobility experiences, not production. We don't want that. We don't need that, and we can't do that."

"How well prepared are we in Germany for this development?" I want to know.

"Not at all! The innovations are coming from China and from here, the western United States. The robot car doesn't fit into German car culture," says Neumann. When people in Germany think of autonomous driving, they think of an S-Class in which you can fold away the steering wheel and read the newspaper. "The Chinese and the West Coast Americans, however, are focused on car robots. That's a completely different approach."

I ask whether Germany could not also take up this different approach. After all, we Germans still build the best cars in the world. "That's just the big trap we're in," Neumann replies. "We build the best cars in the world, but in an outdated business sector." What the Germans can do, fewer and fewer people around the world demand, he said. "We talk about all kinds of things in Germany, but not about what our future should look like. What we need to do to maintain our position in the world. Germany is far too little attuned to disruptive innovation, especially in new business models based on data. Though we have the basics, we still don't feel the competitive pressure."

"What should a company like VW be doing?" I ask.

"It's not my place to give advice to individual companies, I can only give you my impression," says Neumann, "I don't think it's possible to build traditional cars in the morning, constantly improve them in mass competition and under cost pressure, and then develop electric cars and radical new business models in the afternoon, where you have to completely rethink and make huge investments. Strictly speaking, you would then have to creatively destroy in the afternoon what you have refined in the morning! Something like that tears a company apart. That's why I also said at Opel — either or."

"Why didn't you go straight to China, where there is greater pressure to innovate? Because you can surf better in LA?" I ask. "No, that didn't play a role. We find that a car from California is even easier to sell internationally than a car from China," says the manager. That will change quickly, he adds, but that's still the case today. "And this is where we get the best people outside of China."

What Neumann misses most about his old job is that he had an entire office working for him. "I wasn't nearly as flexible then," Neumann says, "but I always had the feeling that I was very efficient." Now, he says, it's the other way around. "I can take a turn faster now and make an unusual decision. That's refreshing. And I can finally say what I think is right. At Opel, I had to say that the electric motor is a good addition. Now, I say that the combustion engine is dead."

This is also the view in Beijing, and it makes it easier for the state planning commission to keep up with the times. In modern urban traffic, it will look something like this: I use an app to order a kind of rolling transverse egg. It arrives and pulls up driverless within three minutes. I get in. The air in the vehicle is filtered. I am automatically connected to the vehicle and can charge my smartphone without contact. It plays my favorite music, knows the lighting that I find pleasant, and may even have some drinks and snacks with it that I can buy without cash using my smartphone. I control everything by voice. The egg drives me to my destination without any traffic jams because all the vehicles are networked and hardly ever get in each other's way. Thanks to the experience of artificial intelligence, the egg knows two hours earlier when it needs to be where. And when the egg isn't needed, it drives itself to an underground garage to recharge.

That this will become reality in China first is more likely than that it will happen in the USA. Europe is lagging behind anyway. The Americans are much further ahead with the software. The cars equipped by Google have already driven around 500 million kilometers. They only need the intervention of a human driver every 9,000 kilometers. However, the Chinese are catching up fast, and they are generating more data. That means the algorithms are learning faster, making them fit for the biggest challenge; an autonomous car that can make it through Beijing's chaotic traffic and so can get through anywhere. The Chinese are faster when it comes to implementing a new technology in everyday life.

The Germans are not bad at basic research. However, they fail because of their skepticism about technology and also because of very practical issues. For example, they need the 5G mobile radio standard for connected traffic. "We won't get there in time," suspects Ferdinand Dudenhöffer, a professor in Duisburg and one of Germany's leading auto-specialists. "The Chinese will outpace the rest of the world in autonomous driving." Germany, after all, is still fully occupied with plugging the radio holes of the 4G standard.

However, the Germans are world leaders when it comes to ethics. Back in the Summer of 2017, at the request of the government, the Ethics Commission laid down 20 ethics rules and justified them in 30 pages. These are the two highest levels of automated driving, four and five, in which humans still have to intervene the least. Five working groups worked in parallel on the rules for nine months. The commission was headed by former constitutional judge Udo Di Fabio, a man who is as practical as he is smart. In addition to lawyers and ethicists, the commission also included engineers, representatives of the German Automobile Association (ADAC), and car manufacturers — as well as the auxiliary bishop of Augsburg, Florian Wörner.

The commission has done a good job. The Germans should take note of rule one — automated and connected driving is ethically imperative if the systems cause fewer accidents than human drivers. That the technology should eliminate accidents as well as possible "goes without saying," Di Fabio said. It is equally self-evident that there is no technology that can "always reliably avoid risks or exclude damage."

Hardly anyone succeeds in leaving one and the other sober. In Germany, the first statement carries more weight. In China, the second. The U.S. is in between. "I have to smile when I see the seriousness with which the Germans set the rules of the game," says Michael Slackman, *The New York Times*' international news chief, at the Chinese–American– German Bosch Media Forum in Silicon Valley in May 2018. "All these philosophers in Germany, we do first things first, and then we think about the rules. First things first." The Chinese are different once again. "Safety first applies here, too," says Hu Xijin, the editor-in-chief of *Global Times*. "But even if the stones are dark, we keep going."

Di Fabio sees another advantage on the side of the Chinese; "If this technology promises a significant gain in safety, then that virtually forces the legislator to be technology-friendly." Here, Beijing would act faster than Berlin. However, it should not only be about security but also "about the possibility of personal free choice and self-determination." As far as that is concerned, Beijing would clearly give preference to security.

The following rule is particularly controversial: In unavoidable accident situations, any qualification of people according to personal characteristics (age, gender, physical, or mental constitution) is inadmissible. Thus, the machine must not decide that it is better to run over the old man than a group of playing children. For the commission, "such an ethical scenario is out of the question." Di Fabio does not want a programmer to write a program that dictates: better old man than children. "Every human life is worth the same." But what happens when technology acts intuitively? When algorithms make an intuitive decision that we can no longer comprehend? This is already possible today. At this point, Di Fabio states, "We can't humanize the technology." This is certainly a line that is drawn more sharply in the West, and certainly in Germany, than in China. The most important insight, however, is that each country, each cultural group, will have to decide this for itself. Above all, however, the Asians will not allow the West to dictate anything to them in these matters because whoever dominates technology has the greatest decision-making power internationally.

The commission headed by Di Fabio had "absolute pioneering work" and developed "the world's first guidelines" for automated driving, meanwhile, the then transport minister Alexander Dobrindt promotes the project, "This means we remain an international pioneer for Mobility 4.0." I wish. Hardly anyone will be interested in our rules if we are not at the forefront of technology. This now seems to have dawned on policymakers as well. During intergovernmental consultations in July 2018, Merkel and Chinese head of government Li Keqiang had self-driving cars demonstrated by top auto industry executives at the former airport in Berlin-Tempelhof. "We both have enjoyed a small journey and have also arrived back safely," said Merkel. "We now understand that it's important to develop the technology, once the car is designed, that will recognize events and objects." That takes lots of data and artificial intelligence. They now want to collaborate. Premier Li Keqiang has promised Merkel it will be a win-win situation. The fact that the premier promises this and not the other way around shows who is the weaker party in this game. Merkel only said that she hoped for a win-win situation and "open, transparent cooperation."

Daimler and Audi are already testing autonomous vehicles in China and BMW wants to cooperate with the Chinese search engine giant and technology group Baidu. Audi and telecommunications supplier Huawei also want to strive toward the networking of cars. Without China, there is no way, "We are striving for uniform technology standards worldwide in order to eliminate regional differences in implementation speed and regulation," said BMW's head of development Klaus Fröhlich. Of course, China will be the determining factor. Whoever has the most data wins.

Baidu alone, China's Google, has established the $1.5 billion Apollo Fund to invest in 100 autonomous driving projects. At the same time,

Chinese network equipment supplier and Audi partner Huawei is pushing ahead with the introduction of the fifth-generation mobile communications standard 5G to provide the necessary high-speed Internet.

And the Chinese have long had the money and the courage to buy into Western companies. If the companies are listed on the stock market then even against their will. The international pioneer in this field is a man named Li Shufu. He owns the car brand Geely. He is famous in China, but in Germany hardly anyone knows the rather inconspicuous entrepreneur with the thinning hair and the gentle smile. Except perhaps at Daimler, after all, Li has ensured that Daimler CEO Dieter Zetsche appeared on the cover of *Manager Magazin* wearing a Mao jacket and Mao cap. The reason was the news that struck Stuttgart like a thunderbolt on February 23, 2018: Li, 54, had secretly bought up 9.69 percent of Daimler shares. A package worth around 7.5 billion euros. The Chinese have thus replaced Kuwait's sovereign wealth fund, which holds a 6.8 percent stake, as Daimler's largest shareholder.

Li is a "long-term oriented investor" with whom "industrial change can be discussed constructively" was the businesslike comment in Stuttgart. The shock, however, runs deep. "The competitors who will challenge us technologically in the 21st century do not come from the classic automotive industry," says Li, as if he were already speaking for both companies. In fact, a collaboration with Geely would be a natural fit. However, this is diplomatically difficult. After all, Stuttgart must not upset its previous partners BYD and BAIC, the two market leaders in e-vehicles last year. The Germans have been working with BAIC, the powerful Beijing state-owned company, since 2003. So, Stuttgart is playing it safe for now. Shortly after Li's entry, Daimler and BAIC announced their intention to invest 1.5 billion euros in new production facilities for electric and hybrid vehicles as a commitment and mutual assurance.

With Geely, Daimler now has a triple competitor in the House — Volvo, which was acquired by Li and successfully reorganized, is a premium brand that competes with Mercedes. Moreover, Volvo trucks want to outperform Mercedes trucks. In addition, Geely is much more successful in e-cars than Daimler in the Chinese market. At the same time, Geely is a competitor of BYD, which in turn is a technology partner of Daimler. BAIC and Daimler have jointly developed a listlessly designed vehicle called Denza, which hardly anyone wants to buy.

Geely is also a competitor of BAIC. Daimler has a production and a sales joint venture with BAIC. China CEO Hubertus Troska would now need an accomplished Go player to go through the various possibilities of how the power nexus can develop. Could artificial intelligence help?

The optimists would say, "Great, Daimler can play the individual Chinese partners off against each other. However, this is a relatively unlikely scenario. BAIC, for example, would not put up with this and would call in the Beijing politicians. BYD, as the largest private player in the Chinese e-car market, is so well established that they need Daimler less than Daimler needs them. And pressuring Geely, its largest shareholder, would not be a good idea either. Geely CEO Li does not need a seat on the supervisory board, as was initially feared; he is powerful enough as it is.

The other extreme would be a catastrophe for Daimler: the politicians give the competitors Geely, BYD, and BAIC a little nudge that they should coordinate their goals with each other in the interest of China. In this way, they would factually determine the direction at Daimler because the Daimler Board of Management can't beat its most important production partner, with whom it produces the most cars in the most important market, and its most important shareholder, if all three of them stick together. It is possible that the Stuttgart company will one day be grateful that the Chinese have forced it onto the path of the new car virtues but that is a baseless speculation.

The most likely scenario is that Daimler will have to forge ahead with limited leeway. After all, all three, most of all Geely, have an interest in Daimler being successful for a little longer.

In China, Li is celebrated for the quiet coup. There, the son of a rice farmer from the eastern Chinese province of Zhejiang is already praised as the "Chinese Henry Ford." Unlike Henry Ford, Li still has to prove that he will revolutionize the automotive industry. In global terms, he is still a fast catch-up — albeit a very successful one. The name "Geely" stands for "luck" or "auspicious" in Chinese. His company is currently the largest private automaker in China and also the fastest growing. The group sold 1.25 million cars there in 2017 — a third more than the year before. This makes Geely the first Chinese manufacturer to clear the 1.25 million hurdle, with a market share of over 5 percent at home alone. Geely has now moved up to third place among the most popular brands behind Volkswagen and Honda, ahead of Buick, Toyota, and Nissan. What's more, Li sells twice as many cars as Audi.

Already in 2013, Li had a fortune of 17 billion US dollars and briefly landed on the *Forbes list* as the richest man in China. In Germany, of course, that is still no reason to deal with him. Rather the opposite. In Germany, success is suspect. Perhaps that is one explanation for the fact that shortly after joining Daimler, Li was on a trip to Germany "only" received by Lars-Hendrik Röller, Angela Merkel's economic advisor, at the Chancellor's Office?

In any case, as a member of the Political Consultative Conference, one of the highest advisory bodies in China, the entrepreneur maintains excellent relations with top cadres all the way to Chinese State and Party leader Xi Jinping. For many Chinese, Li is a role model. At industry meetings, he is sometimes photographed like a pop star and asked for autographs. Only the former English teacher and Alibaba founder Jack Ma embodies the "Chinese dream" more than the self-made billionaire Li Shufu, whose career began in the mid-1980s with a factory for refrigerator parts. It's inconceivable that someone like that would rise to the top ranks of carmakers in Germany.

Li came into contact with Daimler at an early stage. He wanted to build a Chinese Mercedes. So in 1993, he bought an E-Class car and the chassis of an Audi 100, modified both, and assembled them together — and the Geely No. 1 was ready. In China, people still remember this first vehicle well, over which Li placed a huge bow made of red tulle. The car's shell was made of fiberglass and plastic and looked amazingly similar to the E-Class. It was then that Li first attracted attention, albeit unpleasant, in Stuttgart. Former Daimler employees claim that the German car company sent Li a sharp letter at the time. Li did not contest this but conceded that the quality of the Chinese Mercedes was not so good after all. Apart from the prototype, no second number 1 was built. Instead, Li bought a number 1 from a manufacturer of prisoner transporters in the Province of Sichuan and produced small cars.

That was all just 20 years ago. Li sold cars to the growing Chinese middle class so profitably that Geely successfully went public in Hong Kong in 2005. The stock debuted at 0.44 Hong Kong dollars and today stands at 20. Meanwhile, the company can build a million vehicles a year. However, Geely vehicles have not yet been able to compete in Europe and the USA. So Li took a shortcut. In 2010, he bought Swedish automaker Volvo from Ford. Previously, several attempts to turn around the Swedish automaker and make it profitable had failed. Hardly anyone believed that a Chinese, of all people, would manage to save Volvo from ruin. In the end, it was quite simple; Li gave Volvo CEO Håkan Samuelsson all the freedom he needed and drove the modernization of the company forward in the background. Today, Volvo is growing again and, together with Geely, operates a technology and innovation center in Gothenburg with 2,000 engineers. Volvo is selling more cars than ever and making record profits — up 28 percent in 2017. And that's mainly due to the Chinese market.

Li continued his expansion abroad with further acquisitions. Since 2013, he has owned the London Electric Vehicle Company (LEVC), which manufactures the legendary London black cabs. Li also holds 49.9 percent of the Malaysian car group Proton, which includes the British sports car manufacturer Lotus. Meanwhile, Li feels mature enough not only to buy successfully in Europe but also to sell successfully there. That will be the next wave to come.

Who could blame the Chinese manufacturers for concentrating not only on their home market? No, the Chinese want to sell their cars — apart from China — not only in Africa and Southeast Asia, where they are already quite successful but also in Europe and the USA. And they will succeed. After a few failed attempts, the time seems ripe for this. Anyone with an affinity for cars will remember Landwind's SUV, which failed the German crash test with a bang. We never heard from the car again. But those days are over. The Qoros, for example, tested well, although it too has not yet managed to gain a foothold in the European market. However, that doesn't mean that no model will make it. After all, we were also amused by the first attempts of the Japanese in the 1980s, and a decade later by those of the South Korean manufacturers Hyundai and Kia. Today, the group with the two brands is the fourth largest manufacturer in the world, with 7.2 million vehicles sold. In May 2018, *Auto Bild* tested six Chinese SUVs and was full of praise for the first time, "It feels like the Chinese are learning even faster than the Koreans," was the summary. "The times when we smiled at the Chinese with pity are over."

All this should not be forgotten in view of the joy that arose at the beginning of April 2018. That's when President Xi Jinping delivered a keynote speech at the Boao Forum for Asia in Hainan, southern China. It was meant to take pressure off the trade dispute with the USA (see Chapter 8). Xi announced the biggest relaxation of the rules of the game for the foreign auto industry in a quarter of a century. The joint venture requirement for foreign carmakers will be dropped. First for manufacturers of electric and hybrid vehicles, then by 2020 also for commercial vehicles, and by 2022 for the entire passenger car sector. In addition, Beijing is lowering import duties for cars from 25 to 15 percent.

Incredulous amazement. How does this fit in with the development so far? On closer inspection, it is above all a very clever political decision. Opening up markets goes down well in the current global political climate. Xi is positioning himself as a champion of the free economy against U.S. President Donald Trump and he seems to be giving ground in the trade war with Trump.

However, the major Western manufacturers, with the exception of BMW, know immediately that not much will change for them. In some cases, they will not be able to get out of their joint ventures for decades. VW's joint venture with SAIC, for example, runs until 2035, and VW is tied to FAW in northern China until 2041. The contracts for the latest joint venture, which VW founded with JAC from central China to build electric cars, even provide for cooperation until 2042. Even if they want to build new production facilities, it is not politically smart to try to do so alone and leave the partners. The question of whether joint ventures or not does not determine whether one is free or not free, but only where China starts — inside or outside the company. What good is the nicest 100 percent subsidiary if you don't get a production license? Or if you are told which suppliers you have to work with or how many e-cars you have to produce?

The joy of the German carmakers is limited. All hastened to assure that they would not be unfaithful to their partners. So, it is not a U-turn; on the contrary, Beijing is so strong that it can afford to be generous on this issue without risk. The big rules are only replaced by small print. Nothing more.

However, it is now becoming more interesting for small, innovative companies to invest in China. The American company Tesla is the first to benefit from the relaxation. It almost looks as if the rules have been eased as a concession for Tesla. Because whether Elon Musk actually achieves the big breakthrough with Tesla will be decided primarily in China. In July 2018, Musk decided to build a factory in Shanghai that is just as large as the Tesla headquarters in California. 500,000 cars are to be built here at some point. It is the first major foreign investment in the automotive sector without a joint venture partner. The American news agency Bloomberg estimates the costs at up to ten billion US dollars. Money that Musk has to borrow because he is still making too little profit. By approving Tesla, the Chinese are not only showing that they are opening up their market further but that they are also playing a trick on Donald Trump. After all, the American president actually wants to prevent US companies from producing in China. Perhaps the most important reason for the easing becomes clear only after some delay. It is: "Tit for tat." In the meantime, the Chinese also want to manufacture and sell cars in the West.

On the contrary, Premier Li can now take the following stand vis-à-vis Angela Merkel; Chinese cars should be allowed to have a similar market share in Germany as German cars have in China. That's a good 20 percent. We can be happy if they don't insist on claiming the same accumulated profits in Europe that we have made over the past 20 years. That would be fair in any case. Or reciprocal, as we like to say. We would rather not calculate it.

Geely boss Li, at any rate, wants to be the first again this time. The first to establish himself in the West with a Chinese car. To this end, Geely has set up a joint venture with Volvo. Together they have developed a Volvo for young people. In October 2016, the Chinese brand Lynk & Co was already presented to the public. The car is not quite Chinese, because the Lynk's platform is based on the Volvo V40. But that won't bother potential buyers much — on the contrary. In any case, Li is once again presenting a 01: This time it is not a clumsy clone of Audi and E-Class, but a very successful, hip SUV, which of course is also on the market as an electric car. In the meantime, there is already the more compact 02. The vehicles are a successful symbiosis of Chinese innovative drive and European engineering skills. The power struggles in this European–Chinese joint product are manageable. After all, Li owns both companies.

Is it a coincidence that Li was speaking almost at the same time as President Xi announces China's intention to conquer the European market? He has already presented his vehicles in Amsterdam. After that, Li wants to go to the USA. It's not easy to establish a new brand in a stagnating market. But why shouldn't the largest private Chinese manufacturer succeed? That there will be a fourth major player in the global car market besides Germany, the U.S., and Japan is clear. "Geely's dream is to become a global brand," Li says with an ironic smile at the 2018 Beijing auto show, "We have to leave the country for that."

Li believes that in the future, automakers will not just be producers of a commodity, but will have to grow into mobility platforms that offer all kinds of services related to driving. And he has already proven that he can adapt to the new challenges, even in the West and, if need be, very quickly. Since the beginning of 2018, all new London cabs have had to convert to electric motors. 90 percent of the 22,000 cabs in London currently come from the plant of a Geely subsidiary. Li saved it from bankruptcy in 2016. He reacted promptly and invested 340 million U.S. dollars in the factory in the small English town of Coventry, where the legendary Black Cabs have been manufactured since 1948. Since the beginning of the year, the cabs have been running as hybrids. Li has completely overhauled the vehicles, making them fit for the new challenges. The electric motor comes from Siemens and the batteries from LG in South Korea. They now have a 220-volt connection for the computer and a charging socket for the smartphone and free Wi-Fi. You can control the temperature in the back of the car yourself. And at the touch of a button, you can turn off the driver behind the divider when you want to talk privately. It's a service you'd like to see in Berlin, Hamburg, and Munich, too. Li has now set the standards for this in Europe and, what's more, revived an icon of British culture. Why did a Chinese person have to come up with this idea? Why couldn't the British have done it themselves?

Not only the cabs, by the way, are made in Europe, but also the Lynk vehicles. They will be built in Ghent, Belgium, where Li already has a Volvo factory. Production will start in 2019 and sales in 2020. All cars will be offered as hybrids or fully electric. Li also wants to set up a kind of Airbnb for cars. Anyone who doesn't need their car at the moment can rent it out.

As far as international markets are concerned, Geely is the biggest player, but not the only one. Some Chinese start-ups also want to become successful in the West. NIO, SF Motors, and Byton are also among them. BYD is already making electric buses in California. In autonomous driving, Baidu has teamed up with Microsoft. The fact that these cars will also appear in Germany will not only be unavoidable, they will come with offers that make it easy for customers to jump over themselves to buy a Chinese car. Price–performance is the keyword. In summary, the situation looks sobering. E-technology needs less know-how. The Chinese are at the forefront of electric motors, control battery technology, and the raw material deposits needed for it. People in China are more open to new technology. Young people have new ideas about what cars should look like. Their young automakers are not dragging around historical baggage. The government is pursuing a considered, long-term industrial policy. The Chinese only have a good 40 percent market share in China, a market with a still low car density, and they have yet to develop the western markets. In view of the air pollution and the many traffic jams, the pressure to reform is much higher than in the West.

It will be tough for German manufacturers in the Chinese market, on whom they are dependent like no other. And China will probably bring them to their knees. The relegation battle has already begun for some. The weak were hit first. Buick is stagnating. Chevrolet is no longer reaching its 2013 peaks. Ford had its sales peak in 2015. Citroën nearly halved its sales in China in 2017. Peugeot lost a third. Fiat quit. The South Koreans are also slumping. Only the Japanese and the Germans can still hold their own. Only the short-sighted can rejoice that these competitors are exiting in the market. The next to be hit will be Škoda. This will also put Volkswagen under pressure. The impacts are getting closer.

Dear Germans, forget the diesel scandal. The Americans may have been able to annoy you, but the Chinese can do more. They can beat you.

# Chapter 4

# China's Reformers: Radical Retread

## How President Xi Bullies Civil Society and Successfully Reforms China

*China is closer today than at any time in its history to completing the great rebirth of the Chinese nation.*

Xi Jinping, State and Party Leader

The applause of the nearly 3,000 people starts with a thud and ends the same way. One big roar, in between eerie silence. No one coughs. No chair creaks. Only the insistent voice of one man can be heard in the Great Hall of the People in Beijing. Xi Jinping speaks slowly, emphasizing every word. He is 65 years old, has been in office since 2013, and is now the most powerful man in the world. Xi is president of the most populous country on earth. In terms of purchasing power, China is the world's largest economy and the world's number one exporter. Xi leads one of the world's oldest civilizations, one of the few that has survived to this day in its ancient grandeur. He is also party leader of the Chinese Communist Party, the world's largest and most influential party.

Xi stands behind five large microphones and delivers the final address of the first session of the 13th National People's Congress, the world's largest parliament, though not freely elected in the Western sense. "We have strong capabilities to take our rightful place in the world," Xi said. "China will continue to play its part in governing the world," he said "and contribute in a Chinese way to making the world a safer, more integrated, and cleaner place." "The Chinese people are a nation of great dreams. China is closer today than ever in its history to completing the great rebirth of the Chinese nation. We are confident enough and capable enough to do it." Applause erupts again.

After the speech, Xi sits down in the middle of the standing committee of the CP Politburo. The six men next to him form the center of China's power. However, Xi is the only one with the broad red staircase under the party's huge red and gold emblem at his back. It seems to lead directly to communist heaven. Every six-year-old recognizes who is the most powerful man on this stage. And since that speech on March 20 2018, Xi has been more powerful than ever. At that meeting, he had the presidential term limit of two times five years lifted. To do this, the constitution had to be amended. It was a unanimous decision — Xi can now rule for as long as he sees fit. This makes him the third most powerful man in the history of the People's Republic, ahead of his predecessors Jiang Zemin and Hu Jintao. Many observers, especially Westerners, now place Xi on a par with Mao and Deng Xiaoping. Some even speak of a new cultural revolution. Both are exaggerated. Mao Zedong unified and rebuilt the country, and millions of people lost their lives in the process. Deng Xiaoping conquered hunger, opened China to the world, and made the country prosperous. Xi wants China to become a world power that plays a role internationally. At the same time, he must restore confidence in the Chinese political system. He may succeed in all this, but for the time being, that will probably not be enough to put him on a par with Mao and Deng.

From 1943 to 1976, Mao was chairman of the Communist Party. His portrait still hangs in Tiananmen Square. It is very unlikely that it will be taken down and replaced by a picture of Xi. Deng, the great reformer, was, unlike Xi, so powerful that he never needed a top political office. He was temporarily vice prime minister and vice party chairman. For a long time, after all, he was chairman of the Central Military Commission. The army listened to him. In November 1989, Deng retired from this position. He nevertheless remained the most powerful man in China. When he died, his policies were not revised. It was different with Mao.

After all, more than 20 years after Deng's death, Xi can succeed in changing an important aspect of Deng's reform policy. Deng had stipulated that the prime minister, the state president, and the party leader could only rule for two five-year terms each. To be on the safe side, Deng still selected his two successor teams of premier and president himself: Jiang Zemin and Zhu Rongji, and Hu Jintao and Wen Jiabao.

The fact that Xi will never become as powerful as Deng and Mao is not only due to him but also because the party is much more heterogeneous today. Malicious tongues in the party even say that Xi was forced to undermine the five-year rule because he is up to his neck in conflict. He messed with too many people and started too many reforms at the same time. On the other hand, he has proven that he is powerful enough to prevail on this issue. Those who have already warmed up for the time after Xi must now go back to the bench and wait until Xi allows them into the game.

Xi is far from staging a propaganda circus like Mao once did. But his propaganda machine does ensure that the president's images are omnipresent to the point of pain, even on social media channels. In doing so, it uses a visual language that is very reminiscent of Mao's, even though it is no longer up to date. Social Media users retaliate in their own way, for example, Winnie the Pooh. The good-natured, likable bear from the classic children's book *Pooh the Bear* is ideally suited as a parody for Xi. As early as 2013, Internet users had pointed out a resemblance between Barack Obama and Xi Jinping depicting the two of them on a walk with Winnie the Pooh and his friend Tigger and juxtaposed them in picture montages. Since then, Winnie the Pooh has been used repeatedly by China's Internet users as a proxy for China's state and party leader, which is actually a sympathetic counter-program to the stiff propaganda images. But apparently, from the leadership's point of view, they were taking it too far. From mid-2017, search queries for the bear were suddenly answered with an error message: "Illegal content." The Pooh stickers were also deleted from WeChat.

Xi's associates may be petty and Xi may not be as powerful as Deng and Mao. But he is as courageous and as consistent as they were. Xi has taken on a responsibility of historic proportion. In scope and speed, his reforms are a demonstration the likes of which world history has never seen. And one must never forget: experiments can go wrong.

In an incredible number of areas at the same time, the president has begun reforms. Among them are reforms that we in the West appreciate. Others that we resist. Some control individual freedom, for example, the anti-corruption campaign, which is largely not based on the rule of law, the restrictions on freedom of speech, and the complete surveillance of people. Other reforms increase individual freedom, for example, for the new start-up scene, which stimulates the inventive spirit of individuals. The abolition of the *hukou* system, which previously forced people to live in a certain place, also makes people freer. And the Chinese are now allowed to have two children, if they want. The one-child policy is history. Chinese are traveling the world more than ever — but only privately. Business trips by high cadres have been severely restricted. That, in turn, is part of the anti-corruption campaign. At the same time, Xi is keeping the military on a short rein. He has fired most of the old generals, and the new ones are no longer getting any ideas, not when it comes to power or when it comes to corruption. Xi has not necessarily made friends with his reforms.

In addition, the reforms have great advantages and disadvantages at the same time. The anti-corruption campaign has made it much more difficult to be corrupt. At the same time, however, the arbitrariness of the investigators is undermining the still young rule of law. Networking via smartphones has great advantages, especially for people in rural areas. At the same time, however, the state can control people more comprehensively than ever before. In other words, one and the same reform can mean more and less freedoms at the same time. For Western observers, this is difficult to grasp: liberalization, on the one hand, and ideological hardening, on the other. One is unthinkable without the other in this great contradictory country. And that is how it will remain. Xi is not expected to be meek in his old age.

Contradictions confront you everywhere; China is the largest polluter and the biggest environmental protector, at the same time. In the coastal cities, the middle class already attaches greater importance to clean air, clean water, and ecologically sound food than to growth at any price. In the more backward regions, the situation is very different. There, people want prosperity first, environmental protection can come later. The government has to balance these different expectations and constraints every day. A lot of things go wrong in the process, as in the Winter of 2017 when the heating season begins in mid-November, a blanket of smog covers large parts of northern and eastern China. Fine dust levels climb to 20–30 times the limit value that the World Health Organization (WHO) considers tolerable for health.

In said winter, however, the government insists that tens of thousands of smaller and larger factories close. The private coal stoves are to be switched to gas and coal-fired power plants are to be shut down. It was assumed that the measures would work. But the fact that it would happen so quickly surprised everyone including inhabitants, Greenpeace, and even Beijing party cadres. Air quality improved by over 50 percent in

Beijing in the last quarter of 2017. In the northeast region of 27 cities, smog levels were still a good third lower. And these are not the government's figures, but Greenpeace's, "We're seeing a dramatic improvement." Now, again, we have freezing cold days with blue skies.

However, this political juggernaut did not work equally well everywhere that winter. Three million households were to receive new gas heating systems. But only a portion were delivered. Coal stoves were quickly dismantled, but the replacements were a long time coming. In some villages, the gas lines were not completed in time. In others, gas demand was underestimated so prices for propane cylinders went through the roof. Poorer people could no longer afford them. Some schools moved their classes out into the winter sun because it was warmer outside than inside, without the smog. Others continued to heat with expensive corncobs or with coal, which was actually banned. In one village, saying "anyone who continues to heat with coal will be put in jail" was a mantra, but it demonstrates how relentless reforms can be enforced throughout the populous in China.

That winter, the authorities had to back down. Those who still had coal stoves were allowed to heat with them again, but Beijing wouldn't be Beijing if it didn't learn from the bad planning of 2017. The message to the people in the country is that everything will run smoothly next winter because then the new gas pipeline from Russia will be ready. The government will probably achieve its goal of turning four cities, including Beijing and Tianjin, into "coal-free zones" from 2020. The new environmental tax law, which has been in force since January 2018, allows provinces to set their own taxes and keep the money. A system to compensate for environmental damage is also being tested nationwide. At the same time, the government is promoting the introduction of new technologies, such as the world's largest air purifier. Its test results were presented in Xi'an, central China, at the beginning of 2018.

China is the world's largest investor in renewable energy. Such research, investment, and experience are not only worthwhile for China but also benefit the entire world. New Delhi, in particular, but also Los Angeles, Lagos in Nigeria, or the South Korean capital Seoul suffer from smog, and some cities in Germany are groaning under fine dust pollution. In this respect, these reforms by the Chinese ultimately benefit the climate of the entire world.

China is currently transforming entire cities with radical measures. The focus is not only on environmental pollution but also on urban planning, short distances to work, forward-looking traffic management, and last but not least, water supply. Falling groundwater levels and polluted lakes and rivers are causing problems for China's agriculture and industry alike. Both need reasonably clean water, and ironically both are at the same time the ones that pollute the water the most. Mining, steel production, textile industry, printing plants, and oil refineries are the biggest polluters. Farmers use too many pesticides. In the short term, this gives them a higher yield, but in the long term, they no longer have clean water but have contaminated soil. In addition, there is a huge garbage problem: 14 billion tons of waste end up in the Yangtze River alone every year.

Drinking water shortages could worsen in the coming years and could become a serious threat to the country's stability in the next decades. In 2016, the first government report on the water problem counted 50,000 rivers that have dried up in the past 20 years. 70 percent of drinking water is contaminated. Around nine percent of the groundwater is below rating level five. This means it is no longer even suitable for industry or irrigation. The government wants to reduce this value by five percent by 2020. Another reform that is likely to succeed. In the first half of 2017 alone, China invested more than 80 billion euros in around 8,000 water rehabilitation projects, including a gigantic canal system. The 2,400-kilometer network of man-made waterways is the largest construction of its kind in the world. When complete, it will supply some 45 billion cubic meters of water a year from the subtropical south to the parched north. From a small section that has already been opened, more than nine billion cubic meters of water flows from a reservoir in Hubei province, more than 1,400 kilometers away, to Beijing.

But even this project will not be enough in the long run to solve the water shortage. The rivers that Beijing is tapping are partly fed by meltwater from the Himalayas. Soon the world's highest mountain range will be the only source of fresh water not only to China but also to large parts of Southeast Asia. Already, more and more neighboring countries are complaining that China is claiming these reserves too much for itself. Here, too, Xi faces a dilemma; on the one hand, he must guarantee China's supply but, on the other hand, he does not want to spoil relations with his neighbors. They also criticize China for the water supplies of the Mekong River, which Beijing dams and partially diverts before the rest of the water flows on to Myanmar, Thailand, Laos, Cambodia, and Vietnam. Tensions with riparians got so bad that Beijing saw fit to establish the Lancang–Mekong Cooperation in 2015, a forum in which problems are to be addressed and — if possible — resolved. There was particularly big trouble in 2016 when Vietnam experienced its worst drought in 90 years and 1.8 million people and their rice fields suffered severe water shortages. The struggle for the water of the Mekong is the largest source of Sino-Asian conflict after the South China Sea conflict. For us in the West, this means one more factor of unrest that we have to keep an eye on when it comes to stable political conditions in the world. We have known what drought can mean since the German Summer of 2018. For Asia, it is true that whoever controls the Mekong controls Southeast Asia.

China doesn't just consume a lot of water. China also consumes more steel, coal, cement, grain, and fertilizer than any other nation on earth. The Chinese are also at the forefront of oil consumption and greenhouse gas emissions. China has 18 percent of the world's population to feed. But it has only nine percent of the world's arable land and six percent of its freshwater resources, again, a major difficulty facing the Xi government. If China does not want to sacrifice its unique and partly untouched landscape, the Chinese will have to import agricultural products. On the one hand, this means a new market for us, for example, for German milk, but at the same time, it means that certain foods will become more expensive for us as Chinese demand increases.

Besides environmental protection and basic food supplies, the anti-corruption campaign is one of President Xi's major political goals. Here, too, there is a dilemma where, on the one hand, he wants to fight corruption, however China wants to become more constitutional. The vast majority of the 1.3 million corrupt officials arrested in the past five years were not granted the rule of law in the Western sense. Among them were politburo members, vice-army chiefs, provincial governors, and top managers of corporations. One of them is Yu Haiyan. To ensure that no one discovers that he has taken the equivalent of 1.5 million euros in bribes during the course of his career as a civil servant, he submerges his business cell phone in vinegar and throws it into the Yellow River. The vice governor of Gansu Province also dumps luxury watches and other gifts of favor into the clayey water. All this for nothing because Yu cannot escape his punishment. In the meantime, he sits in prison. And he tells his story from behind gray bars for the five-part documentary series *The Sharp Sword of Inspection*. It ran with great success on China's state broadcaster CCTV; co-produced by the Central Disciplinary Commission of the Communist Party of China (CCDI), China's state anti-corruption body, the show is just one of several TV formats. It aims to turn the issue of corruption, once swept under the rug, into prime-time material in a genre of investigative journalism and propaganda. Whether as a TV tribunal or action thriller, the message is always the same: yes, China has a problem with corruption, but the government is leaving no stone unturned to curb it.

Even when he was a member of party leadership in the province of Zhejiang, the fight against corruption was important to Xi. When he then became state and party leader, he immediately announced that he wanted to catch the "flies" just as much as the "tigers," an almost poetic euphemism for the fact that low-level officials and top functionaries would be held accountable indiscriminately under him. His investigators were even active abroad. More than 2,500 suspected corruption criminals have been extradited to China from 70 countries since 2014. The international police agency Interpol has been headed by Chinese Meng Hongwei as president since November 2016. Even high-ranking corruption watchdogs have come under the scrutiny of investigators. Mo Jiancheng, who has headed the supervisory authority at the Ministry of Finance since December 2015, and Xiang Junbo, head of the Insurance Supervisory Authority, were both charged with corruption, serious disciplinary violations, and dismissed from their posts.

The top anti-corruption official, until Spring 2018, is Wang Qishan, Xi's close confidant. From 2012 to 2018, he led the Central Disciplinary Commission. Today, the urbane politician, who ruled as mayor during the Beijing Olympics, is considered one of the most powerful men in China. He may even be, in effect, the second most powerful man after Xi Jinping. He cracked down so hard on corruption that the economy weakened and local politics came to a standstill in many places. Even blameless officials preferred to wait in silence rather than make decisions while Wang was at the helm. As a result, Xi introduced a new rule at Wang's suggestion — those who sit idle will also be punished. In the meantime, Wang has become the country's vice president and is also responsible for the trade war with the United States. And although he is no longer permitted to sit on the Politburo because of his age, he is present at the meetings.

Xi Jinping has made many enemies with his anti-corruption campaign. Only a small circle of the powerful knows whether the delinquents are really corrupt or just politically inconvenient, or, as is so often the case, both. Xi also uses the legal gray area to get rid of his political opponents. In July 2017, for example, Sun Zhengcai, former party secretary of Chongqing, one of the world's largest cities, was ousted on corruption charges and sentenced to life in prison. He admitted to accepting $27 million in bribes. He was the youngest member of the Chinese Communist Party's Politburo and had previously been considered a possible successor to Xi Jinping. Xi's old confidant Chen Min'er has now replaced him in Chongqing. Sun Zhengcai's trial also had nothing to do with the rule of law in the Western sense.

Nonetheless, hardly anyone would have expected much before Xi took office and less likely bet that a CP party leader would ever be able to fight endemic corruption down to the country's capillary ramifications. This is a major achievement, despite the lawless grinding marks, Xi has restored the party's credibility. This is another reason why he is very popular among the population. Not only has he been successful but also *because* he has undermined the mechanisms of the rule of law. The rule of law costs time, is cumbersome, and makes it more difficult to swiftly remove political opponents from circulation. People liked that. The long-term damage to trust in the legal system, on the other hand, cannot be foreseen.

For a long time, investigators only took action against party cadres. Since March 2017, all civil servants have been investigated. A new authority is making the fight against corruption even more effective. The National Commission for Monitoring combines the previously fragmented monitoring offices and should at least help ensure that the monitors themselves are better monitored in the future. The reality now is that suspects can be interned in a secret location for up to six months. They do not have the right to a lawyer or can they challenge their arrest in court. At least they have a right to have their employer and family informed when they have been arrested. And there are other small adjustments; those who are incarcerated can now complain to the superiors of the officers responsible for them. An internal reporting system is also intended to provide some transparency.

This new system resulted in the first fatality in May 2018. Chen Yong, 45, a former driver for the district government in Nanping in southern China's Fujian province, was handed over to his family dead, his face and parts of his body disfigured from beatings. Chen had been "questioned" on corruption charges against a district vice director he had been driving. There was nothing against him himself, an exceptional case, to be sure, but one that tells a lot about the severity with which the authorities are cracking down. At least they promised the family an investigation into what had happened and an autopsy.

However, Xi cannot be accused of ignoring and allowing the big ones to run and the small ones to be punished. He is also taking action against the bosses of powerful corporations, and when they threatened to become overconfident, he cracked down on capital flight. First, however, a gigantic wave of acquisitions by China rolled over the West. Chinese companies bought what they could get: German high-tech companies such as Kuka as well as Portugal's largest insurance company and the Italian tire manufacturer Pirelli. They bought shares in hotel chains such as the Hilton Group and acquired Club Méditerranée and the leading British tour operator Thomas Cook. They also bought soccer clubs such as Inter Milan and Atlético Madrid, as well as Logicor, Europe's largest owner of logistics centers, for a good 12 billion U.S. dollars. They bought Volvo, the Swiss airport service provider Swissport, the British luxury yacht manufacturer Sunseeker, major Hollywood studios, and the largest cinema chain in the USA, AMC Entertainment. They took a majority stake in fashion labels, including the long-established Swiss luxury brand Bally and the oldest French couture brand Lanvin. Yes, they even bought Cirque du Soleil and jewelers like Folli Follie.

The peak of this unprecedented purchasing wave was the year that Xi got fed up and pulled the emergency brake. The not entirely unjustified suspicion had arisen that the entrepreneurs were primarily interested in getting their money out of the country and escaping Xi's control. After all, almost all of those who became rich in this boom left behind traces that the sniffer dogs of the anti-corruption campaign jumped on. In addition, some of the companies were up to their ears in debt. The state banks were ordered to turn off the credit tap.

Investigation teams moved in on the corporations that had "internationalized" most aggressively. These included Dalian Wanda, the world's largest real estate developer and the world's largest cinema owner. HNA was also scrutinized — the group owns Hainan Airlines, the most successful private Chinese airline, and Radisson Hotels, among others. It also holds shares in the Hilton Group and NH Hotels, and just under 10 percent in Deutsche Bank.

Fosun, the largest private business conglomerate, whose founder Guo Guangchang likes to call himself the "Warren Buffet of China," was also investigated, as was the insurance group Anbang. In the meantime, Anbang had bought the South Korean interest in the German Allianz AG as well as 16 iconic American hotels, including the Waldorf Astoria in New York.

Some entrepreneurs got off lightly, such as Fosun CEO Guo Guangchang or Wanda Chairman Wang Jianlin. Wang, however, was forced to sell many of his international holdings in order to reduce the over-indebtedness of his company. But he also sold off his hotels and leisure parks in China for nine billion U.S. dollars. Since Wang did what he was advised to do, immediately, the authorities did not take action against him personally.

Wu Xiaohui, the founder and head of Anbang, was hit harder. He was arrested in June 2017 and in February 2018 the company was effectively nationalized. The Chinese insurance regulator took control. In May 2018, Wu was sentenced to 18 years in prison.

Two months later, Wang Jian, one of HNA's two founders, fell off a wall in France while taking photographs and died. Since then, there have been persistent rumors that it was not an accident, although the French police have ruled out any outside influence. Whatever the case, the Chinese government is very annoyed by the fact that HNA is majority-owned by a foundation based in New York — beyond the reach of Chinese authorities. The shareholders have so far refused to change anything.

We are already feeling the consequences of Xi's policy. While we in Germany are still thinking about which companies we want to sell and which we don't, Xi has long since decided that Chinese companies will now have to make do with the short end of the stick. For many a medium-sized company that had hoped to sell its business for a lot of money, this is a big disappointment. Xi cares little about that. He has the Russia of the 1990s as a warning example in mind when hundreds of billions disappeared abroad and the Russian economy was left hollowed out. China's economic situation is much better, but Xi still wants to ensure that China does not come close to such a predicament.

That is why he is also paying particular attention to the country's financial situation. China must not get carried away.

The figures sound frightening and regularly make it into the headlines of the international media. The total debt of China's state, private households, and companies outside the financial sector rose to a record 282 percent of economic output at the end of 2017. In just five years, the level has climbed by a good 50 percentage points. The International Monetary Fund (IMF) examined the rise in debt in more than 50 boom countries, where the level had increased by more than 30 percentage points over the same period. In all but five cases, the rise in debt led to a slump in growth or even resulted in financial crisis. "The debt-to-GDP ratio is 25 percentage points above the long-term trend, which is very high by international standards and thus indicates a high probability of (imminent) stress in the financial system," IMF analysts write.

Is a financial crisis really looming? If so, China would take half of the world with it. Exporting nations like Germany would feel it first. That's why we have to take notice when the Bank for International Settlements (BIS) warns that the ratio of loans to GDP among China's companies is higher than in the Southeast Asian economies just before the Asian crisis and higher than among American companies before the financial crisis.

All of this sounds spectacular. However, BIS is not falling for the alarmism that some institutions are spreading because they, too, are aiming for a big media response. Even BIS admits in the fine print that corporate debt alone gives a distorted picture. In terms of the sum of *all* outstanding loans — i.e., government and private — compared to GDP, China is around seven percent lower than the eurozone and over 50 percent lower than Japan. Beyond the headlines, the IMF also puts its warning into perspective: "There is every reason to be convinced," says David Lipton, deputy managing director, "that China can manage its problems."

The ratio of debt to GDP alone does not say enough. It is also about the level of economic growth. There is a difference between Japan, for example, which has grown by an average of just over one percent over the past five years, and China, which has achieved six times as much growth. Every year, China generates a GDP the size of Sweden's and thus alone contributes 30 percent to the growth of the global economy. The Americans do not even manage half of that. In the development phase, in which China still finds itself, it is even important to take on debt because that way, debts have a greater chance of being paid off: the first bridge over a river is more useful to the economy than the fifth. The more mature an economy is, however, the more problematic debt becomes. Former U.S. President Obama alone incurred more debt during his term in office than all 43 presidents before him combined, with average growth of just under two percent. Donald Trump's term in office will not look any better. China will come off even better.

In order to be able to realistically assess the risk, it makes sense to simply compare the state with a private household. Let's take the Müllers. They are a family of eight. The six children constantly borrow money from their parents. The children also borrow money from each other. They use it to buy things from amongst themselves and also buy from outside.

It's confusing, but as long as the Müller family can pay their bills and the reserves on the savings account grow, it doesn't matter who borrows what from whom within the family and who buys what. Even if the Müllers were also heavily indebted to their savings bank, no one would worry as long as they paid their interest on time and didn't keep taking out new loans.

The Chinese are in the comfortable position of having the best-filled savings account in the world. And almost no debts to foreign banks or states. The savings book of the countries is the foreign exchange reserves. They are invested internationally in banks. If you want to know how stable China is, you have to look above all at whether its foreign exchange reserves are growing steadily, stagnating, or falling rapidly. As long as they do not fall sharply, you only have to look at who in China owes what to whom.

China has 3.1 trillion U.S. dollars in savings. Even in June 2018, at one of the high points of the trade war so far, the reserves are not in free fall but are still growing by 1.51 billion U.S. dollars. However, and this is concerning, the savings account has been fortified. In 2014, it stood at just under four trillion U.S. dollars. Nevertheless, three trillion in reserves is still a lot, even for a large country like China, especially since China has no foreign debt. With this sum, China could pay its bills, for example, its imports, for around 20 months without having to generate any new revenue.

By comparison, the USA has reserves for just two months. Germany has only 1.5 months. The European Union could get by for 3.5 months. Japan, by the way, has 16 months, which is more in line with China. We can see this from Japan, high foreign exchange reserves and low foreign debt, a mature economy that can remain stable even with very low growth and a high domestic debt ratio. No one asks repeatedly whether Japan is about to collapse.

The Americans are the riskiest in this respect; they have hardly any foreign exchange reserves, plus a high level of foreign debt — and that from the Chinese, of all people. And their market is already much more saturated than that of the Chinese. A crisis in the world economy would therefore hit them much harder.

However, the countries of the world are exposed to a danger that does not exist with the Müllers. Since each country prints its own money, it is tempting for the government to produce more so it can lend more. But this makes the money worth less. It is true that the value of the debt also falls as a result. But it takes more and more money to pay for the same product. Inflation increases. It becomes risky when you have income in a currency whose value is low or declining and expenditure in a higher, more stable currency. That's why it's important to keep an eye on the money supply that's in circulation in China. In fact, the growth of the money supply there, at around eight percent, is much higher than in the EU (plus five percent) and the U.S. (plus 4.5 percent) which is normal in a rising economy. Just how normal this is can be seen from the fever curve of the money supply, inflation: 1.6 percent in 2017. That is not worth mentioning.

In this respect, the crisis comparisons with Japan in the China's financial system may be opaque, but it is stable, much more stable than that of the USA and the EU. This is both good and bad news for Germany. A major crisis that could also drag us into the abyss is not in sight. As a competitor, however, China will tend to become stronger.

What remains is the skeptical view of the international community on the Chinese real estate bubble. Fears that it could suddenly burst are rife not only in the West but also in China. A bubble occurs when properties are built that no one needs. It also occurs when properties built are so expensive that no one wants to buy them or the construction did not cover costs. In fact, since 2001, China's real estate market has gone through a long period of tremendous construction activity and ever-increasing selling prices, with the typical consequences that pointed to an approaching crash; real estate is very expensive, rents too low by comparison. Average incomes are too low for the high real estate prices. And many apartments are empty. This is because, on the one hand, developers in small and medium-sized cities created an oversupply with rapidly erected high-rises and, on the other hand, apartment owners let their property stand empty. They shy away from the hassle of tenants, and the increase in property value is enough for them. In addition, there are few investment options other than real estate. Stock trades, funds, bonds, and investment plans are still not mature. And, of course, young men are often only successful in proposing if they own an apartment.

For all these reasons, a large part of private wealth flows to the gens in the real estate market. Prices here have at least doubled on average over the past eight years. In the inner cities of Beijing and Shanghai, apartments cost more than 10,000 euros per square meter and even 15,000 euros per square meter at the peak even to 20,000 euros. In Munich, the figure is up to 16,000.

Nevertheless, in recent years, more and more real estate loans have been granted to average earners in China, in some cases on very non-transparent terms. This brings back memories of the out-of-control US real estate market, which helped trigger the global financial crisis in 2008. Whereas in China, only just under 40 percent of real estate is loan-financed, in the UK, it is 87 percent, and in the U.S. still almost 80 percent — despite the experience of the great crisis. Nevertheless, in 2016, fears of a crash of the Chinese real estate market was particularly high. The government slammed on the brakes, just in time. "Apartments are built for living, not for speculators," China's state and party leader Xi Jinping warned and pushed through a series of measures. For example, buyers must now pay at least half of the purchase price out of their own pockets to get a loan. The purchase of second homes in cities such as Shanghai and Beijing has been banned. And a property tax is even being tested in the megacity of Chongqing. In Beijing, Guangzhou, Shenzhen, and Shanghai, the overheated real estate market cooled significantly. While prices per square meter still rose by an average of 30 percent in the quarter in 2016, a year later, they were only up by two percent. Fewer loans were granted and fewer apartments were offered for sale. The real estate sector is therefore operating with the handbrake on. Beijing is accepting a slowdown in the construction boom, which is depressing growth.

In the future, the Chinese government wants its owner as a saver and also encourages citizens to rent rather than buy. A state-backed rental market could reach annual rents of $658 billion by 2030, Orient Securities estimates. State-owned banks such as China Construction Bank (CCB) lend a good $200 billion in credits to construction companies, which are not allowed to sell the apartments they build but only to rent them out at reasonable prices. The city of Beijing wants to create 500,000 new rental units in the next five years, and Shanghai even around 700,000. In the tech metropolis Shenzhen, at least 20 percent of the land sold at public auctions is to be used for rental units in the future.

China's tech giants are already in the starting block to serve the new rental market with apps. Tencent, for example, invested in mid-January 2018 in startup Ziroom, which raised $621 million in its latest funding round. Ziroom is similar in concept and structure to the Airbnb platform but is aimed at long-term renters. The start-up already manages 500,000 rooms in nine major Chinese cities, including the most expensive: Beijing, Shanghai, and Shenzhen.

Alibaba is working with Shanghai start-up Mogoroom, amongst others. Rental payments and contracts can be processed on Mogoroom directly via an app. Alipay users with particularly good credit can even get a room without a deposit. Country Garden Holdings Company, China's largest real estate developer by sales, has also announced plans to make one million new affordable rental apartments available over the next three years. Many more will follow. You can see how this looming crisis becomes a business. No bubble has burst, the government has released pressure from the cauldron in a controlled manner. Beijing has learned from the American financial crisis and has tightened the brakes. Politically, this was not easy, as land sales used to account for about 60 percent of local government revenue. Moreover, the real estate sector accounts for about one-third of China's economic output. Of course other sectors of the economy also depend on construction projects: machines have to be bought, steel and cement are needed, and, last but not least, furniture. For the government, this means that, on the one hand, it must get a grip on the overheated real estate market, and on the other hand, the turbulence in the real estate market must not trigger a chain reaction and weaken the economy. In case of doubt, however, it is easier to deal with a dip in economic growth than with a drop in real estate prices. There is nothing the government fears more than that its citizens becoming nervous because their homes are suddenly worth much less.

As we have seen, all these reforms come under one heading: stability at any price. This is also at the core of civil society but in a way that is very strange for us in the West. Xi is in no doubt that order is more important than civil society diversity. He and his comrades-in-arms are concerned that critical lawyers, journalists, dissidents, and civic movements will trigger mass movements that can no longer be controlled. Foreign NGOs, including German party-affiliated foundations, are evaluated according to a point system. Activities that "harm national and public interests" or "endanger China's reunification, security, and national unity" are prohibited. Organizations must not "slander or publish or disseminate harmful information that endangers national security or harms national interests." Deductions are also made for involvement in "political activities" or "illegal" support of religious practice. The heads of the organizations are also specially graded. More and more websites are blocked. So far, however, they can be opened with a little effort via a so-called VPN channel. Depending on the provider, the software is available free of charge or for little money. Again and again, there are rumors that the government wants to ban this software. But that would greatly reduce China's attractiveness to foreigners. And China is not taking such a risk without good reason.

At the same time, the authorities regularly scour the Internet. Even "Rage Comics" are considered dangerous by the authorities. They are mostly childishly drawn faces and stick figures that express different emotions such as amusement, anger, or sadness in the manner of emoticons. One of the most famous is the stylized, exaggeratedly smiling face of Chinese basketball star Yao Ming. On the most important Chinese social media platform Weibo alone, 16 accounts were deleted that specialized exclusively in Rage Comics. It was not uncommon for users to address the challenges of everyday life in their comics, from excessively high rents to the difficulties young university graduates face in finding a job.

However, the platform did not cite this form of subtle criticism for the deletion of the accounts but rather the "Law for the Protection of China's Heroes and Martyrs," which came into force at the beginning of May 2018. Compliance with this law was entrusted to the authorities responsible for public security, culture, the press, and the Internet; these authorities, in turn, called on the operators of web platforms to check their own content in this regard.

Users will find ways to reclaim digital space, for example, by varying names and hashtags. Rage comics, which can be easily made by anyone with the help of web tools, will not disappear by being deleted from individual platforms. On the contrary, China's Internet culture will remain cheeky, becoming even more international and ambiguous. And the Internet authorities, who are otherwise alert enough to recognize new trends, are ultimately wasting an opportunity with their censorship measures. This is because many memes and rage comics are often affectionate jibes that contain humorously packaged suggestions for improvement; their creators are not out to overthrow but want to breathe new life into stiff politics and old familiar figures. It would be wise for the government to use the new wave of irony for its soft power efforts. Imagine if the cultural authority or even Xi himself shared a Winnie the Pooh post or a Rage comic on an official channel. That would be ingenuous but it doesn't fit into the general climate.

The threshold at which critical people can be placed under house arrest and in prison has become lower. These are not people who had broad popular support. There is not a single dissident in China who would have the name recognition of a Nelson Mandela in South Africa or an Alexander Solzhenitsyn in Russia or a Václav Havel in Czechoslovakia.

Even Ai Weiwei or the late Nobel Peace Prize winner Liu Xiaobo is hardly known in China. This cannot be due to censorship. The Chinese are very creative when it comes to circumventing censorship. And the Soviet censorship in the 1970s was much more rigid than it can be today in the age of social media. Nevertheless, Alexander Solzhenitsyn was very well known in the country.

No, there is simply no interest in such lateral thinkers among the general public in China. There may be cultural reasons for this; in a country with so many people, it is understandable that the individual has to take a back seat to the majority. But it may also have to do with the fact that the upswing is taking the vast majority of people with it and that those who have not been taken along so far are more capable of suffering. In any case, it is particularly tragic for the dissidents that they are in prison and are acknowledged by only a few on the outside.

Every now and then, individual governments in Western countries are able to achieve something for Chinese dissidents in individual cases. Liu Xia, the wife of Chinese Nobel Prize winner Liu Xiaobo, was allowed to travel to Berlin in July 2018. She had been under house arrest for nine years, one of them still after her husband's death. No charges were ever brought against her. Since her brother Liu Hui was not allowed to leave with her, Liu Xia is not really free to say what she wants even after she leaves the country. She was released only one day after the Sino-German government consultations in Berlin. The Chinese government has an interest in tying Germany more closely to itself because of the dispute with the United States (see Chapter 8). That is why it agreed to Angela Merkel's request to let Liu travel to Germany. A year earlier, when it was a question of letting the terminally ill Liu Xiaobo leave for treatment in Germany, Beijing still turned down this request. The political situation had been different. Liu is the first Nobel Peace Prize winner to die in captivity since German pacifist Carl von Ossietzky in 1938.

The rules of the game for such diplomatic interventions can be that Beijing is now getting its way — only the Western politician who expresses his wishes and criticism behind the diplomatic scenes has any chance of success. This was already the case before the Xi era, but it has become even more pronounced since then. At the time, this could be seen in the way Norway was handled. After the independent Nobel Committee decided in 2010 to award Liu the Nobel Peace Prize, a political ice age began between the two countries. At that time, 90 percent of the salmon imported by China came from Norway. After that, it was only around two percent.

It was not until April 2017 that Norwegian Prime Minister Erna Solberg was allowed to travel to China again, but by then Liu's cancer had already reached an advanced stage. Since Norway did not campaign for his release, the former head of Amnesty International Norway accused the prime minister of being relieved when she heard of Liu's death. When China and Norway signed a new agreement to supply salmon a month later, they hailed massive criticism. The action was "cowardly" and "embarrassing," Solberg said and made "a genuflection to China." Solberg denies this, but the whole episode since 2010 shows the influence China has in Europe and the consequences of dependence.

The fact that Liu's widow was allowed to leave for Germany does not mean that the treatment of dissidents has fundamentally changed. It may not be a coincidence that just one day after her release, political activist Qin Yongmin was sentenced to 13 years in prison. The 64-year-old was found guilty of "endangering the state." Qin has already spent a total of 22 years in prison. His first imprisonment was in 1981, and 2015 was his last for the time being. At that time, he led the group China Human Rights Watch, which organized discussion rounds and disseminated statements on the Internet condemning the government's policies.

If China has more and more power to determine the rules of the game, what does that mean for the development of civil societies in the West? It cannot be overlooked that authoritarian currents are now gaining a foothold even in Europe. And when it comes to defending European liberalism against the Chinese idea of order, as we saw in Chapter 1, even some EU countries are no longer playing along. The West should not underestimate the fact that China can become a trendsetter not only in the technological field but also in these areas, especially since its rigid ideas of public order are falling on open ears among those citizens who are disillusioned with the current political establishment in Europe.

Xi's biggest push against civil society took place back in July 2015, when a group of 300 activists were arrested. Surprisingly, Mo Shaoping, the lawyer of the imprisoned Nobel Peace Prize winner Liu Xiaobo, was not among them. To this day, he continues to publicly represent critical cases. Most of the arrested activists have since been intimidated but released. However, some are still in pre-trial detention. Others were later convicted. For example, Zhou Shifeng, the head of Beijing's Kanzlei Fengrui, was sentenced to seven years in prison for "undermining state power." Zhou was Ai Weiwei's lawyer but also represented families whose children were sickened by contaminated milk powder. Another lawyer and the head of an underground church, who had previously served 16 years in prison, were also sentenced to long prison terms. A business-man and an activist surprisingly received only suspended sentences. All are said to belong to the "anti-China forces" of an underground Christian church, allegedly financed by American NGOs. There had been "train-ings" in Taiwan. Zhou's law firm had served as a "platform." The aim of the church was to "organize protests" and "spread subversive thoughts," official statements said.

What is true about the accusations unfortunately does not become clearer even with a little distance in time because China's judiciary has made short work of them. There are Christian groups that are not squea-mish when it comes to subversively or violently undermining the social order of people of other faiths. At the same time, Christians have a long and impressive history of courageously standing up against injustice. What was at stake in this case cannot be traced. The families will not know where their arrested relatives are until weeks later. The defendants cannot choose their defense lawyers. The indictment is not made public, and the defendants are not allowed to speak freely in public. The verdict was reached after one day of trial. An appeal is theoretically possible but not advisable. There is no doubt that much has improved in the Chinese legal system over the past 20 years. From a Western perspective, however, these trials appear to be show trials. They are intended to keep the vast majority of Chinese believing that they are getting what they expect: a strong state. Unfortunately, this reckoning may even work out — no one in China yearns for an overthrow.

# Chapter 5

# Inventiveness: Intuitive Innovation

## How the Chinese Are Once Again Becoming Inventive and Germany Is Being Left Out in the Cold

*Europe needs a radical shake-up in the space industry.*

Tom Enders, Airbus CEO

It's storming and pouring with rain at a sultry 26 degrees. It starts early this year, and the first typhoon moves through southern China. The rain lashes down, and in some places, you can only see 100 meters away. Air traffic is restricted on this 8 June 2018. The engineers in the headquarters of the Taishan nuclear power plant are not interested in the weather outside. They stare at the large monitors on the wall, their red safety vests with the words CPR hang over their chairs behind the dark woodwork desks. The curtains at the front window are drawn. Half a dozen cameras hang from the ceiling. Now and then, soft commands can be heard.

Taishan is located a good 140 kilometers west of Hong Kong. The gray domes of the two reactors can be seen far out at sea when sailing from Hong Kong to the new free trade zone of Hainan. French people work here, and Chinese. Today, they are about to start the first chain reaction in this new nuclear power plant. They have been working toward this moment for years, practicing it over and over again with a simulator.

Here, a technology that was actually invented by the Germans and French is making its Chinese debut. In 1989, Siemens and the French nuclear energy company Framatome began developing this pressurized water reactor, the third generation of nuclear power plants with the abbreviation EPR. Originally, they were called *European Pressurized Water Reactor*. The Chinese now consistently call them *Evolutionary Power Reactor*. That says a lot about China's new self-confidence.

Siemens was forced to withdraw from the project in 2011. At the time, Chancellor Merkel had decided to phase out nuclear power following the Fukushima disaster. Four years earlier, the Chinese had joined the project. In 2007, they signed an 8-billion-US-dollar contract with Framatome, and construction began two years later.

When the chain reaction succeeds for the first time on this June day in 2018, Xavier Ursat, the head of new nuclear projects at French power giant EDF, tweets, "This is a great day for the entire nuclear industry." Above all, it's a great day for China because the Chinese have shown that they can consistently and successfully advance this risky technology, which we face with great reservations. The Chinese have finished their power plant faster than the French in Flamanville and the Finns in Olkiluoto, who started two and four years earlier, respectively. The Chinese have not only overtaken the Europeans but they have also learned from their mistakes.

The French now only have a 30 percent share in the two reactors in Taishan. This means that the greatest output now comes from the Chinese. The first chain reaction of the new EPR reactors is an important step for China in becoming a nuclear world power. The Chinese politicians have made a different decision than the Germans. Beijing wants to make nothing less than industrial history in this field. In the next 10 years, at least six new nuclear power plants are to be built each year. In other words, 60 new nuclear reactors. By way of comparison, in the same period, the EU countries have planned 14 new nuclear power plants, of which probably only half will be built.

Beijing has concluded, after weighing $CO_2$ emissions against the risks of a potential GAU (maximum credible accident), that nuclear power is not an option at the moment. Even with the 60 new power plants, the share of nuclear power in Chinese electricity would still be less than 10 percent. In the U.S., the figure is well over 20 percent, in France over 70 percent, and in South Korea, the leader in Asia, just under 30 percent. So, China still has room for improvement. It is expected to overtake the

U.S. in capacity by 2030 at the latest. The Americans have led the world since the 1960s, while in Europe it is France.

Regardless of whether you are among the opponents of nuclear power or an advocate, one thing can be said after the decision in Beijing and that is that the future of the technology, and therefore its safety, will now be decided in China. In 2018 alone, five new nuclear power plants will be connected to the grid there. Construction is to begin on six to eight power plants. At least that is the plan of the National Energy Administration (NEA), which is known for achieving its ambitious targets, even if it still has to get help from abroad for the time being. In June 2018, for example, the Chinese awarded a contract to Russia's Rosatom to build four new nuclear power plants — at $3.62 billion, it is the largest deal between the two countries.

In parallel, China itself is developing. Experimental, networked research platforms that can easily exchange results are to be set up all over the country. China is also working on floating reactors. The first ones are expected to be on the market before 2020. They raise entirely new questions about the risks of this technology. Greenpeace is already warning of a "floating Chernobyl." Their technology no longer has anything to do with the obsolete reactors of Chernobyl, defend the Chinese. What's more, the floating reactors could primarily assist poorer countries along the coast that are hit by natural disasters. The nuclear ships are of course also very suitable for supplying the disputed islands in the South China Sea with electricity in the short term, if, for example, China wants to set up a military base there.

The first reactors to be developed entirely by the Chinese, which are currently being built in the southeastern city of Fuqing, are scheduled to go online as early as 2020. And, in the meantime, a considerable proportion of the world's new nuclear power plants are being built or at least co-built by the Chinese. Their companies offer the best price–performance ratio, including favorable financing. In May 2018, China and Uganda decided to build a nuclear reactor, and in the same year in Argentina, construction began on two reactors. The cost is estimated at $13 billion. The Germans still built Argentina's first two reactors. In Karachi, Pakistan, two third-generation Huanglong reactors are scheduled to go online in 2020 and 2021, and another power plant is being planned. Negotiations are underway with Thailand and with the Czech Republic. There are other bidders in the running, however it is already clear that none of the competitors offers better financing. Warsaw and Beijing are negotiating the first Chinese nuclear power plant in Poland and Hungary wants to follow suit. The new government in South Africa wants to get back on board and the Chinese are set to do so. In September 2017, even the British government gave the green light for the Hinkley Point reactor in southwest England. It is an EPR-type reactor. The Chinese are still building it together with the French. After that, they will stand on their own two feet.

"It's going to be the same story as solar energy," says Fatih Birol, executive director of the OECD's International Energy Agency. "China is gaining more and more experience and can now export its technology cheaply. The Chinese will put pressure on traditional exporters like the U.S., Japan, Korea, and the French." In the long run, Russians and Chinese will probably share the world market. The West will have a small role to play. We may have phased out nuclear power nationally, but we will soon have Chinese nuclear power plants on our doorstep that are very likely not as safe as the German ones we have closed. That's tough.

We no longer have a say in safety standards, either in Europe or worldwide. This is regrettable since German nuclear power plants were the safest of all. What was considered an indispensable standard in Germany is still considered superfluous by many of our neighbors today. As a technology leader and top exporter, we would have had the power to set safety standards, in China too. Every hidden champion in Germany knows how to do this. Even Bill Gates has now outsourced the research for his Terra-Power nuclear project to Beijing. The fact that our nuclear power plants were so safe was not only due to our top engineers but above all to the impressively successful pressure exerted by opponents of nuclear power. Of course, resistance to nuclear power is also forming in China. The largest demonstration in this context took place north of Shanghai in 2015. Several thousand people protested against a repro-cessing plant. However, it is very unlikely that the Chinese resistance will result in the same pressure as in Germany. In this respect, the German withdrawal from nuclear power is a Pyrrhic victory from a global perspective. The chancellor now has the chance to go down in industrial history as the one who abolished the world's safest nuclear power plants and thus negligently relinquished the West's control over the risky technology. Merkel had hoped to lead by example, to initiate a trend toward other forms of energy. But China has put a spoke in her wheel. Another example of how much the Chinese have outstripped the Europeans is set in a particularly interesting area of quantum physics. It is the stuff of a drama reminiscent of Shakespeare because when the foster son grows up to be a rival, things get uncomfortable. Especially when it also involves competition between two great empires. When both are also working on beaming photons with secret information into space that can't be hacked, it sounds like a science fiction movie with Harrison Ford and Matt Damon.

In reality, the main characters are named Anton Zeilinger and Pan Jianwei. The plot takes place in the Lustbühel hills near Graz and in Jiuquan on the edge of the Gobi Desert. The idea is to send data into space via satellites in an absolutely hack-proof manner, using a phenomenon discovered by Erwin Schrödinger in the 1930s. Albert Einstein had doubtfully referred to this as "spooky action at a distance." This is based on the fact that two particles can assume a common state regardless of their distance from each other and thus transmit information massless and at the speed of light. This is difficult to imagine, but it works and is important because it allows information to be sent that is absolutely tap-proof. This is of course indispensable for a world power that is digitizing so quickly and to such a high degree, and it is a decisive advantage in the competition between world powers.

To prove that this is also possible over long distances, a Chinese rocket with a satellite was sent into space in August 2016. The bulky name of the mission is "XD-2-Quantum Experiments at Space Scale" (QUESS).

But let's take it one step at a time. In the mid-1990s, the young Chinese physicist Pan Jianwei was doing his doctorate in Vienna under Anton Zeilinger, the renowned quantum physicist. The student and his teacher compete to prove the existence of entangled particle pairs, whose interrelation is stronger than classical laws of physics actually allow, even over long distances. The two teams succeed in proving this almost simultaneously. However, Pan is slightly ahead, and the British magazine *Physics World* calls it the "breakthrough of the year." The Zeilinger team, in turn, succeeds in raising the record to 144 kilometers as the crow flies. Both teams are each honored with an article in the prestigious scientific journal *Nature*. Pan's achievements, however, are more surprising. In just a decade, he turns small-time China into a world leader in a key area of quantum physics. He is so successful that from now on it makes more sense for Zeilinger's team to work with China. The Austrians don't have enough money and the decision-making processes at the European Space Agency (ESA) are too slow. In China, on the other hand, it is much easier to get billions for research in this area. At the same time, the Europeans' findings are still so valuable to the Chinese that they make a common cause. Rivals become partners.

The Chinese first succeed in creating the first long-range quantum communications link on the ground. It runs between Shanghai and Beijing. The disadvantage is that the photons or light has to be reloaded after 100 kilometers. The light beam is too weak. At these 32 points, the information is not hack-proof. Previously, they were not vulnerable at any single point. Some Chinese banks are already using the route to exchange data.

After that, it's the turn of the Austrians and the Chinese in a joint experiment. The Micius satellite is now to transmit the information to Earth. The research teams are the first in the world to succeed in establishing an absolutely tap-proof satellite link between China and Austria. A huge success. "China is now leading the way," writes the American *MIT Technology Review*. Of course, there are still teething problems. Communicates are only visible in a short space of time when the satellite, which flies comparatively low, is visible. So you would need a satellite chain or very high flying satellites. But then the transmission is compromised. However, this will be resolved in time.

In early summer of 2018, the Chinese government decides to establish a national center for quantum information and increase research funding from \$10 billion to \$20 billion. The Americans are shaken up by the sensational successes of the Chinese. They, too, need hack-proof satellite links. Under no circumstances do they want to fall behind; they must catch up. "We are now in a race as a nation," admits Walter Copan, director of the National Institute for Standards and Technology in the United States. A race, in which the Chinese are already ahead.

The Chinese now feel very much at home in space. In 2016, with 22 rocket launches of two new types of rockets, China was on a par with the USA for the first time, even outstripping the former Russian space pioneers by five successful flights. In September 2016, a Long March 2F rocket launched China's second space launcher, Tiangong 2, into orbit. Only two months later, China completed its longest manned space mission to date on the spacecraft "Shenzhou 11" that docked with "Tiangong 2" space laboratory.

All this is just the beginning. "Exploring the vast cosmos and developing the space industry is a dream we are relentlessly pursuing," the government declared in a five-year plan presented in early 2017. While U.S. spaceflight is increasingly driven by private companies such as Elon

Musk's SpaceX, China has now become the pace-setter in space with major state investment. On board the SJ-10 science probe, for example, the Chinese succeeded in proving that mouse embryos can develop in space. "This is a milestone in space research," says Professor Aaron Shue of the U.S. Stanford University, who researches stem cells. It's a milestone that the Chinese are now more likely to be able to exploit than the Europeans or the Americans.

By 2022, China plans to complete a 66-ton space station in which three astronauts can live and work, including a space telescope similar to the U.S. Hubble telescope but with a field of view 300 times larger. If the International Space Station (ISS) ceases to operate in 2024, as planned, because NASA in particular no longer wants to finance the project, China would be the only nation with a permanent outpost in space. China wants to allow all UN members to conduct research in their space station. Countries in the Belt and Road Initiative, the New Silk Road, however, are to be given preference. The Americans, on the other hand, still stubbornly refuse to grant the Chinese access to the International Space Station (ISS).

Further major steps are underway to setting the tone for the spatial competition. Two unmanned lunar missions are planned for the future. As early as the end of 2018/beginning of 2019, the unmanned landing module "Chang'e 4" is scheduled to touch down with a robotic vehicle near the south pole of the moon. The relay station, which can be used to send information from the radio shadow of the moon, is already flying. In the quiet lunar environment, the "Queqiao" satellite will then also search for silent radio signals from the ends of the universe. Without the Earth's atmosphere interfering, astronomers can better detect signals in the silence of space and hope for new insights into the formation of the stars. They are "well on their way," said Zhang Rong Qiao, chief planner for the mission. The exploration is a cooperative project with the Lowlands, which is building the low frequency radio receiver (NCLE). It is reassuring to know that the Chinese still need us Europeans for one or the other project.

In addition to the lunar mission, China is also planning a trip to Mars, with six lunar rover vehicles to be placed on the red planet in 2020. In the Chinese province of Qinghai, it will be possible to experience the distant planet Mars up close and personal. There, in the northeast of the Tibetan highlands, a replica of a 95,000-square-meter Martian landscape is being built at a cost of more than $60 billion for scientists to conduct research.

But the site can also be visited by tourists. "People dream of traveling to Mars — we're giving them the opportunity to experience what it's like to be in space," explains Liu Xiaoqun, the project's director.

China's space ambitions are comparatively late — the first NASA rover was put on Mars back in 1986. Still, Beijing's push has set off global competition. European aerospace company Airbus, for example, is to design a rover that can collect sample canisters on Mars and return them to Earth. The project is a cooperative effort between U.S. and European space agencies and is scheduled to launch in the mid-2020s. Europeans celebrated their last major success on 24 December 1979, when the European Ariane launch vehicle took off. Since then, there has been no more groundbreaking progress, except for the Copernicus earth observation system and Galileo satellite navigation. Europe's rocket builders are behind the U.S. and Russia in terms of the number of launches and have been behind China for some years. In 2017, 11 European rockets were launched, while the Chinese sent 18 into space, even though they play no role internationally. This is because the Americans have prohibited sending U.S. technology into space with a rocket made in China. Europeans are faced not only with the technical advances of Elon Musk's SpaceX but also with those of the Chinese. "Europe needs a radical change in the space industry," says Airbus CEO Tom Enders. The competitiveness of the European economy depends on it.

Chancellor Merkel and French President Macron took the initiative in mid-June 2018 and commissioned experts from politics and industry to develop a strategy. In addition, the first spaceport on European soil is to be built in the north of Scotland. The first rockets are to be launched into space from the A'Mhoine peninsula as early as the next decade. London is hoping that its own spaceport will provide a boost to the economy of around 4.3 billion euros over the next 10 years — an urgently needed boost in view of the impending Brexit.

China is already the leader when it comes to the fastest way to transport people and goods over land. The latest generation of high-speed trains, called "Fuxing" which means "renewal" or "revitalization," have been in operation since September 2017. Seven times a day, they cover the 1,300-kilometer route between Beijing and Shanghai in four and a half hours. By way of comparison, in Germany, it takes six hours by ICE train to cover the Hamburg–Munich route, about half the distance. So far, Chinese trains have been traveling at a speed of 350 kilometers per hour, however a test at 400 kilometers per hour is scheduled for 2018. Chinese researchers even believe that a speed of 1,000 kilometers per hour is possible.

The route between the capital and the business metropole of Shanghai is the most important in the country. It is used by around 100 million people a year and already generated around one billion US dollars in 2015. If the Fuxing trains prove themselves on this route, China will set new standards worldwide as far as high-speed trains are concerned. The fact that the Chinese have worked their way up to the top of the industry so quickly is astonishing. After all, it wasn't that easy to catch up with the old industrialized nations. This cannot be done with money alone. It is true that around 118 billion U.S. dollars were invested in 2016, and according to the current five-year plan, over half a trillion U.S. dollars in investments are planned in this sector. But China has also needed resourceful engineers who do not let up. The network of high-speed trains now covers more than 22,000 kilometers. By 2020, this figure is set to rise to 30,000 kilometers. A total of eight north–south and east–west lines will then connect 80 percent of all Chinese cities with more than one million inhabitants to the network. Even Hong Kong will soon have a fast connection to the mainland.

At present, around two-thirds of the high-speed rails laid worldwide are in China. There is no better way to sell Chinese trains and rails abroad. The new Fuxing trains are set to become the new export hit. A contract with Indonesia has already been signed. The Chinese are not only building the trains but are also laying the rails between the capital Jakarta and the country's fourth largest city, Bandung. There, starting in 2019, the travel time is to be reduced from the current three hours to 40 minutes. A train connection between Thailand and China is already under construction. The government in Beijing is also looking north, a 6,630-kilometer freight line to Russia was already opened in August 2017. There are also talks of building a high-speed line between Moscow and Kazan, on which trains are to run at speeds of up to 360 kilometers per hour.

High-speed trains have actually always been the domain of the Europeans and the Japanese. How did China's railroad technology become so strong so quickly? One of the reasons is the many years of cooperation with foreign companies. The German, French, and Japanese companies gained access to the Chinese market in exchange for technology. A good decade later, this is paying off for the Chinese.

Today, no German trains are running in China. Even German suppliers have problems, such as Knorr-Bremse AG from Munich. The world's leading manufacturer of braking systems for rail and commercial vehicles has long supplied to China. Joint ventures with several thousand employees were set up, and the braking systems were manufactured in China using German know-how. Knorr-Bremse air conditioning systems and door systems were also installed in Chinese high-speed trains. But when it came to the latest generation, the Munich-based company didn't get a chance. "Our brakes were not even inspected," complains Klaus Deller, CEO of Knorr-Bremse.

"We transferred technology, and China benefited." A Chinese company, once a partner of Knorr-Bremse, won the contract. For German Ambassador Michael Clauss, this is a good example of how China is still protecting its own interests. "There were repeated announcements that China would indeed open up further quickly. However, not much has happened so far. In fact, protectionism has even increased in some areas."

In the end, it doesn't matter who copied what from whom; it can't be changed. It is more important to find out what Beijing wants to do with this technology. If you put the individual projects in an overall context, it becomes clear that they ultimately serve the larger project of the New Silk Road. Whether in Russia, India, or Southeast Asia, the new train routes are intended to create a trans-Asian corridor across China's borders all the way to Europe. From an overall economic perspective, this is a development that Europe can actually be pleased about. Of course, it would be even better if European companies were involved in building this corridor, but it is already clear that neither ICEs nor TGVs will run on these routes. The Chinese have the know-how by now, the practical experience as well, and companies like Siemens are still supplying at best.

In the Fall of 2017, the situation for the former railroad stags from Germany and France becomes so serious that the two fierce competitors decide to merge. Siemens and Alstom merge their rail divisions. But even together, with 15 billion euros in sales and 62,000 employees, they are only the second-largest manufacturer behind the Chinese group CRRC, which is twice as big. Here, too, hope dies last. The employees support the project and in return receive job and location guarantees for four years. The managers cannot look much further. They cannot predict how quickly the Chinese will develop internationally. In this case, China is already making very concrete decisions about European jobs and management commitments. Alstom boss Henri Poupart-Lafarge said that the new group "will undoubtedly shape the future of mobility" but does not sound convinced. Even the prominent reinforcement announced by the group in

Spring 2018 may not be able to help; former foreign minister Sigmar Gabriel will join the new company's executive board in 2019. His thankless job will be to sell trains outside Europe against the Chinese competitor. We wish him the best of luck.

Virtual reality (VR) is already one step ahead. It no longer needs to move in the traditional way. In the middle of Guiyang, the capital of the Chinese province of Guizhou, huge circular structures nestle in the hilly landscape. In the center of the area, which looks like a space colony in the distant future, stands a 50-meter-high statue of a robot pointing to the horizon with an outstretched weapon arm. On closer inspection, the giant, welded together from 750 tons of steel, turns out to be a character from the well-known *Transformers* film series. So, we are in the present after all.

The global future of the entertainment industry will be decided here, in southwest China. The futuristic scenery forms part of the "Oriental Science Fiction Valley," the largest virtual reality theme park in the world. Construction of the 1.3-square-kilometer facility began in July 2016, and the "Alien Base" is now the first section to open to visitors in December 2017. Attractions include movie theaters, roller coasters, video gaming centers, and neon-lit adventure platforms. But that's just the beginning. The real magic unfolds beneath the virtual reality headsets visitors are equipped with. So, although you're doing loops on a real roller coaster, under the goggles the experience is translated into an alien, digitally programmed world. Users jet through space in a spaceship or ride a twisting dragon in a rodeo. In the best experience, the impression is so convincing that the simulated environment is perceived as real, as if in a frenzy.

For a long time, virtual reality technology was a lonely one where geeks and gamers alienated themselves from reality in dark rooms. In VR amusement parks like the one in Guiyang, it's a community experience. VR entertainment centers already exist in many countries, but the $1.5 billion Oriental Science Fiction Valley is by far the most ambitious to date. But, by now, we're used to that from China. It was developed by the publicly traded company Oriental Times Media, which bought Huahua Media, the Chinese partner of Paramount Pictures, in July 2017.

Film companies and filmmakers see virtual reality as the next big step in cinema. Star director Zhang Yimou, for example, who has demonstrated his talent for large-scale productions with films such as *Great Wall* and the opening ceremony at the 2008 Olympic Games, has co-founded a start-up called SoReal. Just about two blocks from Tiananmen Square.

It opened a 3,000-square-meter VR hall in Spring 2017. By comparison, the biggest western competitor at the moment is VR World in New York, which is located in a building in Manhattan with around 1,500 square meters on two floors.

China is also currently the most promising growth market for virtual reality. One-third of the VR headsets sold worldwide go to Chinese customers. Industry experts estimate that sales of VR devices, services, and software in China will increase from 520 million US dollars in 2016 to almost 12 billion US dollars by 2021.

There are many reasons for this success. Since Chinese Internet users are primarily mobile, domestic manufacturers such as Ritech focus on lighter, economical hardware and less on high-performance consoles and desktop devices, such as the Oculus Rift and PlayStation VR, which are well-known in the West. High-end devices are used in China primarily in the country's more than 5,000 game arcades and "VR experience booths," which can be found in many large shopping malls. In addition, when it comes to technical innovations, the Chinese once again focus on the opportunities rather than on the dangers.

The loss of reality that VR applications could result in, as Western critics fear, is far less of an issue in China. Since much of the technology and equipment, such as headsets and 360-degree cameras, are manufactured in China anyway, early experimental fields for virtual reality start-ups emerged in Beijing, Shanghai, and Shenzhen. Currently, more than 200 PRC companies and start-ups are working on new solutions for fields as diverse as sporting events, theme parks, cinema viewing, exhibitions, social media platforms, and video games. Other areas of daily life, such as shopping tours, real estate inspections, and vacation travel, are benefiting, especially from new applications in so-called augmented reality (AR) technology. This combines the virtual and the real. For example, as in the film *Terminator*, users can have information, directions, or product details displayed in their field of vision via a pair of glasses. In industry and education, artificial intelligence is already successfully minimizing the effort and risks involved. For example, the company Superb Medical Skills, together with a Shanghai hospital, has developed an app that can be used to practice difficult operations under VR goggles. 3,700 doctors are already using it for training purposes.

While cell phone manufacturers, such as Xiaomi, are launching high-end yet low-cost headsets, such as the MI VR, Chinese tech companies

Alibaba, Tencent, and Baidu are pursuing their own VR initiatives. When it comes to shopping, e-commerce companies, such as Alibaba and JD.com, are experimenting with virtual shopping experiences, such as 3-D shopping malls with a panoramic view, catwalks, shopping baskets, and dressing rooms, where detailed programmed products can be examined in advance and paid for online.

On the country's most important shopping day, known as Singles Day, where Alibaba turned over the equivalent of $25.3 billion in 2017, the company was already experimenting with a mixed reality game where people could use their smartphones to hunt for virtual discount vouchers outside their doors, similar to the popular Pokémon Go.

As bizarre as all this may sound to us in the West, consumers are happy to accept the new shopping concepts, and sooner or later these concepts will also be available in Europe. In China, 84 percent of young people can already imagine shopping in virtual spaces in the future. So, China is well on the way to becoming the first mass market for virtual reality. Just imagine being able to stop by the stand of your favorite market woman on a rainy day and get advice from her without having to leave the house, while the market is in full swing. The market woman can also stay at home and does not have to set up her stand early in the morning. The virtually purchased vegetables are then delivered to your home by courier in time for lunch.

Would something like that be well received in Europe? So far, it doesn't look that way. VR has not yet been able to establish itself beyond the gaming niche. The industry is struggling with a chicken-and-egg problem in the West. Hardware manufacturers are hoping for spectacular content to sell their products, while content manufacturers are hoping for the one big hardware blockbuster to sell their content to the largest possible audience.

In China, this question no longer arises, as VR has long since found its way into many areas of life and is already more than just a futuristic gimmick for people of all ages. The VR park in Guiyang could reinforce this trend and could even become a kind of Disneyland for virtual reality fans. Then, the Chinese will perhaps feel like the wise Zhuang Zhou from the Chinese philosophical classic *Zhuangzi*, who, after waking up, no longer knew whether he had just dreamed of being a butterfly or whether he was a butterfly who had just dreamed of being Zhuang Zhou.

Today, all it takes to immerse yourself in virtual reality is a smartphone and a pair of glasses. In both areas, Chinese products are increasingly leading the way. When it comes to smartphones, the most important utensil in our daily lives, China has long been competitive.

It seems longer, but it was only 10 years ago that Steve Jobs introduced the world to the first iPhone. At that time, three companies led the world market — Nokia from Espoo, Finland, Sony Ericsson from Tokyo and Lund, Sweden, and Motorola from Schaumburg, USA. Companies from Asia, Europe, and the USA thus shared the market. Then, there were three big surprises. The first: Apple revolutionized the smartphone and the Nokia phone disappeared from the scene.

The second surprise: Samsung replaced the iPhone with its Galaxy back in 2011 and now has a market share of a good 20 percent, 5 percent higher than Apple's smartphone. In other words, the American iPhone was only the world market leader for a short time, in a sense between the European pioneers and the current Asian players.

The third and biggest surprise: Huawei phones from Shenzhen in southern China have only 0.7 percent less global market share than Apple in the first half of 2017. In July 2017, Huawei overtakes Apple for the first time. But in the Fall, Apple can push ahead again with the new iPhone X. By mid-2018, Apple has a global market share of over 14 percent, while Huawei maintains a good 10 percent. That is still astonishing; Huawei launched its first smartphone only five years ago. If anyone had predicted back then that Huawei would make it to third place in the world rankings in such a short time, no one would have believed them. And certainly not that the Chinese manufacturers would serve one-third of the world market.

China has caught up much faster than the world thought. Not only is Huawei an outlier but only the vanguard of a trend. In the world rankings, Samsung, Apple, and Huawei are now followed by two more Chinese providers: Oppo and Xiaomi with a good 7 percent global market share. Xiaomi is now represented in 74 countries. In July 2018, Xiaomi raised over five billion US dollars in Hong Kong when it went public. Although it was only half of what the self-indulgent Xiaomi managers had hoped for, the company is now worth 55 billion US dollars.

While Samsung and Apple are stagnating, the Chinese are growing at double-digit rates. This also applies to companies like Transsion Holdings, which is unknown even in China, but which is the market leader in Africa, the fastest growing mobile communications market in the world, with a share of 40 percent, and has even outperformed Huawei.

In China, the situation looks even more serious for the West: Huawei, Oppo, Vivo, and Xiaomi have a combined market share of 73 percent. The iPhone has slipped to fifth place and the trend is continuing downward. At least Apple's profits per smartphone are still unbeatable. The chipmakers are also catching up, with more and more premium models that promise a higher profit margin. Oppo offers a device for 999 euros that has the largest touchscreen of all cell phones available on the market. Oppo's "Lamborghini Edition" costs 1,599 euros. You will pay just under 700 Euros for the best Vivo smartphone. Huawei's competitor to the iPhone, which is better than the Apple smartphone in some features, such as the camera, sells for 800 euros. The Chinese will dramatically expand their global market share. Huawei only has a market share of around 5 percent in the USA so far.

Some revolutions take place quietly — almost as a matter of course — and yet they turn everything that has gone before upside down. One such revolution in China is payment platforms through WeChat or Alipay. These are apps for smartphones that, in the case of WeChat, you can use not only to pay but also to make free phone calls using applications like Facebook and WhatsApp. Before the credit cards so coveted in the U.S. could even establish themselves in China, along came WeChat & Co. Within a few years, they have ensured that cash has largely disappeared from everyday life in China. This is just as true for the market woman and the bicycle mender as it is for supermarkets, restaurants, and now even for buying a smaller car. Simply scan the code with your cell phone, confirm the amount, prove your identity with a thumbprint, and you're done. What you spend where is clearly listed on the cell phone. Food deliveries, electricity bills, and even credit and stock transactions can be conveniently handled with the fast payment method. Even the rare beggar in China now holds up a cardboard box with a barcode, just like the street musicians. The days of the open guitar box into which coins and small bills could be thrown are over in China.

In China, credit cards are considered a strangely old-fashioned Westerners system. You have to lug these clunky readers to the customer in the restaurant, which then usually have connection problems. The customer has to enter a PIN into them. Then, these little pieces of paper come out of the machine, which the customer also has to sign. One slip is given to the restaurant and one to the customer. These slips have to be collected somewhere because four weeks later, they have to be compared with a bill. The Chinese just shake their heads with a smile when they hear what the Americans have come up with. WeChat now has more than one billion users and Alipay more than 780 billion. In 2017, transactions worth more than 15 trillion US dollars were made — over 50 percent by Alipay and just under 40 percent by WeChat. So, over 90 percent of those transactions are in the hands of two tech giants — Alibaba and Tencent. The two are in fierce competition for customers, which they fight out via discount battles.

Even more valuable than the transaction fee is customer data. Knowing who buys what and when opens up opportunities for companies to tailor their offerings to customers. However, most Chinese are not bothered by the fact that they are becoming transparent. According to a study by Penguin Intelligence, 92 percent of Chinese made mobile payments in major cities in 2017. The wallet belongs to a past century in China. However, as Chinese are becoming more and more familiar with not carrying bills and coins, the chances of getting suitable change are getting worse. This can be a problem for tourists from abroad. Up until now, a Chinese bank account has been required to use the virtual wallet of Alipay & Co.

The competition between Alibaba and Tencent is like that between Pepsi and Coca-Cola in the past. The caffeinated fizzy drink that started its triumphal march around the world was American in every way. From Europe, or more precisely from Germany, came BMW and Mercedes. A duo that shaped the world of premium cars. At the end of the 1990s came Apple and Google, also American.

Today, mobile payment systems are triumphing around the world — and the big players are Chinese. The West has little to counter this. Apple Pay has 127 million users worldwide. U.S. provider PayPal came up with 7.6 billion transactions worth a total of $451 billion in 2017. Alipay, on the other hand, recorded orders for around nine trillion US dollars in the same period. The Americans no longer have a chance to prevail globally on this issue. Not to mention Europe and Germany.

The industry behind this is called FinTech, short for financial technology. It's not just about mobile payment systems but also about other areas in which people "take money in their hands" virtually, for example, in digital banking and insurance or in asset management. In short, FinTech is about nothing less than the future of money.

In China, market leader Ant Financial, the company with the blue ant in its logo, is growing immeasurably. In Spring 2018, the Hangzhou-based company raised $14 billion from investors — the largest known round of financing by a private company ever. Analysts now estimate the company's value at 150 to 160 billion US dollars.

In addition to its payment service, the Group also offers loans and microcredits. It is a subsidiary of the omnipresent Chinese tech giant Alibaba. Alibaba was founded in 1999 by former English teacher Jack Ma, who is now considered a kind of Chinese Steve Jobs, if you will. In 2004, Ma founded the payment service Alipay through his Internet platform Alibaba. Ant Financial, whose advisors include Deutsche Bank, spun off from Alibaba in 2014, shortly before the parent company went public in New York and raised $25 billion at its initial listing. Next year, Ant Financial plans to go public itself, presumably in Hong Kong. The company could even outperform its former parent company.

It's a fruitful collaboration: Ant Financial is the world's largest FinTech company and Alibaba operates China's largest online trading platform, Taobao. The two companies can therefore sell customers to each other. Compared to traditional banks, Ant Financial has another advantage; due to lower security concerns in terms of data protection in China, the company has access to its customers and their consumption and user behavior. Discounts can also be granted much more easily with Alipay and Taobao than with a credit card, for example. This also puts the Chinese in a better position to compete with the Western top dogs: Google Pay and PayPal. The Chinese central bank is already taking care not to undermine its power. In order not to endanger the stability of the financial market, it recently imposed transaction limits of 10,000 yuan ($1,560) per day. So for larger purchases, you need an exemption.

Beijing's politicians are far more skeptical with other innovations in financial technology. At the beginning of September 2017, for example, the Chinese central bank made good on its threat and with immediate effect banned so-called Initial Coin Offerings (ICO), digital IPOs with which companies generate capital via digital cryptocurrencies. For Beijing, the unregulated financing model is a disruption of the economic and financial order. In a statement, the central bank described ICOs as "illegal public fundraising related to criminal activities such as fraud and snowball schemes." The ban made international waves, not least because China had emerged as the world's fastest-growing ICO market. Shortly after the decision was announced, the value of Bitcoin, the most popular online currency, plummeted by 7 percent, but later recovered.

However, Beijing does not want to put too much of the brake on cashless payment. Domestic consumption, rather than exports, is now the most important pillar of China's economic growth. So, smooth purchasing is important. More and more companies that were previously too refined to offer their products via WeChat are now buckling. French luxury brand Christian Dior, for example, offered handbags on WeChat for the first time in August 2017, just in time for Qixi, the Chinese Valentine's Day. The "Lady Dior Bag" special edition with decorative "cannage" topstitching inspired by Napoleon III-style chairs sold for the equivalent of 3,800 euros. This is no longer a shopping event, lament traditionalists, even at Dior. In fact, the bag is then delivered to the door by a musty driver of an electric tricycle who might be delivering Chinese cabbage and metal on the same trip. The French are the first of the major haute couture brands to jump over themselves. Others are likely to follow.

The people who have been denigrating an old festival for years should also regret the commercial denigration of it. The Qixi Festival is much older than Dior. It has been celebrated since the Han Dynasty, which began 200 years before the birth of Christ. According to legend, on that night a shepherd boy and a weaver girl looked at the stars together, separated by the Milky Way. Also separated for a long time were the new world of the Chinese and the old world of the West. Ant Financial is now bringing the two together, with a Dior bag, thus reducing the traditional Qixi festival to a shopping event. This may be regretted, but consumers are happy to take this opportunity, just like the "cash-free week" initiated by Alipay, a campaign with numerous discount promotions.

With the help of the newly raised 14 billion US dollars, Ant Financial wants to increase its market share to two billion users in the coming years. In India, Alibaba and Ant Financial together already own 36 percent of Paytm, the Indian version of Alipay, which already records around one billion transactions per month. Ant Financial also wants to gain a foothold in Indonesia as soon as possible and has already, in 2017 established a joint venture with the Indonesian media group Elang Mahkota Teknologi. Together, the companies are planning a mobile payment system specialized for the huge Indonesian market. "In developing countries, including those through which China's New Silk Road passes, up to two billion people live without bank accounts. Seventy-nine percent of these people rely on loans that their countries' financial systems cannot provide," says Yu Shengfa, vice president of Ant Financial. It's an opportunity you don't want to miss out on.

In the U.S., on the other hand, the probability is low that the Chinese get a foot in the door. The Americans are closing their markets. When Ant Financial wanted to acquire the American money transfer specialist MoneyGram for $1.2 billion in 2017, Donald Trump said no.

In the Europeans' thoroughly regulated financial system, it's not easy either. The "enforce first, regulate later" method that Ant Financial uses in developing countries does not work here. In Germany in particular, the familiar is preferred to the innovative and has been for some time. So Alipay first migrates with its customers setting up at airport stores, at popular tourist destinations, such as the Palace of Versailles, or in upscale shopping centers. Stores such as Harrods in London can be paid using WeChat Pay. In Germany, Alipay has been cooperating with the drugstore chain Rossmann since April 2017, where Chinese tourists, students, and business travelers can now use the app to pay for goods such as powdered milk or shampoo from the Bielefeld-based brand Alpecin, which is extremely popular in China. Cooking pot manufacturer WMF is co-operating, as is Munich's upscale department store Ludwig Beck and Munich Airport. And Alipay has signed a contract with the German company Concardis, which operates 470,000 card readers in Germany.

While Germans do not notice it, Chinese tourists passing through recognize the small blue Alipay logo at the checkout from a distance. The same goes for the green WeChat logo. Around one million Chinese now travel to Germany every year; they spend an average of 4,700 euros.

Since 2018, around 70 stores at Munich Airport have been accepting WeChat Pay. The transactions are processed by a German company called Wirecard. The company could soon appear on the Dax and be worth more than Deutsche Bank. The TecDAX-listed group, headquartered in Aschheim near München, is one of the biggest profiteers from Internet commerce.

The company, which is listed on the Munich Stock Exchange, has had incredible success. In the Summer of 2018, the company's stock market value of around 20 billion even exceeded that of Deutsche Bank. Then, at the beginning of September, with its China business behind it, Wirecard kicked Commerzbank out of the DAX. In the first quarter of 2018 alone, the transaction volume processed via the Wirecard platform increased by 50 percent to a good 26 billion euros. Alipay and WeChat will boost the company's success even further because they haven't really arrived in Europe yet.

In response, Tencent invested in Berlin-based flagship startup N26 in Spring 2018.

It is one of the highest financing rounds in a FinTech company in Europe and the highest in Germany so far. Still, things won't go as smoothly here as elsewhere. The fact that something is convenient, fast, and inexpensive can't easily overcome local concerns about data privacy. Germans do not want to become "transparent citizens" as a result of the data collected in the digital payment process.

However, WeChat and Alipay could soon be cold coffee: There seems to be nothing unusual about the women at this Beijing party. Perhaps a little too perfectly made up, but well-dressed and self-confident, in long dresses and pantsuits. The scene could be set in New York or Paris. It's one of those countless events, another new venture, you can hardly keep up with. This time, it's the launch of the tech start-up Megvii in northwest Beijing. The guests stand together in groups, a glass of champagne in their hands. But then a face scanner detects the first group of women and, immediately, it recognizes them as men. The company's software, called Face++, is not fooled; it can clearly determine the gender in all cases on the basis of the face alone. When it comes to age, the program also proves to be impressively accurate, with a deviation of only one year. Ten years ago, such accuracy in the field of facial recognition was still a thing of the future.

That evening the creators of Megvii have hired a team of male actors and dressed them up as women to demonstrate the progression of their programs. Megvii is well on its way to setting global standards in future technology of facial recognition. What is technically a major challenge can be summed up in a few words. For facial recognition, computers measure key features such as eyes, nostrils, chin, and mouth areas and their distance from each other. In the sum of the data collected from ever new angles captured physiognomies, a digital biometric pattern is created that is unique to each person. Deep Learning, the supreme discipline within artificial intelligence, is indispensable to produce good facial recognition software. The algorithms have to learn what kind of faces there are and what distinguishes one from the other. They must be able to distinguish real faces from artificial ones and include factors such as angular distortions, light influences, or details such as sunglasses in their calculations. A large database of faces and images is the basic prerequisite for this. China is therefore an ideal experimental field for the development of such software. Unlike in Europe or the U.S., developers here are hardly restricted in their research by data protection laws and privacy discussions. On the contrary, selected companies are even allowed to draw on government data pools. And these are enormous. In China, more than 176 million cameras currently ensure close-meshed surveillance in public spaces. In addition, every Chinese over the age of 16 has an identity card with biometric data, which can also be fed into the deep learning programs. This is not just about police surveillance, as we often reflexively believe. There are also other milder forms of control. In retail, for example, sophisticated facial scanners could help generate personalized advertising for customers based on their gender, age, and facial expressions and send the advertising via smartphone. In this way, a morose-looking person could be made to feel good about a trip to the sunny Caribbean. Whether we really want that is another question.

At the moment, however, the greatest economic potential lies in authentication processes in which the user's own face becomes a personal universal key, for example, when withdrawing money from the bank, checking passports at the airport, or unlocking a smartphone. Of course, the technology is also available to the police for tracing and surveillance purposes — the area that sends shivers down our spine in the West and brings us very close to Aldous Huxley's "Brave New World."

Megvii and its company Face++ are also pioneers in this field. Since 2016, 4,000 suspects have already been arrested with the help of the software, the company proudly announces, with the aid of the police goggles that we uncovered in the chapter on artificial intelligence. The glasses have a face scanner, which is used to scan crowds at the East Railway Station in the central Chinese city of Zhengzhou. Connected to a huge database, it can recognize a person of interest in seconds. The pilot project in Henan province is already considered a success by the police. In just a few weeks, thanks to the glasses, more than seven suspected criminals wanted on arrest warrants have been arrested and 35 people have been caught with false ID cards.

Megvii was founded in 2011 by three graduates of Tsinghua University in Beijing. It was the first start-up in the industry to join the exclusive club of "unicorns," i.e., companies that are no more than 10 years old and already worth more than one billion US dollars. A success story that shows the potential of facial recognition technology in China is as follows: While Megvii employed only 30 people in 2014, it now has around 530. Major customers, such as Alipay, China Merchants Bank, CITIC Bank, smartphone manufacturer Xiaomi, and computer giant Lenovo, are already using or testing the newcomers' software.

Qi Yin, the company's chief executive, is just 29 years old. He says 90 percent of the top 200 Internet companies in China now use Face++ and its Face ID facial recognition platform. The programs are especially popular with digital financial service providers such as online banks, which use them to identify users more securely. Loopholes are gradually being plugged. No one can disguise themselves with a mask or similar since Megvii has integrated "vividness tests" into its applications, for example, in which the user has to speak or move their head in certain directions. To fool the program, even plastic surgery wouldn't get you far, as Qi says, "You'd have to have your facial bones ground off."

In the last financing round, the young company once again raised 460 million US dollars. Of course, Megvii is also supported by the government in Beijing. In November 2017, the start-up received the equivalent of 400 million euros from a state fund. Megvii can also access the state data pools to feed the company's own deep learning program (subsequently christened Brain++), with huge amounts of data. Megvii is convinced that the software will completely change people's everyday lives. With Megvii facial recognition, a shopping trip will be possible without a wallet, credit card, or ID. Customers will be scanned when they enter a store. They can leave the store with their goods without having to go to the checkout or even put their purchases down. In restaurants, too, people would only pay with their face. And even the door to your apartment will unlock automatically via facial recognition.

In the future, the company intends to use its competencies to contribute to the success of its customers. The company is also expanding its activities into the field of robotics. Among other things, Megvii is currently working on an assembly line robot for Apple supplier Foxconn, which is intended to make the production of the iPhone X, which has been particularly complex up until now, even more efficient. Ironically, the very device that made the big push into the market with facial recognition technology in the West at the end of 2017. Coincidence? Apple had to overcome a few teething problems with its face scanner. For example, the detector could not clearly distinguish between certain Asian women's faces. That wouldn't happen to Megvii. After all, fingerprint recognition, which Apple made popular just five years ago with the iPhone 5s, has since been adopted worldwide. It could be similar to Chinese facial recognition. As it looks at the moment, the Chinese have set the global standard. This is because Megvii is not the only company that is successful in this area. Sense Time from Hong Kong also joined the league of unicorns in the Summer of 2017 and, in addition to facial recognition, specializes in environment analyses of autonomously driving cars. Or CloudWalk, which was able to collect 301 million U.S. dollars from the local government in Guangzhou in late Fall 2017 — just two years after its founding. Its applications are used in the financial and aviation sectors, amongst others.

Since 2017, Alibaba has been operating a supermarket in the eastern Chinese city of Hangzhou, where customers are identified by facial recognition and automatically pay the bill with their Alipay account when they leave the store. There are no checkout counters, no queues, and no cash. Whether this is a dystopian surveillance scenario or a vision of a brave new consumer world is literally up to the eye of the beholder.

At 1,000 ATMs of China Merchants Bank, a glance at the camera is already enough to withdraw money. According to the inventors, photo fraud is ruled out by the "vividness tests" mentioned above. Faster admission checks at soccer matches or rock concerts are made possible by facial scans. This considerably increases the quality of life in a country where huge crowds of people are constantly on the move. At least that's how the inventors advertise it.

The airline China Southern Airlines is already testing the use of facial recognition in the city of Nanyang. Instead of boarding passes, a facial scan has been sufficient here since 2017 to allow a passenger to pass through the flight gates. In the future, you won't even need to bring a passport, the developers promise.

As is often the case with new developments, the technology is also being used for peculiar applications. In Beijing's Temple of Heaven, a UNESCO World Heritage site, face scanners have been installed in the public toilets to catch paper thieves. If someone helps themselves to more than 60 centimeters of toilet paper within nine minutes, the machine politely informs them that there is no extra toilet paper. No information is currently available on how long it will take for the expensive face scanner to pay for itself through reduced toilet paper consumption.

# Chapter 6

# The New Silk Road: Skillful Belt

## How Beijing Is Pulling Off the World's Largest Infrastructure Project and Europe Doesn't Want to Find Its Role in It

*In the meantime, it's okay to state: This is a great idea, That has helped our country a lot.*

Nursultan Nazarbayev, President of Kazakhstan

The lecture hall looks like a small parliament. Dark wood, dark walls. The heavy lecterns for the audience rise upwards row by row in a semicircle. Daylight enters the room from the gallery between Ficus benjamina. This is where it all began with the New Silk Road, the Belt and Road Initiative, or BRI for short. On 7 September 2013 at 10:30 a.m., the hall is full of students, politicians, and journalists. "Nazarbayev University" is written in gold letters above the stage. Sitting below is the university's namesake, Nursultan Nazarbayev, the president of Kazakhstan. We are in Astana, the new capital of the largest Central Asian country, a city that is "younger than Google," as Nazarbayev likes to emphasize. It turned 20-years-old in 2017. The former capital was Almaty (Alma-Ata).

Kazakhstan is one of the 10 largest countries in the world in terms of area and one of the 15 countries with the most mineral resources worldwide. Optimists say that oil worth five trillion US dollars lies under the Caspian Sea that forms Kazakhstan's western border. Its 18 million

133

inhabitants have two powerful neighbors: China to the east and Russia to the north. Between the three million population of Kiev, Ukraine, in eastern Europe and the 15-million metropolis of Istanbul, Turkey in the west of the Silk Road and Ürümqi, the Chinese metropolis of three million in the east, Astana is the only modern city.

Today, the audience has not come for Nazarbayev. Chinese President Xi Jinping is standing at the lectern. Dark suit, light blue tie. "Shaanxi, my home province, is at the beginning of the ancient Silk Road," Xi says. "When I think of that time in history, I can almost hear the calls of camels in the mountains and see the dust blowing in from the desert." Kazakhstan played an important role in exchanges between East and West more than 2,100 years ago, he said. "A close neighbor is more valuable than a distant relative," Xi cajoles the Kazakhs. Exchanges between East and West, he says, led to learning from each other. "This has made a decisive contribution to the progress of human civilizations," Xi says. It shows that countries with different cultural backgrounds can work together for the benefit of all, he adds. "Therefore," he says, "the Eurasian region must reinvent itself and jointly build an economic belt along the Silk Road."

Xi had only been in office for six months at this point. He arrived the day before from St. Petersburg, where he attended his first G20 summit as president. There, he made no mention of his plans for the Eurasian continent. That he wants to initiate the largest infrastructure project in world history, the largest since the construction of the Great Wall, which is more than 20,000 kilometers long and whose first ashlars were placed on top of each other as early as the 7th century BC.

These are the dimensions in which Xi wants to think as a politician.

Eurasia is home to 70 percent of the world's population. It is home to 75 percent of the world's energy resources and already accounts for 70 percent of the world's gross domestic product. Nearly 30 percent of world trade is conducted between Asia and China. It is Xi's plan that in around 10 years, China wants to more than double the volume of trade with the partners of the New Silk Road to 2.5 trillion US dollars.

It seems to Xi that Kazakhstan is the right place to announce the initiative. The country has a key position in the New Silk Road, which was officially called the Silk Road Economic Belt at the time, The initiative is intended to aid the participating countries to achieve an economic upswing. Xi wants Central Asia to boom in such a way that "terrorism, separatism, and extremism" have no chance. He believes that terrorists — from Afghanistan and Pakistan, for example — are tolerated or at least not adequately combated in some Silk Road countries, and fears consequences for China as well. In fact, terrorists are already infiltrating Xinjiang province in western China.

Of course, China is not Caritas. Building bridges to the West will bring new orders to China's construction companies and thus keep growth in its own country stable above 6 percent. And, in the end, the new middle class along the New Silk Road should, of course, buy Chinese products. Above all, however, is the prize of consolidating China's status as a world power. Part of this strategy is that China does not want to transport products it manufactures or the natural resources it purchases exclusively by sea, through the Strait of Malacca near Singapore. A dangerous bottleneck that can be blocked by terrorists or hostile states. For China, this would be like cutting off the jugular vein of its booming country. A world power cannot take that risk.

However, Xi also knows that such a project of the century will only be successful if the people in the countries involved benefit from it. Then, in the end, the region's politicians will be so grateful to Beijing that they will stand united with China on issues. That is why Xi keeps repeating, "We want a big chorus, not a Chinese solo." The countries along the New Silk Road must become more independent, secure, and stable, he says.

The governments of the countries involved are under little illusion that Beijing will listen and, in case of doubt, ignore objections and criticism. And their people are wavering between the lure of economic recovery and political dependence on China. This is the price they will pay for the anticipated boom — because the money for the initiative comes mainly from China.

Beijing, on the other hand, knows very well that it must not act too recklessly; tact is required. That is why Xi wants the countries along the route to be treated not as vassals but as customers. Of course, like any service provider, Beijing tries to make the customer as dependent as possible and establish many of its own standards. In the best case, the enthusiastic customer does not even notice the dependence. But only in the best case.

Xi has already made clear his geopolitical intentions through the sequence of his first foreign trips as Chinese president. His first trip was to Russia, much to the delight of Vladimir Putin. Xi was the first foreign statesman to be allowed to visit the Russian Military Command Center. After that, Xi traveled on through the countries of Africa with the grand finale being the BRICS summit in South Africa. Besides China, the

BRICS are the up-and-coming countries of Brazil, Russia, India, and South Africa.

His second major trip was already that of the "Silk Road speeches." From Central Asia, he made a detour to the G20 summit in St. Petersburg, then went straight on to Kazakhstan and finally to the summit of the Shanghai Cooperation Organization (SCO) in Bishkek, the capital of Kyrgyzstan. The Central Asian countries have joined forces in the SCO, and Pakistan and India are also members.

Only then was it the turn of Europe, the USA, and Japan. It was a clear signal that Xi does not want to chase after the large established states, but rather ally with the small emerging countries and together, as the majority of the world, rebuild the world order. "Let's do something innovative and build this economic belt together," Xi entices in Astana. Initially, however, Xi has a slight problem; his speech has virtually no global resonance. This announcement of changing the world is simply overheard or deemed unnoteworthy. I myself only stumble upon it weeks later, by chance, and I too am not struck by it at first. Even the Chinese media do not cover the topic. True, the foreign ministry's website speaks of an "important speech," and it was even broadcast live on Chinese television. But that alone means nothing; after all, every speech by Xi Jinping is important in some way. Party newspapers rather dutifully comment on their party leader's plan. Journalists and commentators apparently thought that the plan for a "common economic belt" was more of a friendly "green light" gesture towards the Kazakhs.

The review in the Kazakh media is equally restrained. The initiative is reported in the *Astana Times*, but already in the second sentence, the author feels compelled to emphasize "that China does not interfere in the internal affairs of the Central Asian nations." Enthusiasm sounds different. What President Nursultan Nazarbayev thinks of this is not mentioned. Only the Chinese Foreign Ministry emphasizes that the Kazakh President fully agrees with the "strategic version of a New Silk Road."

In the weeks that followed, not much happened. Most people have long since forgotten about the issue, although Xi gives a similar speech to the parliament in Jakarta, in which he speaks of a maritime Silk Road. But then, in the fall of 2013, the term "New Silk Road Economic Belt" appears in the document of the annual meeting of the Central Committee of the Communist Party. It is the first under the leadership of the new state and party leader.

Now, it is clear to everyone that the issue is important. What is not yet clear is *how* important. Only gradually is it becoming apparent that Xi Jinping does indeed intend to build a series of economic belts from China to the West. One axis is to go north through Mongolia and Russia to Moscow and from there to Western Europe. A second route through Kazakhstan via Moscow to Rotterdam. A third through Kyrgyzstan, Uzbekistan, and Iran to Istanbul and from there to the Greek port of Piraeus. A fourth from China diagonally through Pakistan to Iran. A fifth via Myanmar and Bangladesh to the Indian Ocean. And a sixth practically perpendicularly to the south via Vietnam, Laos, Thailand, Malaysia, and Singapore to Jakarta in Indonesia. The Maritime Silk Road, which Xi spoke of in the Indo-European capital, will primarily integrate Africa, but also Central and South America.

Skepticism is high in China. At home, Xi is pushing the issue with all his propaganda power. Special pages appear in the Chinese newspapers, one event after another is organized. Funds are set up. The cities in western China must now get involved in the construction of the New Silk Road.

To ensure that Europe also gains momentum in this respect, Xi will be traveling to Duisburg in March 2014. This is where Europe's largest inland port is located. A quarter of a century ago, heavy industry still dominated here. A ThyssenKrupp steel mill stood directly on the Rhine. At the end of the 1980s, thousands of workers demonstrated unsuccessfully against the planned closure. Today, the site is being used again — as a port and logistics hub. 20,000 ships and 25,000 trains are expected to pass through here annually.

Xi is on-site to welcome the first of the trains that are to run regularly from the Chinese metropolis of Chongqing to Duisburg in the future. The train took around twelve days to cover the 10,000 kilometers; a ship would have taken around 40 days.

Four years later, in 2018, the line is part of everyday life on the New Silk Road. Twenty-five trains run each week. "The train is more expensive than transport by water, but it is faster and in any case cheaper than by air," says Erich Staake, CEO of Duisport AG, explaining the success. Compared to what can be transported on a ship, however, 25 trains are still very few. A train can only carry a maximum of 60 containers per trip, while a single ship can carry around 10,000 containers. But it is a first step in the right direction. Business already grew by 10 percent in 2017.

"If we reduce the time between China and Duisburg from twelve days to eight days, there will be even greater demand for this rail service," says Staake. This has also convinced the Chinese project developer Wang Yiao. She and her company want to invest 250 million euros to build a German-Chinese trade center near the port. The plan is to accommodate 300 Chinese companies which will arrange their sales in Central Europe from here. This would create 2,000 new jobs.

Other cities are now following suit. Nuremberg now has its own train connection to Chengdu in western China. BMW has parts from Leipzig and Regensburg transported to China by rail. The environment also benefits: co2 emissions from rail transport are lower than from road transport. Mannheim, however, has the best chance of becoming perhaps the most important German hub. After Duisburg, it has the second-largest inland port in Europe and also one of the most important railroad hubs on the continent. If you want to get from Vienna to Paris, you have to go through Mannheim. The same applies if you want to get from Rotterdam to Genoa. In addition, Mannheim is only half an hour by train from Germany's largest airport and has not only major companies, such as Daimler, Roche, SAP, and BASF, in the immediate vicinity but also the private brewery Eichbaum, the largest German beer exporter to China. The first train between China and Mannheim will run in the fall of 2018. "We definitely want to make this happen, as a city with an export quota of 65 percent," says Lord Mayor Peter Kurz, "and we have the best prerequisites for this: politics and business play hand in hand on this issue." Kurz is probably the most international German mayor. He is the only German mayor to sit on the EU Committee of the Regions, where he can promote networking between the EU and Asia. "That's very important to me."

The New Silk Road is now taking shape in all corners. Relentlessly, the Chinese are building highways and railroads through rough terrain, welding oil and gas pipelines together, building power plants, and developing new trade centers in regions that were previously unconnected to the global economy. "The New Silk Road is shaking up existing paradigms by which the world operates," writes the American business magazine *Forbes*. In all, it involves investments of $900 billion to a trillion in more than 70 countries, Beijing says. 140 billion has already been invested by 2018. It's difficult to do the math because whether it's Cuba or Nepal, Nigeria or the Philippines, everything now somehow relates to the New Silk Road with the following three exceptions: the U.S. and Japan are not invited. And India doesn't want to because it feels surrounded by the Chinese Silk Road, so China has forged alliances with India's neighbors: Pakistan, Bangladesh, Nepal, and Sri Lanka. Japan and India now want to create a "free and open Indo-Pacific region" as a counterweight, in which Delhi and Tokyo play a central role. But this is not yet much more than a plan.

Moscow, on the other hand, is torn. After all, one of the New Silk Road routes passes through Russia, and there are many opportunities for cooperation with China. On the other hand, China's involvement in Central Asia is an attack on Russia's sphere of influence. Long before President Xi proclaimed the New Silk Road, in 2009 the Chinese and Kazakhs built a pipeline from the Caspian Sea through Kazakhstan to China, breaking the Russians' monopoly in the region. Putin does not have the money to counter this. If cities like Moscow and Kazan in the east of the country are to be connected by a high-speed train over a distance of 770 kilometers, it will cost 22 billion euros. This can only be achieved with foreign investors.

The route is the first section of the nearly 7,800-kilometer long Moscow–Beijing line. At a speed of 400 kilometers per hour, the train is to reach Beijing from Moscow in 33 hours. The entire line will cost around 100 billion US dollars. Chinese and German investors are vying for the contract, with a decision expected before the end of 2018. The German High-Speed Rail (HGV) Initiative, in which Siemens and Deutsche Bank are among the investors, wants to invest 2.7 billion euros in the project. It would be an important order for German industry. But the West's sanctions policy makes it unlikely that the Germans will get a chance. Putin has already hinted at this.

This would not be the first large-scale Chinese project in Russia. In recent years, China has invested heavily in the expansion of the Russian port of Zarubino in the far east of the country. Since 2016, Moscow has been China's most important crude oil supplier. A year later, both countries established the Russian–Chinese Investment and Cooperation Fund. In addition, Moscow and Beijing are planning to jointly build long-haul aircraft and civil helicopters.

However, the main axis of the New Silk Road will not pass through Russia, but through Kazakhstan. The hub is the world's largest dry port, on the border of China and Kazakhstan. Khorgos is the name of the Kazakh side of the border town, Korgas the Chinese. Both are located near the so-called Pole of Inaccessibility, the point in the world furthest from the world's oceans. A good place for a dry port, then. One of the world's largest shipping companies, the Chinese state-owned company Cosco, and the Jiangsu Lianyungang Port Co. have jointly held 49 percent since Summer 2017. This is intended to boost business over land. So far, only 1–2 percent of the goods transported between Europe and Asia pass through here.

At Khorgos Gateway the containers have to be reloaded. In Kazakhstan, which was once part of the Soviet Union, the trains have the wider Russian gauge. Therefore, the containers have to be transferred from Chinese to Russian wagons. The Chinese have already built a large logistics center in the steppe, the Khorgos East Gate Special Economic Zone. All in all, this represents an investment of 200 million US dollars. In 2020, 500,000 containers are expected to be handled here, five times as many as in 2018. So far, things are still quite tranquil. That's not surprising; up until Xi's Silk Road initiative, there were only a few nomads here. In the meantime, 1,200 people live here, most of them Chinese. The number is expected to reach 100,000 when the new test-tube city called Nurkent is completed. The climate is likely to be a challenge for the new residents; in winter, it can reach –20 degrees and in summer, it is over 40 degrees, on the edge of the Taklamakan Desert, on the "Sea of Death" as the Chinese call it.

The dry port is crossed by a four-lane road. There is still hardly any traffic here. It will one day become the West China–Western Europe Route, a highway that will extend continuously from western China to western Europe. The success of the New Silk Road will be measured against this project in particular. And with it, Xi's success. The containers are still allegedly subsidized by the Chinese government at 1,700 U.S. dollars each. Only when more trains are running will the business become profitable. So there is a lot of room for improvement. After all, at the last meeting between Nazarbayev and Xi in June 2018, 40 economic contracts worth 13 billion U.S. dollars were concluded.

The New Silk Road is nothing less than a geostrategic model attempt at globalization in the 21st century. While Western policy is currently tamping down the concept of isolating disagreeable states in some places, as in Iran and Cuba for a time, it is currently being revived in dealings with Russia. China, on the other hand, wants to integrate countries with very different political constitutions and levels of economic development. If Xi succeeds in this, the New Silk Road will make 130 years of misfortune and mishaps in China pale into insignificance. Then it will pick up where the good old days left off, without getting bogged down in the past, and help regions that were previously excluded from globalization to prosper.

Hardly any president in recent decades has succeeded in spreading so much hope globally. "China is catapulting the Silk Road into the 21st century," writes *Die Welt*. "A grandiose project," comments *Die Zeit*. "World History with audacity that takes one's breath away," one reads in the *FAZ*, "the largest investment program in the world," sums up *Manager Magazine*.

The German economy has hesitated for a long time about how to position itself. Questions upon questions. Will the project even be implemented? Is there enough money for it? What are the rules of the game? Will the Chinese companies be subsidized by the state? Are the tenders transparent? Are the German companies only suppliers to the Chinese or will they be independent partners with the countries in question? Do the countries in question want to cooperate with China at all? Does the West have access to Chinese sources of financing, or do the Europeans have to bring their own money? Many of these questions remain unanswered.

It is clear that Beijing has no interest in transparent rules of the game, but wants to decide on a case-by-case and country-by-country basis. The Europeans, on the other hand, want to determine the rules first — for the whole game. For Beijing, the game is quite simple. Whoever co-finances, co-determines. But there is no EU Silk Road Fund. And so what happens is what has to happen; the Chinese get started. The Europeans wait. Years will pass. When 29 heads of state and government and top representatives from 100 countries meet in Beijing in May 2017 at the historic launch of the Belt and Road Forum for International Cooperation to set the world's course in a new direction, top politicians from Europe are absent. Chancellor Merkel is at least sending her Economics Minister Brigitte Zypries. However, she is very reserved about the initiative. She obviously does not want to make a mistake in the Bundestag election campaign. Meanwhile, the Chinese just keep on building.

In the Fall of 2017, World Bank President Jim Yong Kim said that the World Bank wants to provide eight billion U.S. dollars for the infrastructure of the New Silk Road. That's not much yet, but it's a signal. The Americans under Trump are not interested. The Europeans still can't bring themselves to take a position. At the beginning of 2018, Sigmar Gabriel, still Foreign Minister, could not hide his skepticism at the Munich Security Conference. "The New Silk Road initiative is not what some in Germany think it is. It is not a sentimental reminder of Marco Polo," he warns, "but it represents an attempt to establish a comprehensive system for shaping the world in China's interests."

The rise of China will lead to a massive shift in the balance of power. China is developing a comprehensive alternative to the Western system that is not based on freedom, democracy, and individual human rights like our model.

One can share this assessment. But wouldn't that have been a good reason to get together three years ago to find a political position?

The new German coalition's stance on the issue remains hesitant. "China's Silk Road initiative is an example of opportunities and risks. We want to develop a European response to this in order to protect our interests and to better equip and bundle German and European financial instruments," reads the coalition agreement. To date, this response has not been forthcoming. And in the meantime, almost five years have passed since Beijing launched the initiative.

A joint European response would be important. Brussels and Berlin criticize the lack of transparency in tendering procedures and corruption along the Silk Road, the lack of environmental requirements, and the fact that Beijing does not care about respect for human rights in partner countries. In addition, the EU observes with concern that China is undermining the European periphery and forming alliances. "Depending on the rules governing this project, it will be a project of cooperation or domination," warns France's Prime Minister Édouard Philippe. This criticism is justified. But one question begs asking: Why does the World Bank nevertheless go along with it? The answer is simple. The Chinese are not waiting. Why should they? China pioneer and former Siemens CEO Heinrich von Pierer formulates the most flaming appeal on the part of the business community, "Do we continue to remain in a passive spectator role and wait to see what happens next? Or do we clearly define our own interests and strive for a partnership at an early stage — a strategic partnership, I guess you'd call it — with the Chinese? The question is, what can we gain, what can we lose? Isn't the risk of not being part of this project of the century greater than the undoubted risk of active participation? Let's take the Chinese at their word!"

At the same time, the associations are finally positioning themselves. "It is better for the German economy if we participate at an early stage," says Volker Treier, head of the German Chamber of Industry and Commerce (DIHK). This is also "interesting in the short term," after all,

90 percent of global growth will take place outside Europe in just ten years. "In the medium to long term, the focus will then also shift to opening up these newly connected markets."

"There are considerable opportunities for the German economy," agrees Jürgen Friedrich, Managing Director of Germany Trade & Invest (GTAI), which is tasked with marketing Germany as a business location. And BDI head Joachim Lang demands, "Europe needs a strategy for coexistence with China."

In any case, in June 2018, Siemens CEO Joe Kaeser no longer likes to wait for Brussels and Berlin. He organizes his own BRI conference and positions himself clearly: The New Silk Road has proven to be a "prudent and powerful force to accelerate infrastructure development in many participating countries." For him, the Belt and Road Initiative is an opportunity for more business in the region. It's a "milestone movement," the Siemens CEO enthuses. And because it's better to have a say in the rules of the game than from the sidelines, Siemens is signing ten contracts with Chinese companies for orders from the Philippines to Zimbabwe. Kaeser even opens his own Siemens Silk Road office in Beijing.

BASF CEO Brudermüller agrees with him, "From the Chinese perspective, this is a clear, clever concept to expand its own global sphere of influence. This is not only necessary for a country of this size — but also legitimate for a country of future great power." Brudermüller is surprised that many in the West are very critical of the concept. They are quick to speak of colonization. "But I see it above all as an opportunity for Asia and Europe to become more closely aligned. Why aren't we more self-confident and say that the Silk Road has two ends and two beginnings, depending on which side you look at it from? Why don't we accept the challenge and help shape the Silk Road according to our own ideas? This is something we should discuss. It should be part of our long-term strategy."

At the beginning of 2018, Kaeser even described the BRI as "the new world trade organization." However, the common rules of the game are missing for this. BRI is not an association or club or even an institution like the WTO rather the initiative is actually a loose collection of bilateral trade and development agreements between China and many countries. There is no coordination required at the meetings, not even a joint communiqué like at the G20, for example. This has one major drawback — there are no common rules of the game. However, the decentralized structure of the initiative also has an advantage in that no one is forced to formulate a soft-washed consensus of common interests that can hardly be reconciled, as at the G20 summits, for example. And if conflicts arise between individual partners, the entire network is not destabilized. However, decentralized does not necessarily mean transparency. And this is where one can start.

But what does everyday life look like on this New Silk Road? That's what I want to find out during my visit to Astana. On the day I arrive in the Kazakh capital, it is rush hour in the morning and I arrive 40 minutes late at the small beer garden where I will meet my interlocutor. It will be the last summer day of the year, in the evening the weather will turn and the long winter will begin. At nine o'clock in the morning, we are the only guests. Coffee is served, not beer. I apologize for being late. "No problem," says Jörg Hetsch. He was still expecting me, despite the delay. "Astana is a city where you can already see on Wednesday who's coming on Friday," he says with a grin, alluding to the city's steppe location. Hetsch is the longtime delegate of German business for Central Asia and chairman of the Association of German Business in Kazakhstan (VDW). Bald, mustache, smoker, and a man who feels at home here. The East German lived in Ukraine as a child. He has more than 20 years experience in Central Asia under his belt. He is the man that no German planning team dealing with Central Asia and the New Silk Road can afford to ignore. So no one in politics or German business can say there was no one who knows the ropes.

Hetsch still knows the region from the days when the Russians had control here. Despite all the China hype, one should not forget that "the Chinese are relatively new in the business, even though they have been really active for over a decade," he says. About a quarter of Kazakhs are Russian, and High Russian is spoken here, not Chinese, "but that doesn't mean people are any less suspicious of Russians," Hetsch adds. "The two big neighbors have always been a choice between plague and cholera," although the Chinese have never been underestimated. As early as the 18th century, the Kazakh Khans, having no other choice, asked the Russian crown for protection. "To be a prisoner of the Chinese is a narrow knot — with the help of the Russians it is a wide open road," says a proverb from that time.

I ask Hetsch if that still applies today. "What was said by the Russians are coming for the region," he explains, "is — to put it mildly — less conclusive. And the Americans are no longer there." Due to that, the

Chinese would have an easier time gaining influence. "You don't like them, but you can't get around them. Besides, the Kazakhs really expect a lot from the Silk Road initiative." Kazakhstan may have been a bridge between China and Europe before, he says, but now the child has a name. "And with the name comes a pot of money and political strokes on top."

Kazakhstan, he says, is strategically interesting for Beijing — it is rich in mineral resources and has a large land area that lies almost exactly halfway between Europe and Asia. "Here, the New Silk Road can gain land without constantly encountering new borders." 4,500 kilometers as the crow flies. That's halfway to Europe. "So you don't have to be a clairvoyant to see how important Astana is," says Hetsch.

Europeans would nevertheless find it difficult to invest in Kazakhstan. "Of course, it's not easy here." Eradicating corruption is improving considerably, but it is still a major problem. It is also not that easy to start a business. That scares off many Germans. "They liked to operate on a playing field with clear rules." Chinese managers and entrepreneurs, on the other hand, are used to such imponderables at home. And they have a government that has their back.

"The Kazakhs would be happy if more investment came from Europe," says Hetsch. That would reduce their dependence on China. "There is a fear that too many Chinese are coming to Kazakhstan," Hetsch says, "that they will buy land, take over businesses, open restaurants, and marry away the Kazakhs' wives. A while ago," he says, "a marriage bureau that specialized in placing Kazakh women with Chinese men had to close after protests." And several years ago, land sales to Chinese were already severely restricted after tempers between Chinese and Kazakhs grew increasingly heated. "But the greater the economic success, the more likely people are to come to terms."

Hetsch invites me to the first major Silk Road Conference of the Chamber of Foreign Trade in Berlin a few months later. I am looking forward to seeing him again. Unfortunately, it did not work out in terms of scheduling. The fact that Hetsch retired in March 2018 is bad news for the German economy. They would still have needed him. As he leaves, he tells me: "The Chinese have already achieved one thing. They have woken up Central Asia." And what about us? "We'll just go back to sleep."

Only a few German companies have settled in Kazakhstan. Of these, at least half judge the business climate as positive or slightly positive. However, around 40 percent are still talking about stagnation. This was the result of the first survey of this kind in Spring 2018. 41 companies were surveyed, which employ around 5,000 people and have a turnover of over 830 million euros. The bilateral trade volume with Kazakhstan grew by almost a quarter in 2017 to around five billion euros after all. "While media reports often point to authoritarian political structures, Kazakhstan at the same time commands a lot of respect as the most socially stable and economically successful country in Central Asia," says Michael Harms, Managing Director of the Committee on Eastern European Economic Relations. However, German companies fear competition from China. "Chinese state-owned enterprises are increasingly confident to operate in Central Asian markets, driven by the Chinese government's Silk Road Initiative." For 70 percent of the German companies surveyed, concern about China as a competitor is still greater than the hope of building something together. A visit to Astana would surprise many Germans.

Room 3a, a conference room that could be anywhere in the world. Light gray floor with black lines. White walls, a glass wall on one side through which light shines into the room. Downstairs, three stories below, people crowd around the lunch buffet in the spacious lobby of the spectacular convention center. It is located just a few kilometers from Nazarbayev University, where President Xi announced the idea of the New Silk Road.

Now, five years later, a lot has changed even in Astana. The men and women in Room 3a don't care that the building was designed by Adrian Smith. The man who designed the Burj Khalifa in Dubai, the tallest building in the world, as well as the icon of modern Chinese architecture, the Jin Mao Tower in Shanghai or — in the old world — Rowes Wharf with the Boston Harbor Hotel at its center. Interestingly, someone like this is now building in Astana.

The men and women in Room 3a sit around a square of white tables. They are engaged in intense and controversial discussions. Most of them are tired from the big reception the day before and the jet lag. They come from all over the world — Nobel laureates, former politicians, top managers, representatives of NGOs, and lateral thinkers. Gathered around the tables is the steering committee of the Future Energy Forum, a series of international conferences held in Astana's new convention center in the Summer of 2017. It was built to coincide with Expo, and Kazakhstan hosted the World's Fair that year. Internationally networked institutions, such as the European Union, OECD, UNESCO, UNIDO, and UNITAR, are represented at the unique conference series, where the New Silk Road played an important role. 500 renowned speakers from all over the world devised a kind of master plan for Kazakhstan's development during dozens of conferences throughout the summer. Now, it is a question of how to summarize the many ideas and present them to the president in such a way that he can act immediately. There has never been anything like this before in Central Asia.

The thought leaders include two Nobel laureates. They are Rajendra Kumar Pachauri, 78, the Indian economist who won the Nobel Peace Prize in 2007 along with former U.S. Vice President Al Gore. The former Vice President wears a beige shirt, dark tie, and his long black hair sticks to his head. It is warm in Room 3a. His eyes sparkle with a zest for action. He sees a bright future for Kazakhstan if the reforms take effect now.

And then there is Professor George Smoot, an American astrophysicist who is now 73 years old. He was awarded the Nobel Prize in 2006 for research that proves the Big Bang theory. "I am the Big Bang guy," he introduces himself.

Also on the panel is CDU veteran Klaus Töpfer, former German Environment Minister and for many years Executive Director of the United Nations Environment Programme (UNEP) based in Nairobi. Tanned and slimmer than ever, he does not look his 79 years. He is one of the few German politicians who is still being asked for international advice at an advanced age. He hopes that the New Silk Road will also become an example of "how Beijing closely combines economic development and integration efforts with sustainability and environmental care."

Jamal Saghir, the former Director of the World Bank's Department for Sustainable Development in Africa, is also on the team. On the Kazakh side, physicist Dr. Kanat Baigarin is coordinating the project. He is responsible for research and innovation at Nazarbayev University. Baigarin has advised the Rockefeller Center on environmental issues as well as the United Nations and the World Bank.

And finally, Lutz Engelke, the founder of TRIAD, came up with the conference format for Kazakhstan. His Berlin-based company developed the highly acclaimed environmental pavilion for the Chinese government at Expo 2010 as well as Fifa's soccer museum. "TRIAD puts ideas into space" is the ambiguous slogan of the German medium-sized company, which has long since found its role in the world having inserted itself into new world trends, including those in Central Asia, with all the challenges associated with being active in such countries. "Without the New Silk Road, this conference would never have happened," says Engelke.

The panel members agree. Since Kazakhstan has a lot of sun and a lot of wind, it can be very warm and very cold, and it wants to reduce its dependence on oil, gas, and coal, it should become a pioneer in new energies. "Future Energy" is therefore also the theme of the World Expo, on the occasion of which the conference is being held. The question now is how they can achieve this.

There is to be a green fund to finance the restructuring of the Kazakh economy and an environmental institute to guide the restructuring. At the same time, a new ecological master plan for the development of the young capital Astana is to be drawn up. Barcelona, Copenhagen, and Dubai are the role models. Dubai, for example, has already decided to put solar cells on every house roof by 2030.

However, the two Nobel laureates are not in complete agreement about how strongly the project should be integrated into the strategy of the New Silk Road. The American Smoot thinks that this will give the project a boost, while the Indian Pachauri believes that the project will then disappear in the slipstream of Chinese activities. Both, however, advise the Kazakhs to manufacture high-tech products in the green energy sector in their country and not just shoes and clothing.

I talk to Smoot about the development pressure in the green energy sector from China to Central Asia. "What the Chinese have done is exemplary," he says. They have built solar cell factories on a large scale, he says, with the result that the cells have become cheaper and cheaper and better and better because they have learned in production. "The learning curve was very steep." They actually did this, he said, to be able to provide decentralized power to their rural areas. "And then they found that you can sell the solar cells internationally."

I object that this has become a problem for German industry. "That's true," counters Smoot, "but it's a good development for the environment. Kazakhstan can now profit from this." I confront him with the accusation from Germany that the Chinese solar plants are state-subsidized. "Were the Chinese smart or unfair?" I ask. Smoot says that from an economic point of view, China can be accused of being unfair. However, that's quite a stretch, he says, "Why shouldn't the Chinese state be allowed to support its industry?" From an ecological point of view, at any rate, this is smart. The bottom line is that the development is "exclusively positive" because it means that there will be more solar installations more quickly.

This is also why Smoot is in favor of Kazakhstan integrating the restructuring of its economy into the New Silk Road initiative. China, he said, is further ahead on these issues. "Latching on to China increases the pressure for Kazakhs to reform."

In addition, the work could be divided up. For example, Kazakhstan could focus on improving batteries for solar cells. This research could also be done in Astana.

"Are authoritarian systems — in terms of such innovations — more advanced than democracies?" I ask him.

"That's a tricky question," Smoot replies, grinning. "A system like this is a huge advantage when it comes to building infrastructure. It's extremely impressive. But the transition to a consumer society is difficult. China has to get through that first. Not to mention countries like Kazakhstan."

While we are talking, the message appears on my smartphone that Uzbek President Shavkat Mirziyoyev, 1,000 kilometers to the south in Tashkent, is allowing the Uzbek currency sum to be released for the first time since independence in 1992. A sensation. The sum even surpasses the black market rate. Just two days later, on September 6, the 61-year-old president travels to Turkmenistan. It is the first summit meeting between the neighbors in 17 years.

Central Asia is on the move. Whether in architecture, the economy, ecology, or politics, the competitive pressure between China and Europe is setting reforms in motion that seemed improbable just ten years ago. As always, there are many reasons why things are now on the move — a change in the leadership of a country, a president who wants to go down in the history books, discontent among the population, the crisis in mineral resources — but what holds everything together or, better, gives it direction, is the New Silk Road initiative.

Uzbekistan's President Mirziyoyev is now taking care to open up his country, that is to do what the Chinese did in the 1980s. The artificial fixing of the currency, which he has now freed up, had led to fewer and fewer international businessmen being interested in investing in Uzbekistan in recent years. Mirziyoyev's predecessor, Islom Karimov, nevertheless stuck to it ironclad. He died in 2016. Mirziyoyev now wants to do many things differently. The fixed exchange rate had created an "inefficient system of privilege," he acknowledges.

But he also wants to improve relations with his neighbors. For a long time, Uzbekistan and Kyrgyzstan fought over 250 kilometers of border, ethnic problems, and access to water. That is now over. "High growth and the international competitiveness of the Uzbek economy are now top priorities," says Sodiq Safoyev, the former Foreign Minister and Ambassador to the United States. The 63-year-old is Mirziyoyev's most important advisor on foreign policy issues. And he is supposed to ensure that foreign investment grows. The chances of this happening are not bad. The Uzbeks' foreign debt is less than 20 percent of GDP. The budget has not been in deficit for ten years. The European Bank for Reconstruction and Development (EBRD) has meanwhile returned to the country, making it Eurasia's latest economic reboot.

In addition, Uzbekistan — unlike Kazakhstan — has a long tradition of craftsmanship and is therefore a good location for production. Now that "the New Silk Road is taking shape, a lot of things are moving," says Safoyev. In fact, Germany is also benefiting from this. Trade with Uzbekistan has climbed by a good 30 percent to a volume of 600 million euros. That is still very, very little, but "the interest of the German economy in entering the Uzbek market has increased by leaps and bounds," says Michael Harms, Managing Director of the Committee on Eastern European Economic Relations. "Uzbekistan is currently reforming at a fast pace, which is unanimously viewed positively by German companies. A market rich in opportunities is just opening up here with a population of over 30 million."

Nothing is more conducive to "the development of civilized manners and learning than a number of neighboring and independent states bound together by trade and political relations. The competition that naturally arises among states is a good source of progress." This was not said by Xi Jinping, nor by Nursultan Nazarbayev or President Shavkat Mirziyoyev. This sentence dates back to 1741 and was written by David Hume, the most famous philosopher of the Scottish Enlightenment. It obviously applies to Central Asia as well.

But of course, the devil is in the details there, too, for example, with the approximately 500-kilometer-long railroad line that is to be built from China through Kyrgyzstan to Uzbekistan. The Kyrgyz rightly believe that it has only one major flaw — it does not stop in Kyrgyzstan.

The biggest problem of the Silk Road, however, is that border controls in western China are very costly and are still being expanded. In 2018, a German group of 50 tourists on route to Shanghai from Kyrgyzstan experienced six hours of clearance time at several control stations — despite the latest body and vehicle scanner technology. In the Chinese border town of Kashgar, strict security standards now also prevail — the bazaar, public buildings, and large hotels can now only be entered through security gates. And these are protected by massive red-and-white steel barricades that terrorists cannot break through even with trucks. There are checkpoints with heavily armed police at practically every major intersection. Beijing's price for protection is high. Tourism in beautiful Xinjiang has plummeted. Entire new city quarters stand idle in the shell. Now, Beijing must make another of those uncomfortable choices. Economic exchange with the risk of terrorists pouring into China. Or security with the risk that economic cooperation will be thwarted.

In the west, on the other hand, it progresses with great strides. The rail line from Baku via Tbilisi to Kars in eastern Turkey (BTK) was officially opened at the end of October 2017. The approximately 850-kilometer line connects Azerbaijan, Georgia, and Turkey and plays an important role in the Belt and Road Initiative. From Baku, on the west coast of the Caspian Sea, the train will be in the Port of Mersin, Turkey, in four days.

So, one route now goes via Russia, one through Kazakhstan. The third runs further south. New routes are urgently needed. In 2017, 3,200 trains traveled back and forth between Europe and Asia. It is true that the trains are often only full in one direction. At peak times, however, the slots are fully booked.

"The BTK is the shortest and most reliable route between Europe and Asia," says Azerbaijan's President Ilham Aliyev. Reliable, in Aliyev's view, because this route is not dependent on Russia. When the train enters the new section of the route in Baku, it will already have traveled 3,000 kilometers from China to the Caspian Sea. There, it will finally cross the sea on a rail ferry. The new Baku–Tbilisi–Kars route could actually have been even shorter. But it goes around Armenia, which is at loggerheads with Turkey and does not even maintain diplomatic relations with its neighbor — because of the genocide of up to 1.5 million Armenians by the Ottoman Empire. These, too, are the pitfalls of the New Silk Road.

However, Beijing's politicians have learned over the past 30 years what power a well-functioning infrastructure can unleash. Now, they are taking the Chinese success story to the world, not out of missionary impulse but to fuel China's upswing and make the world more accessible — through closer economic cooperation.

No president since the great reformer Deng Xiaoping has had the power to push through such an ambitious project. In the meantime, no country other than China is financially and politically able or willing to undertake such a project as the New Silk Road. Xi is following up on a development that began during the Han Dynasty. Back then, 139 years before Christ, the imperial envoy Zhang Qian was sent to Central Asia for the first time with a delegation of about 100 men to establish trade partnerships in the West. At that time, the undertaking seemed as hazardous as it is today, and it also went wrong at first. On the way, Zhang was captured by the Xiongnu. This was a tribal confederation of equestrian nomads that controlled much of eastern Central Asia between the 3rd century BC and the late 1st century AD. The Xiongnu Empire was the earliest and at the same time the longest-lived steppe empire. They held the imperial envoy captive for over ten years. In order to continue his mission, Zhang had to assimilate. He took a Xiongnu wife and won the trust of the tribal leader, whom he convinced of the importance of his journey for the Xiongnu as well. In the end, he was allowed to move further west as a friend.

Only the good news from his trip found its way into the official history books. "The emperor learned of Dayuan, Daxia, Anxi, and other countries rich in unusual goods, whose people cultivate the land and lead their lives in many ways like the Chinese. All these states, he learned, were militarily weak and appreciated the kindness and benevolence of Han," Sima Qian writes in the *Shiji*. The *Shiji is* considered the first significant example of Chinese historiography and is the first of the 24 dynastic histories. It comprises 130 scrolls or volumes.

Zhang's journey initially gave rise to trade relations between China and Persia. From now on, six to 10 delegations, some of them with several hundred members, traveled to Persia every year. Cultural exchange and trade flourished. Together, the neighboring states secured the routes against hostile tribes and expanded the common infrastructure.

Xi also thinks in such dimensions. For him, the New Silk Road is one of his most important political goals. He will also have to take responsibility if the project fails or remains unfinished. Because Xi is taking a big risk with it, it must not fail. And that is why much more has already happened than is thought in the West. Although there are always rumors that Xi is gradually running out of money and that resistance to the initiative is growing, it is safe to assume that Xi will persevere. At best, he will slow down now and then.

One of the many Chinese starting points of the New Silk Road is Xi'an, the city of eight million inhabitants that was the capital of China in the days of the Old Silk Road with its famous Terracotta Army. Today, the Chinese aircraft industry is based there and is working on another spectacular project for the future. China is in the process of establishing its own globally active manufacturer of large aircraft alongside Airbus and Boeing. The company is called Comac. The Aircraft manufacturers and their suppliers will benefit greatly from the New Silk Road.

From Xi'an, the route runs to Lanzhou. This city of 2.5 million people is world famous for its meter-long fresh noodles. Here, the New Silk Road is already a reality. Since the beginning of 2014, a high-speed train has been traveling 1,750 kilometers from Lanzhou deep into western China. No other high-speed train in the world can reach such altitudes; the line spirals up to 3,860 meters at its highest point. And outside the windows, the Chinese Bedouins are still pulling camels along sandy paths. An elaborate tunnel and concrete pillar system was necessary so that the train can travel at 250 kilometers per hour all the way to Ürümqi. With 1.7 million inhabitants, this is the largest city deep in western China. From there, the train travels through Kazakhstan or via Kyrgyzstan, Uzbekistan, Kazakhstan, and Russia in the direction of Europe.

A lot has also happened in the south of the Silk Road. The one route runs from Chongqing through Myanmar into the Bay of Bengal. Two oil and gas pipelines almost 2,500 kilometers long are already in operation. The oil pipeline alone has a capacity of twelve million tons per year. The other route first runs overland deep into western China to the Muslim city of Kashgar. From there, it crosses a 4,600-meter pass into Pakistan to Karatshi, a city of nine million people, and on to the city of Gwadar, not far from the border with Iran. In June 2017, the first freight train on a new rail link traveled from northern China to the Iranian capital of Tehran. It was loaded with 1,150 tons of sunflower seeds and started in the city of Bayan in the Inner Mongolia Autonomous Region. After 15 days, it reached its destination of Teheran — a saving of at least 20 days compared to the sea route.

The route via Iran also opens up a new route to transport goods to Africa. From Iran, it would go via the sea route to Mombasa. The Chinese are already building the East African rail network. They are investing 3.8 billion US dollars there. In May 2017, the Mombasa–Nairobi train line was inaugurated. It's the first new line in more than 100 years since the English colonial rulers built a narrow-gauge railroad there. A milestone for Africa's development (see Chapter 9).

Such milestones are also possible in Central Asia. While the Eurasian economic belt is economically the more interesting one, the axis from China via Pakistan and Iran to Africa not only poses the greatest political challenges but also promises the highest political return if Beijing actually succeeds in stabilizing the region through an economic upswing.

71 countries are now part of the New Silk Road. At least that is how the Chinese count them. Xi must not disappoint them. That is why he speaks of a "community of shared interests, destiny and responsibility." At present, however, this is still more of a wish than a reality. On his way to the West, Xi has to negotiate with governments that are not considered reliable and countries that have no functioning administration. Islamist terrorists will try to tear down the projects. The populations' opinions in the respective countries fluctuate between great skepticism and great enthusiasm. Even in China, there are critical voices demanding that the government should first build up China before helping Central Asia and the Middle East get on their feet. There is also criticism from Germany — entrepreneurs and managers are still very skeptical, and they are calling above all for transparent tenders that would also enable German companies to win contracts. A joint German–Chinese steering committee, they say, would be a good thing. But by the time it comes, the Chinese will have finished investing. From the Chinese point of view, haste is the order of the day. Beijing is driven by the fear of being cut off from its export and supply routes. In any case, preventing terrorists or even rival powers from being able to cut off China's economy by not letting Made-in-China products out and natural resources in. For this reason alone, Beijing will do everything it can to make the New Silk Road a reality as soon as possible.

As far as the initiative is concerned, the EU obviously has more time. Brussels is, once again, first concerned with the rules of the game. In Spring 2018, an internal EU paper is intentionally leaked to *Handelsblatt*, in which all 27 EU Ambassadors in Beijing, except Hungary, complain to the Chinese Government that the Chinese requirements for participation in New Silk Road projects are not transparent. The Silk Road initiative runs "counter to the EU's trade liberalization agenda and shifts the balance of power in favor of subsidized Chinese companies," the ambassadors formulate. "We do not want to refuse cooperation but politely and firmly state our conditions," says one EU Ambassador. This response looks a bit like the EU slept through the issue first and now wants to get into the game with a loud roar.

There is a simple way to get into the game — the EU co-finances. If there were a 30-billion-euro Silk Road Fund to finance individual projects, the EU could also make demands depending on how much it invests. Just like the World Bank. EU politicians, however, dream of having a say in the rules of the game without investing. Of course, China won't put up with that. Why should they? And even if they were to participate financially, Brussels would have to remain realistic. The EU simply does not have as much money as China for the New Silk Road. So, it will also have less to say, unless the countries along the Silk Road side with the EU, but that is very unlikely.

After all, in July 2018, at the 20th EU–China Summit, it is decided to "form synergies between the BRI initiative and EU initiatives." It sounds like the EU and China have equivalent initiatives on the table. However, the EU Investment Plan and the Trans-European Transport Network are still paper tigers. The cooperation is to be based on "shared principles of market rules, transparency, and equal opportunities for all investors." It is not only to "comply with established international standards" but also to "comply with the laws of the countries benefiting from the projects, taking into account their policies and the individual situation of the countries."

So, the EU can insist on international standards, but China can at the same time insist on regional specifics when it comes to implementing the short-term EU–China Connectivity Platform action plan. It could hardly be more ambiguous.

There has been some progress, however. Barely five years after China's President Xi Jinping launched the New Silk Road project, the EU is now ready to set up a joint investment fund with China. Each side will contribute 250 million euros. The fund is primarily intended to help small and medium-sized enterprises to profit from the Silk Road. However, it is still unclear when the first joint project will begin. Once again, it is to be feared that important time is being wasted while China continues to put its money where its mouth is and is in the process of putting entire countries back on their feet. Stumbling countries are enormously important for the stability of the world. First and foremost is the nuclear power of Pakistan. It would be important to create a counterweight to the major investors from China, but neither Brussels nor Washington seems to have any serious interest in this at the moment.

Meanwhile, along the Silk Road, things are moving in leaps and bounds. In Kazakhstan, foreigners concerns around uncertain investment conditions have been taken to heart. They have been thinking for a long time about how to solve the problem. The fact that they were looking in the direction of China and not in the direction of the West, should no longer surprise anyone. Finally, in July 2018, the Astana International Financial Centre (AIFC) was founded. It is to become a Central Asian including Hong Kong financial center, following the Chinese model of one country, two systems. In the AIFC, English Law now applies to all companies based there. Cynically, one could now say that Europe is represented after all, in the form of English Law. In order to enforce this, President Nazerbayev even had to change the constitution. In the future, disputes will be settled before a court of arbitration composed of international judges.

The AIFC is really a project that fits in well with the New Silk Road, learning from China in order to implement European standards that will help Kazakhstan move forward and not snub its Russian neighbors. So, fruitful exchange for everyone's benefit is possible after all.

# Chapter 7

# Asia's Crisis and China's Neighbors: Special Space

## How Beijing Is Using Asia's Trouble Spots to Annex China's Neighbors

*A Good Prelude to Peace.*

> Kim Jong-un, head of state of North Korea, after
> meeting with U.S. President Donald Trump.

There is something unusual about the flags in the background. It strikes me just at the moment when Donald Trump and Kim Jong-un shake hands for the first time after having insulted each other for a long time. When Kim called Trump a "mentally deranged U.S. moron" and an "old crank," Trump tweeted back at the "Rocketman" saying, "Why does Kim Jong-un insult me as old when I would NEVER call him short and fat? So, I'm trying everything possible to become his friend — maybe one day it will work out." Back in November 2017, such a meeting seemed unimaginable. But it was actually to happen. For the first time in history, an American President and a North Korean Head of State shook hands in Singapore.

"It's going to be the first minute that decides whether we're going to get along with each other," Trump said before the meeting. The tension is correspondingly high as the two approach each other. Kim has stopped too soon and has to extend his arm a little longer; Trump, however, narrows the gap and they shake hands, and Trump puts his other hand on Kim's upper arm. A gesture of power, but one that also has something appeasing about it. It will work out. The solution to one of the world's great conflicts suddenly seems possible.

As the two pose in front of the flags, I consciously notice for the first time that they have the same colors. Red and blue and white. The symbols are also the same, stripes and stars. It almost looks as if one flag has emerged from the other. And that's kind of how it is. North Korea is the result of the last war between China and the USA. A war that was fought on Korean soil. It ended in a draw, the country was divided in 1953. There is no peace treaty, only an armistice. Now, the flags, which have never been officially hung next to each other, contribute to the harmonic picture of the first meeting between an American President and a North Korean Head of State.

After shaking hands, the two walk through the white Arcades of Raffles Hotel, built in 1887 by four Armenian brothers when the British still ruled here. Raffles is where the drink Singapore Sling was invented, a mix of gin and cherry liqueur. And around the corner, in the Bar & Billiard Room, Singapore's last wild tiger was supposedly killed in 1902. The two state leaders stroll down the corridor to the meeting room, where they take their seats on two leather armchairs in front of a wall of books. When Kim has to speak to the international press, he appears surprisingly confident, almost a little casual. Resting one arm on the backrest, the other on his knee, he says, "While we've done a lot to get this far, the past suddenly feels light as feathers on our limbs. The old prejudices that stood in our way in the past have been cleared away, and we are here today."

This is the only public sentence Kim says in Singapore. However, word quickly leaked out after the meeting. Donald Trump and Kim Jong-un have agreed on the dismantling of all nuclear weapons on the Korean peninsula. In return, the U.S. guarantees the security of the isolated country. In addition, they are suspending their joint military maneuvers with South Korea. The sanctions are to remain in place for the time being. Trump invites Kim to the White House and in turn looks forward to the prospect of a trip to Pyongyang. The meeting went "better than anyone could have expected," he says, and, "I met a very talented man." Kim, in turn, calls the meeting a "good prelude to peace."

Later, Trump holds the press conference alone for more than an hour. Kim is already on his way back. The American President enjoys this appearance. Almost casually, he drops a sentence that will make history: "I want to bring back our soldiers."

It must be clear to him that he is messing with his military with this statement because if this plan were actually implemented, Donald Trump would be giving up a large piece of American world dominance. 32,000 American soldiers are stationed in South Korea. 50,000 in Japan. That is significantly more than in Europe. Peace with North Korea would mean that hardly any U.S. troops would be needed in the region. The military in Washington will try to prevent the withdrawal. They will remind Trump that he would be making a radical departure from the policies of his predecessors: Under George W. Bush, there was the "Axis of Evil," and under Barack Obama, "Pivot Asia." For Reagan and Bush Senior, there was no question that the USA had to ensure order and stability in Asia.

Donald Trump is not interested in any of this. For him, something else counts — he has the opportunity to resolve the last major open conflict from the 20th century. That secures him a place in the history books, which is why he doesn't like to build up unnecessary time pressure: "I have signaled to North Korea. We can move quickly, but we can also move slowly," the U.S. president said of the announced end to Kim's nuclear program. Above all, Trump's attitude is well received by the population. He is cleverly tapping into the mood in the United States. The majority of Americans, on both the left and the right, are less and less willing to send their husbands, wives, and children into the world to keep order militarily and thus cement America's world power status. "We're going to stop playing war games and save an incredible amount of money," Trump says with reference to Asia.

There, too, the mood has already changed. The majority of South Koreans want to do without the U.S. military presence if there is peace between North and South Korea. American security costs South Korea at least $800 million a year. In addition, Seoul will pay a one-time payment of around ten billion US for a new airbase. Nevertheless, politicians were surprised by the halt to joint military maneuvers, which are an important part of the alliance with the United States. North Korea's neighbor China, on the other hand, is highly satisfied with Trump's considerations. So is Moscow. What is often forgotten is that not only China but also Russia share a border with North Korea, albeit one that is barely 20 kilometers long. The Russians don't want U.S. troops in their backyard. Although the road to an agreement with Pyongyang may be long, the withdrawal of the

U.S. military is very convenient for the other two major players on the world stage.

In the case of North Korea, Donald Trump is pleased that he was the one who directed the rapprochement. His praise for President Xi after the Singapore summit should be understood in this way: No one should forget "the great help that my good friend, President Xi, has given to the United States, especially on the border with North Korea. Without him, it would have been a much longer and tougher process." It's praise from a man who considers himself the most powerful politician in the world. Trump is convinced that he has the power and decides when to tighten the reins. And he also decides when it's time to move toward each other.

The reality is a bit more complicated. Before meeting with the U.S. President, Kim traveled to China twice in the Spring of 2018, for consultations with President Xi. The first time by train and the second time by plane. He made the trip to Singapore — well briefed — on an Air China plane that was made available to him by the Chinese Government.

The outcome of the meeting was not a foregone conclusion. In previous years, relations had been so strained that President Xi did not travel to Pyongyang after taking office. Until then, it had been customary. And until 2006, Pyongyang would inform Beijing about upcoming nuclear tests. The fact that this was no longer done was seen as a provocation by Beijing. Just as it regarded the missile policy of Kim Senior and Kim Junior as an imposition. Both Kims could still depend on one thing though: No matter how difficult relations were or how tough UN sanctions became, Beijing would prevent North Korea from collapsing. If North Korea collapsed, American troops would be on the Chinese border. That had to be prevented.

However, Beijing has other interests as well. Beijing would prefer that no nuclear weapons were stationed on the Korean peninsula at all. Beijing wants Pyongyang to obey and open up economically. After all, North Korea has mineral resources. The country has reserves of an estimated 1.8 billion tons of anthracite coal, has 400 million tons of iron ore, and, at 490 million tons, is one of the largest and highest-grade magnesite deposits in the world. In addition, there is gold, silver, zinc, copper, lead, limestone, and iron. In total, the mineral resources are probably worth four trillion US dollars. Natural resources that China can make good use of and to which the People's Republic could probably gain the easiest access. This is another reason why Beijing has never been interested in a violent regime change or even a collapse. While China has supported the sanctions, it has always ensured that they do not completely cut off Kim's air. For example, the Dandong-Sinuiju pipeline from China to North Korea, which is only 30 kilometers long and through which about 90 percent of the oil exports to North Korea have flowed since 1975, has always remained in operation. Beijing's argument to critics is that the crude oil transported through the pipeline contains a high percentage of wax. If the flow of oil were stopped, it would block the pipes, resulting in costly repairs. In an extreme case, the pipeline could even become permanently unusable. Beijing has also ensured that North Korea has enough power plants for coal-fired generation. Pyongyang had been banned from exporting coal under the sanctions. However, burning the coal and converting it into electricity, which then supplied across the border to China, was not.

Whatever happened, the two world powers knew what they wanted. The USA did not want peace with North Korea. The Chinese did not want the country to collapse. The Chinese had their limits. So did the Americans. So did the provocations of the North Koreans. This dispute over North Korea even cut through the UN Security Council. The USA, France, and Great Britain are on the one side and Russia and China on the other.

Nevertheless, both sides tried again and again to play fair. At the end of January 2006, for example, Beijing even allowed Kim Senior to travel to China's booming south to show him what an economy opening policy can achieve. Kim was delighted. A "long-cherished wish" had come true with the visit. "We are deeply impressed by the outstanding achievements in technology," he said. The "rapid transformation" of the south and the "stirring everyday life" had "deeply moved" him. In a sentence, "Our visit to southern China convinced us once again that China has a rosy future as a result of the right path taken by the Chinese Communist Party."

For most observers, this was a clear sign that Kim Senior wanted to open up his country. In the end, the will to reform failed because of Washington. The Americans did not want to give Pyongyang a guarantee that they would not stab the regime in the back if the country opened up — a guarantee that U.S. President Richard Nixon had given Mao Zedong in the early 1970s. At that time, however, the Americans had other interests. They wanted China as an ally against the Soviet Union. In the case of North Korea, such a concession never came because the American military needed the enemy North Korea to justify its presence with over 70,000 soldiers in Asia.

Even then, it was said in Washington that a peace treaty could only be discussed if Kim gave up his nuclear missile program. Of course, Kim Senior was not prepared to do that. The missiles were his life insurance, for good reason. As early as 1994, Washington had entertained the idea of bombing North Korea. US President Bill Clinton had already ordered the planning for a first strike and the evacuation of South Korea. The U.S. could afford to play these muscle games because Moscow was no longer playing a role at that time and Beijing was still too weak to oppose the Americans. At the last moment, former President Jimmy Carter traveled to Pyongyang as a mediator. And he succeeded. In the same year, the North Koreans renounced the production of plutonium. The USA undertook to lift the sanctions and, among other things, to build light-water reactors for the production of plutonium. The most dangerous moment so far in the conflict with North Korea seemed averted. But shortly thereafter, the Republicans took over the majority in the U.S. Senate and a domestic dispute erupted over the North Korea issue. As a result, Washington did not deliver the light-water reactors or delivered them only after a long delay. Pyongyang therefore no longer felt bound by the agreement.

The two summits between the two Korean presidents in 2000 and 2007 also failed to bring about a real breakthrough. The first meeting of the two leaders in half a century went down in history as the "Sunshine Summit." South Korean President Kim Dae-jung, who had met his counterpart at the airport, was even awarded the Nobel Peace Prize for his efforts to open up the North and achieve further rapprochement. But later it turned out that Seoul had bought the summit. 150 million U.S. dollars had been transferred in advance without conditions. Of course, Kim Senior was happy to pocket the money.

The fact that a few weeks later, in October 2000, U.S. Secretary of State Madeleine Albright visited Pyongyang, and later also the former President of the European Commission, Jacques Santer, was politically spectacular, but also remained ineffective. The Europeans could not persuade the U.S. to do anything, and even Albright did not have the power to entice with a peace treaty. The Washington hawks did not want peace and Albright could not get past them. The fact that Germany established diplomatic relations with North Korea in March 2001 made perfect sense, however it did not change much. Germany never acted on its own behalf in the Korean conflict. Consideration had to be shown to the

United States, it was said, long before Trump decided to stop showing consideration for Germany.

Perhaps, over time, Washington and Pyongyang would have started slowly moving toward each other. The attack on the World Trade Center in New York on September 11, 2001, however, put an end to these hopes. The USA was shaken to its core. The military and the hawks took over air supremacy in Washington. President George W. Bush devised the "axis of evil." It was to reach as far as Asia, which is why North Korea was put on the list, even though the country had nothing to do with the Islamist attacks. Kim Senior had no choice but to retreat into his shell. Kim Jong-il died in December 2011, a good 10 years after September 11, and his young son Kim Jong-un took power. He was confronted with several problems — he was only in his late twenties, had no stable power base in Pyongyang, and the global situation had still not shifted in favor of North Korea. Kim Junior, first and foremost, had to build a power base in the country. Some of his relatives had the idea that they could turn Kim into a kind of puppet. They were badly mistaken. Similarly, the well-meaning rich uncles from Beijing were convinced that Kim would do well if he followed their advice. However, Kim had his own ideas and Beijing was very annoyed. There was talk of an "ungrateful, difficult partner." Kim was not swayed by this and stubbornly carried out his plan that was to consolidate his power at home and at the same time to establish North Korea in the eyes of the world as a country that cannot be pushed around.

Barely two years in office, in December 2013, Kim had his greatest mentor, his uncle Jang Song-thaek, executed. It is rumored that Jang suggested to the then Chinese President Hu Jintao to oust Kim and exchange him for his China-friendly half-brother Kim Jong-nam. Jang enjoyed great trust in Beijing and hoped to make a lot of money in business deals with China. What is true about the rumor, however, can hardly be verified.

However, in February 2017, Kim's half-brother was murdered by two women with a chemical poison in the airport of the Malaysian capital Kuala Lumpur. Since that incident, it is clear to everyone who holds the reins in North Korea.

The new authority was also evident in foreign policy. Kim increased the frequency of missile and nuclear tests. Between 2011 and 2017, he conducted nearly 90 missile tests, three times as many as in the last six years of his father's rule. Kim is convinced Americans can only be deterred from attacking if North Korea is capable of nuking an American city. Nuclear strike power has never been directed against South Korea. But Kim thought Seoul was a puppet of the Americans. The North Koreans wanted to ensure they had a reliable second-strike capability against the United States. Experts argue to this day about whether or not they were actually capable of doing so.

In February 2018, shortly before the Winter Olympics in South Korea, Kim launched his first charm offensive, he reached out to Seoul. He was very lucky that this step suited South Korean President Moon Jae-in's political concept. This would probably not have been possible under his predecessor. The rapprochement was successful. North Korean athletes entered the Olympic stadium in Pyeongchang together with their South Korean competitors.

At this point, Kim needed a counterweight to ensure that Washington would not get cocky. So, he set off for Beijing after the Olympics — his first-ever trip abroad. The point was to revive the relationship with his closest but temporarily disgruntled ally. And indeed, China and Pyongyang are now cooperating again. This was the message sent to Donald Trump, who now knew he was stepping on Beijing's toes by being too hard on Kim.

Then, in May 2018, the first summit meeting between Kim Jong-un and South Korean President Moon Jae-in took place. When the two met, the highly armed border between the hostile neighboring states seemed almost like a garden gate through which one can walk in and out at will. Kim appeared relaxed and charming at his sister's side and joked that he would never again deprive his South Korean colleague of sleep with unannounced nuclear tests. In South Korea, people followed the meeting like a soccer match via public viewing. A new "era of peace" should now begin, they said. By the end of 2018, the current ceasefire agreement is to be transformed into a peace treaty. Kim then traveled to China again to regroup with Xi. It was high time for Trump to get back in the game. History was threatening to pass him by. Trump accepted the proposal for a summit between Kim and himself. He then canceled it and then agreed to it again.

For a long time, the eccentric American basketball player Dennis Rodman was the only direct U.S. contact with Kim. The North Korean ruler is a basketball fan and has invited Rodman to North Korea several times. In retrospect, it is clear that this was also part of Kim's strategy to approach the West. It is almost like "ping-pong diplomacy" between the Americans and the Chinese. During the 1971 World Table Tennis

Championships in Nagoya, Japan, the American player Glenn Cowan and the eight-time Chinese world champion Zhuang Zedong became friends. Sung Chung, the General Secretary of the Chinese Table Tennis Association, then invited the American players to Beijing in April 1971. A few months later, Henry Kissinger accepted an invitation to Beijing. And finally, in July 1971, Mao Zedong and U.S. President Richard Nixon met in Beijing to discuss the end of the war in China, some 20 years after the end of the Korean War to end the enmity and to cooperate from now on.

Although the parallel was obvious, half of America made fun of Rodman's political naiveté. It was the time when the American missionary Kenneth Bae was in captivity in North Korean and later also the U.S. student Otto Warmbier. Both were accused of espionage and both were released shortly after Rodman's visit. Warmbier, however, died shortly thereafter as a result of his year-and-a-half imprisonment.

The first meeting between Kim and Rodman had already taken place in 2013. On the day of the summit between Trump and Kim, Rodman burst into tears during a CCN interview so that he could hardly be understood. He had received death threats because of his initiative. All he wanted, he said, was more peace. Trump publicly thanked Rodman.

Before the U.S.–North Korea summit in Singapore, Trump's spin doctors were spreading the word that Kim begged for the summit. And that he had to grovel because of Trump's tightened sanctions. Since it is difficult to obtain precise economic data from North Korea, the notion that North Korea is economically up to its neck cannot be substantiated. What can be proven, however, is that Kim has reformed the North Korean economy since coming to power. He has opened 13 new development zones to attract foreign investment. Raising the standard of living was declared a national policy under him. The central bank in Seoul, South Korea, estimates that the economy already grew by 4.2 percent under Kim Junior in 2016, the year before the new sanctions. That would be the highest growth in the past 17 years. Imports and exports are also increasing significantly. China's share of that is well over 80 percent. Even in the year of the tough sanctions, trade between the two countries only plummeted by 10 percent. And the World Food Programs (WFP) reports that "hunger and malnutrition have decreased a great deal." There is "a hopeful mood" among the population.

Visitors to Pyongyang also notice that the cityscape is constantly changing. For example, Uwe Kräuter, the German who has lived in China the longest. He came to the Middle Kingdom in 1973 as a lecturer. He has been traveling to North Korea regularly since 2005. In 2016 and 2017, he was in the country for several weeks each time. "People have become much more open to foreigners," Kräuter notes. "And there was and is a basic trust in Kim's policies." Surprisingly, the sanctions had hardly any effect.

The geopolitical situation is more favorable than ever for opening of North Korea. The Chinese and the Russians support the cause. Unfortunately, the Europeans hardly play a role. During a visit to Beijing in September 2017, former SPD Foreign Minister Sigmar Gabriel put himself forward as a mediator for the North Korea conflict after accusing the Chinese of adopting a "skewed position," but no one really took this seriously. German Chancellor Angela Merkel also spoke out in favor of Germany's involvement in the North Korean's nuclear power dispute before the federal election. "If our participation in talks is desired, I will say yes immediately," she said, "Europe and especially Germany should be ready to play a very active part in this." For the German economy, such involvement would not be the worst thing. But so far, no one has been willing to accept the offer from German politicians. The Europeans have attempted to get into the game before. In 2012, for example, a group of former government officials from Great Britain, Sweden, and Switzerland visited Pyongyang at North Korea's invitation. Wolfgang Nowak, Head of Planning in the chancellor's office under Gerhard Schröder, was there from the German side. Nowak traveled to North Korea a total of seven times. Initially, he was met with internal hostility. The Foreign Office under Guido Westerwelle had "no interest in the beginning of the talks," Nowak told *Der Spiegel* in an interview. "The German Ambassador there was totally against our visit, almost to the point of rudeness." That changed only when Frank-Walter Steinmeier became Foreign Minister, he said. "On the one hand, of course, they didn't like amateurs such as me," Nowak summarizes the situation. "But on the other hand, they didn't want to close off any channels of communication."

The last time Nowak was in Pyongyang was in November 2017. Amongst others, he met Ri Su-yong, one of the five politicians who determine the country's course. They talk about the Olympic Games. Nowak recites South Korea's wishes for the talks and is invited by Ri to the government building for dinner, to the North Korean Kremlin, so to speak. "Then in the course of the conversation, he told me, 'We will not disrupt the Olympics.' And I reported that to my friends in the South." But then developments between North and South Korea occurred and overtook the meaningful diplomatic initiative. At least, thanks to Nowak, the Germans can now hope that, in the event of an economic opening, the North Koreans will remember that Berlin has always had the time for Pyongyang. And perhaps it will also help that Kim Junior, who went to school in Switzerland, speaks a little German.

Another Korean specialist is Hartmut Koschyk, longtime Member of the Bundestag for the CSU, Chairman of the German-Korean Parliamentary Group, and former State Secretary in the Ministry of Finance under Wolfgang Schäuble. He has maintained constant contact with North Korea for years. His assessment of the summit meeting in Singapore: "Kim has dared a lot with this. He had to push through many skeptics in party and army circles. Now, he must also deliver, with an improvement in living conditions."

Now that Trump wants to send his soldiers home from South Korea, an American invasion or another military intervention seems increasingly unlikely. With the Chinese as a protective power, Kim can now in fact dispense with his nuclear missile program. To be sure, he would have to pay for his opening policy by becoming dependent on China. But he is realistic enough to see that he will never be able to open up his country and fulfill his political promises on his own, either politically or economically. In that case, he would prefer to make a pact with a country that is not only closer to him geographically, but also ideologically, than Washington.

Kim Jong-un is thus currently well on his way to becoming the Deng Xiaoping of North Korea. The South Koreans are on his side, even if they have to carefully maneuver back and forth between the interests of the two superpowers, the U.S. and China. In Seoul, they know exactly how it feels to act against the interests of their big neighbor. In 2017, Seoul was in Beijing's stranglehold for months after the South Korean government agreed to install a U.S. missile defense system. China felt this threatened its sovereignty. The so-called THAAD missile defense shield should provide South Korea with better protection against attacks from North Korea, Washington said. However, Beijing feared that the radar system belonging to THAAD could spy on the airspace far into China.

Beijing is acting decisively to enforce its will. Without bombers and aircraft carriers, but with economic pressure alone. In protest against the deployment of the defense system, Beijing banned domestic travel agencies from selling tours to South Korea. Charter flights were canceled, and even the cosmetics from South Korea that are so popular in China got stuck in customs despite the free trade agreement. The number of Chinese tourists in South Korea fell 61 percent from March to August 2017 to just two million. The supermarket chain Lotte, whose owner had dared to use one of its golf courses for the stationing of THAAD batteries, came under particular pressure. Lotte ventured into the Chinese market early on and operated more than 100 stores there until the beginning of the year. Now, Beijing has ordered the closure of most Lotte department stores. The official reason given was fire safety deficiencies. Fire safety deficiencies.

Only after South Korea's new President Moon Jae-in relented and promised Beijing not to install any further units of the system did the dust settle. At the first meeting between China's leader Xi Jinping and South Korea's President shortly before Christmas 2017 in Beijing, both sides agreed to normalize their relations. Moon thus called for a "fresh start" based on "friendship and trust." To ensure that nothing goes wrong, a direct hotline was even set up between the two leaders. Nevertheless, South Korea will probably not be among the big winners of a North Korean opening. For Seoul, its dependence on the U.S. will decrease and its dependence on China will increase. And this also makes it clear who is the winner and who is the biggest loser in this power game. Trump's policies will make him look like a hero in the short term, but in the end, the Americans will dramatically lose influence in Asia. The vacuum they leave behind will be filled by the Chinese. That this may be a move that makes sense for the U.S. is another matter. Nations can also shrink healthily.

Meanwhile, Beijing is preparing to put its money where its mouth is in another crisis region. Beijing is in the process of building the China–Pakistan Economic Corridor (CPEC). It is arguably the most difficult route of the New Silk Road, but also the one that can change the world the most. The 3,000-kilometer corridor runs diagonally through Pakistan from the narrow common border strip across the Karakoram Highway. In the capital Islamabad, it splits into two major roads. The one includes the coastal city of Karachi and ends in the port city of Gwadar on the Iranian border. The other runs more westward and ends in Karachi. The following map shows where and to what extent Beijing is investing in this important corridor.

**Investment in the China-Pakistan Economic Corridor**

Kyrgyzstan

Disputed territories between Pakistan and India

— Existing highways

•••••• Planned and under construction highways and railway lines

\* Estimates

Kashgar ○

**China**

Tadschikistan

Uzbekistan ◉ Dushanbe

Turkmenistan

○ Mary

Khunjerab ○

○ Kunduz

Afghanistan

○ Herat

Kabul ◉

Peshawar ○

◉ Islamabad

**8.2 billion US-Dollar\*:**
Reconstruction of the railway line
Karachi–Peshawar; Length: 1872 km

**1.6 billion. US-Dollar\*:**
New coal-fired power plant in Sahiwai,
Punjab, built by one
Chinese consortium

D.I. Khan ○

○ Lahore

Quetta ○

○ Multan

Sahiwal

**Pakistan**

○ Kalat

**230 million. US-Dollar:**
New airport for the
Port of Gwadar

○ Sukkur

**2.8 billion. US-Dollar\*:**
Karachi-Peshawar highway

Panjgur ○

Iran

India

○ Hyderabad

Gwadar

Karachi ○

*Arabic sea*

**Three coal-fired power plants are
being built in Thar, a joint
Chinese-Pakistani project.**

0   100   200 km

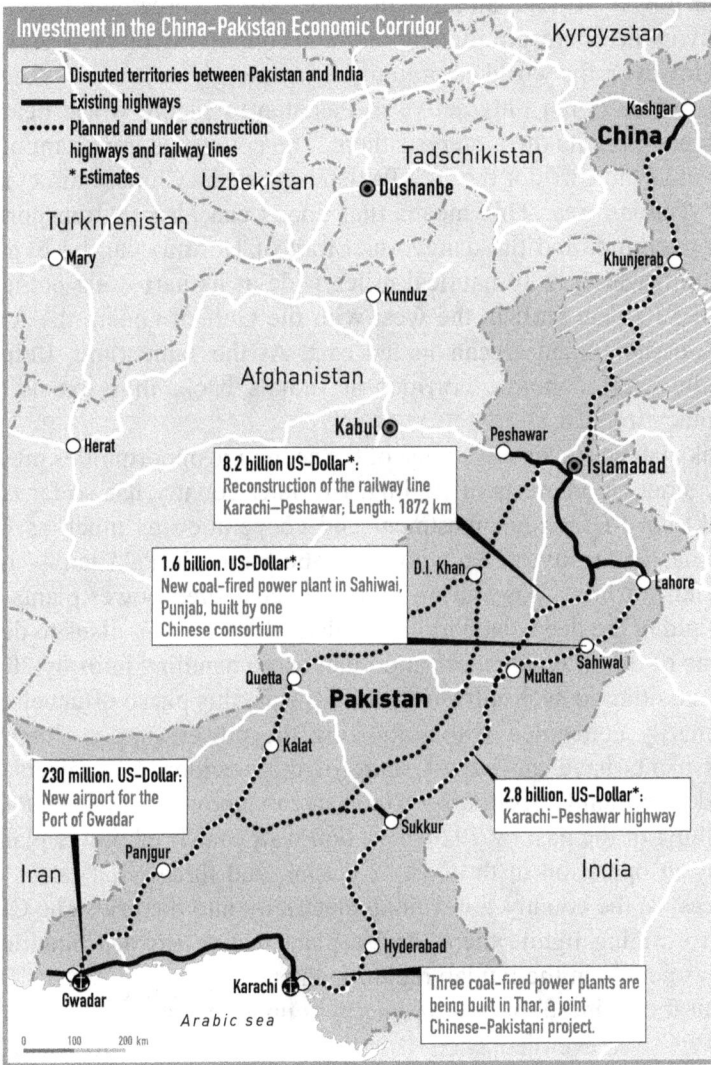

With its 200 million inhabitants, Pakistan is a decisive factor for the stability of the entire region. Only when peace reigns in Pakistan, when Pakistan prospers economically, can the situation in Afghanistan be stabilized and a rapprochement with its eastern neighbor India, from which Pakistan seceded in 1947, become possible. Pakistan is the fourth nuclear power in Asia, along with India, North Korea, and China. It is actually in the interest of the international community that Pakistan prospers. However, the world community is irritatingly reticent — except for China, which is not only active in Pakistan to secure world peace but also in pursuing its own interests there. The country is important primarily because the corridor through Pakistan gives the Chinese direct access to the Arabian Sea. This means that goods can also be transported to China overland, and the dangerous Strait of Hormuz can be bypassed. The strait, which is 30 nautical miles wide at its narrowest point, connects the Persian Gulf in the west with the Gulf of Oman, the Arabian Sea, and the Indian Ocean in the east. At the same time, Beijing is expanding its economic corridor at India's back, thus extending its supremacy in Asia.

Pakistan has taken advantage of the economic opportunities presented by the strategic interests of Beijing. No other country has so far opened up Pakistan to foreign investment and cooperation as much as China, which has so far invested a whopping $60 billion in Pakistan — in new road and rail links, gas and oil pipelines, coal-fired power plants, wind farms and in the deep-sea port in Gwadar, which Beijing plans to develop into one of South Asia's most important cargo handling hubs by 2022.

In addition to such infrastructure projects, this phase of development is primarily concerned with stabilizing the power supply. That's why power plants have the largest share of the corridor. 17 projects worth around 20 billion U.S. dollars are to ensure that power outages in Pakistan are a thing of the past by 2020. Two 660-watt coal-fired power plants are already in operation in the Port of Qasim, and three wind farms in the southeast of the country are feeding electricity into the grid. The Chinese are also mining lignite there. And a plant that re-gasifies liquefied gas supplies people in the Punjab region with energy.

But the Chinese' biggest project was under construction long before the CPEC was even launched. It is the 750-megawatt Karot Dam in the east of the country, which China is building for two billion U.S. dollars. The Chinese will operate the dam for 30 years, after which it will belong to the Pakistanis. The dam is being co-financed by the World Bank to the tune of $125 million. The Chinese had to provide the World Bank with a comprehensive environmental and social impact study, which was approved by the bank. The project is scheduled for completion in December 2021.

The new Islamabad Airport was opened in May 2018. It can process 12 million passengers a year. The Chinese built facility cost nearly 100 million U.S. dollars to build, around three times more expensive than planned. And at eleven years, construction also took twice as long as planned. Compared to Berlin, however, Pakistan is not in such a bad position, the *Neue Zürcher Zeitung* scoffed. The headline of the article: "Pakistan beats Germany."

Of course, even the Chinese don't succeed in everything. In the case of the large Gadani coal-fired power plant, the Pakistanis were unable to raise their share of the financing. The Quaid-e-Azam solar power project has been halted because the Chinese and Pakistanis are arguing about the price at which the electricity should be sold. China's flagship project, the Gwadar Port, is also developing rather sluggishly. Chinese media were already talking about the "new Dubai." The Pakistanis now hope that the port will be added to the list of COSCO destinations, one of the largest shipping companies in the world.

In any case, a corresponding declaration of intent was signed in January 2018. In addition, further industries are to be located at the port.

Even though not everything is running like clockwork, it is amazing how far Pakistan has come with the help of the Chinese. In the past 15 years, the poverty rate has been cut in half and a middle class is emerging. In 2017, economic growth was 5.8 percent — the highest figure in a good decade. Meanwhile, Pakistan's stock market has been included in the MSCI list of the world's 23 most important emerging markets to date. The last country to be included in this index was Qatar in 2014, and the number of victims of terrorist attacks has fallen by two-thirds in just a few years. "The security situation has improved significantly," also says Ines Chabbi, the representative of German Trade and Investment in Pakistan. In Karachi, even foreigners can now move around safely in most areas. In some other regions, it is more difficult. To ensure that construction continues to run smoothly, Islamabad has deployed a 15,000-strong army division to protect the Chinese infrastructure projects from Islamist attacks.

Of course, the upswing in a country like Pakistan is still unstable. In the first half of 2018, Islamabad had to deal with a currency crisis and borrow a billion U.S. dollars from Beijing on short notice. In this way, Islamabad was able to prevent the Western-dominated International Monetary Fund from having to come to the rescue. The other side of the coin is that dependence on China is growing. Beijing is already Pakistan's largest creditor, and its foreign debt has increased by 50 percent in five years. U.S. Secretary of State Mike Pompeo already warned that the U.S. would ensure that the IMF would not give Pakistan money so that the country could repay its debt. The response from the Treasury Department in Pakistan was prompt: "Third countries cannot undermine our joint efforts to make the Economic Corridor a success story."

Nevertheless, Islamabad is now acting somewhat more cautiously. Negotiations on the construction of the Diamer Basha Dam, for example, were terminated on the grounds that the Chinese conditions were unacceptable. Moreover, Islamabad refused to introduce the yuan as a currency in the Gwadar Port Free Trade Zone because this would undermine Pakistan's "economic sovereignty." Despite all its weaknesses, this is one nuclear power talking to another. Nevertheless, the Pakistanis are under no illusions about their position. "Pakistan was not part of the world for a long time," says Economy Minister Khurram Dastgir Khan. "We were in a dark bubble and are just waking up. The fear exists that China will sell us cheap products and services. But they are the only player here."

The public does not seem to be bothered by this. In 2017, the Washington-based Pew Research Center concluded that 78 percent of the population wanted closer relations with China and only 14 percent wanted closer relations with the United States. That result has likely worsened since then. For Donald Trump also began 2018 in an attack mood toward Pakistan, "Nothing but lies and deception" the U.S. has experienced from ally Pakistan over the past 15 years, the U.S. President complained in a tweet posted in January. Despite billions in U.S. aid, Pakistan has remained a "safe haven" for terrorists, he said.

The angry New Year's greeting to Islamabad was more than just hot air. Three days later, Washington suspended military aid to Pakistan until further notice. Prime Minister Shahid Khaqan Abbasi declared that he was "deeply disappointed." Beijing immediately agreed with Islamabad — Pakistan has already achieved enormous success in the fight against terrorism and has made great sacrifices.

The Chinese know how to save face. A little later, it became known that Pakistani companies would henceforth denominate their trade with China in yuan.

In July 2018, the heads of the foreign intelligence services of Russia, Iran, China, and Pakistan met for the first time in Islamabad. They spoke about the rising threat of the "Islamic State" (IS) in Afghanistan; IS forces that had previously fought in Syria would now try to make their way into Afghanistan. The U.S. was no longer invited. In the heyday of the Afghan war, Pakistan was still the main country through which U.S. troops organized their supplies. The meeting was further evidence that Islamabad's military contacts have been moving toward China for some time. More than 60 percent of new weapons for Pakistan come from the Middle Kingdom. That is one-third of China's total weapons sales. In 2011, China and the U.S. were still tied with just under 40 percent of shipments to Pakistan. Even though Beijing sells weapons to Pakistan, it has no interest at all in the conflict with India coming to a head. Together with Russia, Beijing lobbied for India and Pakistan to join the Shanghai Cooperation Organization (SCO). In June 2018, the time had come. At the SCO meeting, India's Prime Minister Modi and Pakistan's President Hussain shook hands in front of cameras. President Xi, standing behind them, looked discreetly to the side. It was better that way. Because Beijing is not as neutral as it would like to be in this conflict. Just a year earlier, the Indians and the Chinese had a tangible border dispute. To this day, India refuses to become part of the New Silk Road because Delhi rightly feels encircled by Beijing's activities, especially the economic corridor in Pakistan. President Xi is therefore very careful not to overstep the mark.

The SCO is a good framework for India and Pakistan to gradually come closer. The *Indian Times* already writes, "the SCO can bridge the distance between India and Pakistan. The organization was founded in 2002 by the Chinese as a security alliance, but it also deals with economic issues. The most important goal is to make the region more stable through economic cooperation. In addition to Pakistan, India, Russia, and China, Kazakhstan, Kyrgyzstan, Tajikistan, and Uzbekistan are also members. Other states such as Iran and Afghanistan have observer status. Incidentally, it was also Beijing that initiated a series of mediation talks between the foreign ministers of Pakistan and Afghanistan in December 2017. China's Foreign Minister Wang Yi wants to integrate Afghanistan into the joint economic corridor as soon as possible. Pakistan has already signaled its agreement.

One can debate for a long time about the usefulness of what Beijing is attempting to do in Pakistan as part of the New Silk Road. But one thing you can't deny Beijing and that is that they have a plan. And it is worth a try. One hears little from the West, which has determined the rules of the game in the world for centuries, in this context. It is preoccupied with itself. The Europeans and the Americans are not mediating, and their economic involvement — if any — is hesitant and once again based on the watering-can principle. For example, the European Investment Bank and the French Development Agency are each investing $75 million in a $600 million project of the Japanese–American Asian Development Bank (ADB). The project involves a rapid bus corridor with 31 stations and bicycle paths in the city of Peshawar.

Apart from that, in the West, Pakistan is considered a country where one would not voluntarily invest. Yet nothing would be better for Pakistan than to be able to draw on more offers from the West to build up the country. But here too, with their lack of foresight, Brussels and Washington are only driving Pakistan further into the arms of the Chinese. A small ray of hope comes from Berlin. In 2017, the government made 109 million euros available to intensify economic relations between Germany and Pakistan. Unfortunately, results are hardly visible. Ironically, it is in part the Chinese who are opening the door to German companies — in 2017, they bought gas turbines and generators worth around 200 million euros from Siemens for a power plant. It is the largest order ever for a German company in Pakistan. Siemens will maintain the power plant for 12 years.

The Europeans who do too little themselves, however, still have enough strength to criticize those who do get involved. The former British colonial masters in particular, who would have a special moral obligation to help the country they once exploited, use terms like neo-colonialism or conquistadorship. Yet China's strategy in the region is more civilized and peaceful than that of the colonial powers and later of the Americans in Iraq or Afghanistan ever was.

The West should turn its anger at the Asian upstarts into positive energy and action. It has long been clear that Beijing is already reaping the political dividends of its involvement in Pakistan. Not only the economic dividend. Pakistani Prime Minister Nawaz Sharif has steadfastly refused to support the Saudi–American coalition in Yemen in the fight against the Iranian-backed Houthi rebels with fighter planes, warships and ground troops. Islamabad said it would rather remain neutral and mediate. That is exactly the Chinese position. And an attitude that suits the new world well.

This may have come as a surprise to the Saudis, who had granted Sharif exile after a coup. In the end, his pragmatism was stronger than his gratitude. In the meantime, that no longer helps Beijing. In the Summer of 2018, Sharif was voted out of office and exiled. His successor Imran Khan will stop one or two projects, he will discover a little corruption, and then it will be business as usual.

Pakistan is a particularly clear example of how the West is losing political and economic influence in Asia day by day. The same trend can be observed in the third major flashpoint — the dispute over the islands in the South China Sea. The Philippines play a decisive role in this.

You rarely see him with a tie. And if he does, the top button of his shirt is open. Even when he meets Chinese President Xi Jinping. Like in April 2018, when he travels to China for the Boao Forum for Asia, a high-level meeting of political and business leaders modeled on the World Economic Forum in Davos.

We are talking about Rodrigo Duterte, who speaks as openly as he wears his shirt. "I just love Xi Jinping," he says quite undiplomatically shortly before his trip. "He understands my problem and is willing to help." Duterte's biggest problem? He needs an economic boom for his country's stability. Duterte's second-biggest problem — at least in international politics? His big mouth. The day before his meeting with then U.S. President Barack Obama in the Fall of 2016, he called the latter a "son of a b****" because Obama had announced that he would take Duterte to task over the human rights situation in the Philippines. "If you do that, we'll both be rolling around like pigs in mud," Duterte threatened. That went down well at home, but Obama subsequently canceled the meeting.

Duterte's populist outbursts would not be worth mentioning and he would not be a central figure in one of the most dangerous flashpoints between rising and declining world powers — the dispute between China and the United States over the islands in the South China Sea. "The Tongue" is what the Americans call the area claimed by the Chinese.

The area extends along the Philippine and Malaysian coast in the east like a tongue deep into the south almost to Indonesia. In the west, Chinese territorial claims come very close to the Vietnamese coast. One-third of the world's shipping traffic is handled there. Large oil and gas deposits are believed to exist in the region. China claims 90 percent of the 3.5 million square meter area for itself, including islands and reefs, some of which are more than 800 kilometers from the Chinese coast, but only about 220 kilometers from the Philippine coast, for example.

There is hardly an issue on which Beijing acts so unbendingly and so brazenly as with these territorial claims in the South China Sea. Duterte's predecessor, Benigno Aquino III, therefore joined the Americans in a confrontational course with China. The situation had come to a head after Beijing claimed the Scarborough Shallows in the South China Sea in 2012, to which Manila also laid claim. When the People's Republic's navy rammed a Chinese flag into the bottom of the South China Sea with the grappling arm of a submarine on 26 August 2012, Aquino concluded a new defense pact with the United States. He did not allow the Americans to open a new military base, which would then be de facto U.S. territory, but U.S. troops were again allowed to visit permanently and to store weapons and provisions in numerous Philippine ports. This was a major success for Washington after Manila decided to send the Americans home in 1991. The country was formally granted independence on 4 July 1946. However, the Americans had secured sovereign rights over 23 military bases for a period of 99 years. At Clark Airbase near Manila alone, 14,000 soldiers were stationed and 24,000 civilian jobs depended on the airbase. In 1991, therefore, not only did an important military cornerstone of the U.S.–U.S.S.R. alliance collapse but also a new military base. Manila also emancipated itself economically from the United States.

In this respect, the Pentagon had sensed fresh air when Aquino sought to close ranks against the Chinese. Joint maneuvers increased. Moreover, Manila fulfilled Washington's wish and refused to negotiate bilaterally with Beijing over the disputed islands. It was a multilateral issue, Aquino said, and the United States had a say in it. And Aquino followed another of Washington's ideas: Manila sued China in 2013 at the Permanent Court of Arbitration in The Hague, claiming Beijing was blocking access to international waters. The court ruled in Manila's favor three years later, but international courts are largely toothless institutions. This also applies to the Court of Arbitration. Although it was founded in 1899, it still has no way of enforcing its decisions — unless the international community decides to intervene. That was not very likely in this case. In addition, the reasoning of the verdict was on shaky ground. The judgment was based on the United Nations Convention on the Law of the Sea, which had been ratified by the Chinese but not by the Americans. Why should China submit to a judgment, Beijing rightly asked, whose basis is not even recognized by the other world power, the United States? Moreover, an arbitration court could only take action if both sides agreed to agree on arbitration. However, there was never any talk of this in Beijing. The arbitration award came to nothing.

Moreover, when the ruling was finally handed down in 2016, the domestic political situation in Manila has changed. Aquino has been voted out of office, and his successor Duterte has taken power. His view of the world situation is different. At his first public appearance, he was surrounded by diplomats from his powerful neighbors Japan and China. He does not want to talk to the Americans for the time being: "I don't feel comfortable with that yet." Arguably, though, he is looking for dialogue with Beijing: "If the door is still open, we should talk."

His negotiating position on the disputed maritime areas is that of a real politician. "Do you want to exploit the mineral resources? Let's do it together. We just don't insist that this is our territory, and neither do you." Duterte cares more about his country's economic prosperity than risky and futile international disputes and a shoulder-to-shoulder relationship with the world power, the U.S. "We can't afford war," he says bluntly. If the Chinese build and finance highways and express trains for his country, then "they can have one of our coral reefs." The de-elected political and economic establishment around the Aquino family is seething with rage. Behind the scenes, they are spreading the word that Duterte received financial campaign aid from Chinese businessmen.

In October 2016, Duterte traveled to China for the first time. Hardly had he arrived when he said, "In this place, I announce my separation from the United States." It was a thunderclap that would pay off for Duterte; by the time he leaves, he'll have a $9 billion low-interest loan in his pocket, plus agreements worth more than $13.5 billion. That's a lot of money for the Philippines, where more than 25 million of the 100 million inhabitants live below the poverty line. In China, with 1.4 billion people, the figure is only 70 million. Beijing is to build a rail network in Duterte's homeland, the province of Mindanao, and also a direct train line to the capital, Manila. In addition, Duterte wants to draw investment money from China's "One Belt, One Road" pot. He also wants to become a member of the AIIB, the development bank founded by Beijing, in order to apply for infrastructural development funds for his country. Washington had fought the bank for a long time but was unable to get its way.

China's President Xi Jinping speaks at the meeting with Duterte in Beijing of "two neighbors by the sea" who "have no reason for hostility or confrontation." There is agreement. Duterte had already proclaimed before his trip that it would be nonsensical to start a war over the South China Sea dispute. "It is always better to talk than to threaten each other." It's a major setback for the U.S., indeed for the West as a whole.

Actually, it would have been tactically wiser for Duterte to negotiate with both the U.S. and the Chinese in order to get more for his country. But that is taking too long for him. What Duterte wants is a good infrastructure for the Philippines, and in return, he will leave the Chinese alone with the disputed islands.

In November 2017, Donald Trump comes to Manila for the ASEAN summit. Once again, the world looks eagerly to Duterte. The two bullies get along. At Trump's request, Duterte sings the song *Ikaw Ang Mahal Ko (You are my love)* together with pop diva Pilita Corrales. A perfect staging, the differences are simply left out. In the run-up, Western media and especially American politicians had called on Trump to address the human rights situation. And also the fight against the drug war by questionable means. Duterte boasts that nearly 4,000 criminals have been executed since mid-2016 and Duterte is popular with the population because of it. However, his methods are anything but constitutional. More than half of the murders are said to have been carried out by death squads. This can hardly be proven. Trump, at any rate, thinks Duterte is doing a "great job with the drug problem." But basically, the American President is not interested in Philippine domestic politics or in the dispute over the islands in the South China Sea. These issues only bring trouble and no votes.

A few months later, Duterte has a problem. At the beginning of 2018, there is still not much Chinese investment. The population is slowly becoming restless. In 2017, Manila posted record foreign investment of 10 billion U.S. dollars. However, the Japanese still played first fiddle. At the same time, Duterte also recorded a large trade deficit. However, Beijing has no interest in leaving its new partner out in the cold.

Vietnam's negotiating position is similarly weak. There, the Chinese are not popular, and there are repeated protests. In June 2018, for example, thousands across the country demonstrated against three special economic

zones in which foreign investors could lease land for 99 years. On plac-
ards, protesters demanded, "No leasing to Chinese. Not for a single day."
It was the largest protest since 2014, when three Chinese died. At the same
time, however, the neighbors are working ever more closely together economically. In 2018, trade between the countries is expected to climb to
$100 billion. Four million Chinese vacation in Vietnam annually. On the
one hand, the Vietnamese government condemns the Chinese actions in
the South China Sea as a "crime and serious violation of our sovereignty."
On the other hand, they said in Spring 2018 to cancel a joint $200 million
project with Spain's Repsol to extract gas and oil. Beijing had put pressure
on it. The "Red Emperor Block," where drilling was to take place, is
located in disputed waters in the South China Sea. Beijing now knows that
Hanoi will not fall into China's arms.

The same applies to 92-year-old Malaysian Prime Minister Mahathir
bin Mohamad, who surprisingly won the elections in May 2018. As soon
as he came to power, he expressed skepticism about the New Silk Road
and stopped the construction of a railroad line that was to run from the
Thai border in the west to the coast off the capital Kuala Lumpur in the
east and from there on to Singapore. In addition, he announced a tougher
stance in the dispute over the islands in the South China Sea. But only a
few weeks later he retracted. It is true that "some things are happening that
cannot be in Malaysia's interest," the Prime Minister said, but, "We are a
trading nation. We can't mess with a market as big as China." The fact that
he is stopping one or two projects for the time being and seeing what he
can squeeze out doesn't change the observation.

So Beijing can continue to test its limits. In May 2018, the first
Chinese bombers trained landings and takeoffs on Woody Island, the largest of the Paracel Islands. The planes have a combat radius of about
3,500 kilometers. The islands are claimed not only by China and the
Philippines but also by Vietnam and Taiwan. South of the Spratlys,
Beijing has built seven artificial islands and equipped them with runways,
hangars, and radar stations. On three reefs, Beijing has stationed ground,
air, and anti-ship cruise missiles for the first time. As recently as 2015,
President Xi denied to Barack Obama that Beijing was planning to build
military facilities on the islands. Washington responded by sending two
B-52 bombers over the islands. In addition, the Chinese People's
Liberation Army was disinvited from the biennial RIMPAC military
maneuver held by Pacific Rim countries. The reason was the "continued
militarization of the South China Sea," according to a Pentagon

spokesman. Since then, the odd U.S. Navy ship has been cruising in the area. But not much more is happening.

In the meantime, pressure from the opposition in Manila has been reduced and Duterte warded off the attacks, "I want to do business. I will not start a war," he made clear once again. "We can postpone the war for 100 years. In the meantime, I need Chinese resources so people can have a good life, so children can get an education and there's food on the table." Xi, he said, had given Duterte a personal assurance that he would help the Philippines and "not let it go to the dogs." The former colony would never again become a "vassal of Washington," declared the Filipino President. "China said, 'We will be there.' I'm not so sure about the U.S., though, because they've lost their will to fight. They only have weapons, cruise missiles, and maybe they have some supersonic thing, but fighting boots on the ground they don't have. The United States is afraid. They are afraid of death and they don't want the war," Duterte sounded off. Perhaps the assessment is not so wrong. The Americans no longer want to be the world police force they appointed themselves to be. If so, however, it would be clear who will control the islands in the South China Sea in the long run.

In any case, one thing is already becoming clear: not only in North Korea and Pakistan but also in the South China Sea the Asians want to resolve their conflicts on their own in the future and are prepared to make corresponding compromises. In August 2018, after more than a decade of negotiations, China and the ASEAN states agreed on a joint draft for rules of conduct in the dispute over the islands. Singapore's Foreign Minister Vivian Balakrishnan calls it a "milestone." Asia is coming of age.

# Chapter 8

# China and the USA: Unrestrained Commercial Agents

## How China Is Getting Better at Playing Off the U.S. and Thus Puts Germany in a Quandary

*Protectionism is like locking yourself in a room. Although you are protected from the rain and wind, you get at the same time no more air and light.*

Xi Jinping, President of China

When Barack Obama, then still U.S. President, lands in Hangzhou, China, for the G20 summit in September 2016, he cannot leave the plane. To the right and left of the red carpet, the honor guard was waiting, but the staircase was off to the side. Down on the tarmac, an American diplomat in a short-sleeved dark blue dress and a Chinese diplomat in a suit are arguing. It's hot. The sun is blazing, casting harsh shadows under Air Force One. "This is our president, this is our plane," she says heatedly. "This is our airport, our country," her counterpart replies calmly.

It had been agreed with the Americans that Obama — like all other heads of state traveling to the G20 summit — would leave his flight via a Chinese staircase. 20 minutes before his arrival, however, American protocol disagrees, the driver of the mobile staircase doesn't speak English. The Chinese protocol agrees to provide the Americans with a translator to assist the driver. The U.S. diplomats do not agree. They want an

English-speaking driver. It goes backward and forward. Then the Chinese put their foot down — Obama gets the staircase that everyone gets. With the driver that everyone has. The Americans refuse.

In the end, Obama decides to take his own stairs. The honor guard is brought over. The welcoming committee rushes in, and the door in the belly of the blue presidential plane opens. The President of the United States exits Air Force One through the rear exit, so to speak. He doesn't wave as usual. He doesn't smile. He doesn't try to hide his annoyance. It's not the only condemnation that day. Earlier, there had been an altercation because U.S. diplomats had wanted further special treatment. Actually, it had been agreed with all G20 participants that the arrival of the various heads of state would only be accompanied by one photojournalist and one cameraman each, due to time constraints. They were then to share their footage with the colleagues who did not get a chance. Only the Americans did not want to accept this. They insisted that all journalists from the White House press corps should be present. In the end, they were able to push this through but were bullied by Chinese diplomats. "China, charming as ever," the U.S. Defense Department tweeted after the incidents. Officials later deleted the comment.

The little scene at Hangzhou airport and its aftermath — as bizarre and grotesque as it is — are also telling. It testifies to the shift in the balance of power between the United States and China. Twenty years earlier, when then-President Bill Clinton visited China for nine days, Chinese security guards were still being pushed around by American security officers in the Great Hall of the People. The world power was a guest in a developing country. Today, the Chinese no longer put up with the Americans' tone.

The new self-confidence permeates the capillary ramifications of U.S.–China relations. And it also shows up in small gestures. "That's how today's power game works," says an American diplomat who was present in Hangzhou; his smile looks a little pained.

The episode is more than just a dispute over diplomatic protocol. It is the expression of a global conflict, the struggle for a new world order between the old superpower, the USA, and the new superpower, China. Who decides the rules, who has to put up with what, and who gets their way — what was foreshadowed on a small scale in Hangzhou now dominates the media day after day in the ever-escalating trade war, for which new superlatives are found, until it was most recently described as the "biggest trade war in world history." A war whose consequences are being felt by Europeans and especially Germans at an early stage. At the end of June 2018, before the tariffs between China and the USA had even come into force, the Stuttgart-based carmaker Daimler was the first company to issue a profit warning. For the first time in a long time, profits will be below the previous year's level. The dispute between China and the USA is primarily to blame. Beijing wants to impose tariffs on the import of cars from the USA. The Stuttgart-based company produces 290,000 vehicles at its U.S. plant in Tuscaloosa, including particularly large SUVs, which are mainly supplied to China. Since Daimler cannot afford to pass on the tariffs to customers on a one-to-one basis in the fiercely competitive Chinese market, the profits will fall.

The intensification of the power struggle between the USA and China is also due to the character of the incumbent U.S. President Donald Trump. One does not need imagination to envisage how he would have reacted if he had been snubbed like that at the airport in Hangzhou. Trump, then still a presidential candidate, tweeted from the other side of the Pacific: "Under these circumstances, I would have stayed on the plane and flown back home." For Beijing, this was already an indication of what would happen if Trump became president.

But the conflict with China is not purely a matter of Donald Trump's character. It was already on the horizon long before he took office. The tone of his predecessors was only more polite, and the attempts to contain Chinese superiority were more delicate and moderate. In fact, this conflict is much larger than the power of individual presidents. It has been building slowly but has long been masked by a deceptive hope. After the 2008 financial crisis, Washington and Beijing still believed that interdependence was only a passing symptom of crisis. Both sides did not like to look too closely at the implications of the shift in power. For a long time, the supposed radiance of the U.S. did not allow Washington to recognize the upstart and aggressor China in its shadow. Beijing, for its part, shied away from realistically assessing the trouble it would cause if it were to assert itself piece by piece against the still reigning world power.

But it is now clear that the USA is becoming weaker and weaker. China is getting stronger and stronger. And Europe is watching this development like a rabbit facing a snake. The rise of China and the conflicts that will arise in the process will be the big issue of our generation. The new normal of the world. For the West, it will be a new experience — the oppressive experience of being dependent on others. This is the flip side of globalization, where no one can do without the other, where everything is interconnected. Either the majority prevails or the strongest prevails. China is already both.

Donald Trump exploited the fear of decline, of losing power, in the election campaign. He is vociferously and more vehemently opposing the loss of power and prosperity in the United States than his predecessors. He is behaving as if the old times can be restored, the times when the United States could do whatever it wanted and almost single-handedly defined the rules of the game in the world when it also set the direction for Europeans. "Make America great again," "America first" — with this policy, Trump is primarily longing to turn back the clock. In the short term, he may actually be able to get something out of it for the USA. There is only one thing he cannot do and that is to stop or even reverse the trend of power shifting toward Asia. Whatever he does, China will become more powerful, the U.S. powerless.

The fatal thing is that the more the U.S. stands up to China, the more it relies on confrontation instead of cooperation, and the more America also loses influence in the rest of the world. The collateral damage of the U.S.–China trade war is that Asia and Europe are being forced to reorient themselves. If Europeans still had the certainty under Obama that he was also representing their interests, this feeling has evaporated with Trump. His "America first" policy is equally disparaging and is accelerating a development that cannot be in Trump's interest. He is driving Germany and Europe into China's arms and thus reinforcing the trend he wants to stop that is China's rise as a world power and Europe's emancipation from the United States.

After the U.S. turned its back on them, the countries of Asia have of necessity decided to move closer to China — a step that is not easy for them considering China's dominance in the region. Europe, on the other hand, is undecided and at a loss. Despite the trouble with the U.S., the EU is hesitant to approach China. Just as it is hesitant in general to put its relationship with the other Asian states, but also with Africa, on a new footing and to move forward decisively. The European Union is paralyzed by the refugee and budget crises, Brexit, and the rise of autocrats of the caliber of Erdoğan or Orbán.

It is vital for the future of a country like Germany to be soberly aware of these interrelationships and to react accordingly. Almost every fourth German job depends on exports. And here, too, China is becoming increasingly important: German exports to China rose from around 14 billion to 86 billion between 2002 and 2017. However, the reverse is not true,

China's export ratio, i.e., the share of exports in its economic power, fell from 34 percent in 2000 to less than 20 percent in 2017. And it will continue to fall, approaching the ratio of the U.S. that is 12 percent. By contrast, the German export ratio was around 47 percent in 2017 — and rising. By way of comparison, in France, it is 30 percent and in Japan 17 percent. The way in which the balance of power is shifting is depicted by the following perspective. In 2022, China's share of the world market in terms of purchasing power will climb to over 20 percent, while Germany's share will fall to below 3 percent and the USA's to below 15 percent. Like a medium-sized company that is dependent on a large corporation as a customer, we will have to focus on which products we specialize in and with whom we ally ourselves. The fact that we actually seem to believe that we can take on the Chinese, the Americans, and the Russians at the same time is astonishing. Even if Europe were to unite at this point, which it is not, that would be presumptuous. That's why we have to analyze our opportunities and risks in the conflict between China and the United States very carefully.

For a long time, well into the second half of the 20th century, wars were the means by which rising and falling world powers fought out their power struggles. War hasn't become less brutal but now the weapons do not destroy immediately. These days the great powers are fighting almost exclusively in the economic sphere for political domination. There are only one or two regional proxy wars, such as in Syria. Otherwise, the U.S. and China are at loggerheads over trade issues, exchange rates, access to each other's markets and which international institutions should balance the global economic playing field.

Trump didn't invent trade conflicts either. There has been such a thing before, for example in 2002, when George W. Bush imposed a 30 percent tariff on imported steel to appease his Rust Belt voters. A year later, he was forced by the World Trade Organization (WTO) to retract his decision. When his successor Barack Obama later imposed a 35 percent tariff on Chinese car tires, Beijing did not even wait for a WTO response but countered directly with tariffs on chicken feet. The result was around one billion U.S. dollars in damages for American chicken farmers, whose votes Obama was relying on. The tire tariff was soon history, but the pressure of the conflict increased.

This tension can already be felt during President Xi Jinping's first trip to the USA in September 2015. Xi was in a dark gray Mao jacket with a pocket in turquoise, the color of his wife's dress. Obama was in a tuxedo,

his wife in an off-the-shoulder black dress. In the welcome toasts, pleas-
antries are still exchanged. But at dinner, the differences become visible
again. Obama accuses Xi of shaking up the world with his chaotic stock
markets; Xi replies that American economic growth on credit is destabi-
lizing the world. In passing, he briefly shows his muscle by referring to
the enormous amount of American government bonds in Beijing's books.
In plain language, we are your biggest creditor. Obama takes refuge in the
argument that the capital is for China's American customers. Xi counters:
"Our cheap "Made in China" products create your prosperity." And when
Obama threatens to raise interest rates, Xi responds by devaluing the
yuan.

Western politicians obviously tend to see emerging countries as
rivals that must be weakened at all costs in order to remain strong themselves. The first response is often that of a knight in his castle: Close the
gates. Whether in Europe or the U.S., policymakers act with varying
intensity and crudeness, but with the same spin. Trump imposes tariffs.
Merkel calls for regulating the purchase of German companies by
Chinese. Juncker opposes market economy status for China. With all the
drawbridges being pulled up, they don't ask an insightful question and,
if you will, assess the battlements of their own fortress. How can I integrate the other, more powerful one out there in such a way that I benefit
from it?

In the U.S., at least, no one has asked the question yet. Exclusion
instead of inclusion is the motto. The best example is TPP, the Trans-
Pacific Partnership, Obama's major trade agreement with the Asian states
excluding China. With the TPP, he wanted to regain influence in the
region and, in a sense, beat China at its own game. It was an agreement
that was supposed to bring the USA and Asia closer together again. An
agreement from which China was excluded — which was to prove to be
the concept's greatest weakness.

In the Golden Week around China's National Day on October 1, when
hundreds of millions of people are on the move and Chinese politics
briefly come to a standstill, Obama's negotiating teams reached an agreement on free trade with eleven Pacific Rim countries in the Fall of 2015.
This was a major success for the U.S. President, who has been pursuing
the "Pivot to Asia" foreign trade campaign since 2011. This is also a turning point for Europe. The turn toward Asia (without China) marks the
beginning of a move away from Europe.

Obama is very pleased this Monday. Not only has he struck a trade deal between the U.S. and Asia unlike any before but he has also scored a strategic victory over China. That's because the trade agreement effectively encircles China. In addition to the economic powers of the USA and Japan, the Trans-Pacific Partnership includes Australia, Brunei, Canada, Chile, Malaysia, Mexico, New Zealand, Peru, Singapore, and Vietnam. Together, the 12 members account for 40 percent of global economic output. Taiwan, the Philippines, Colombia, Thailand, Laos, Indonesia, Cambodia, Bangladesh, and India are also interested in joining at some point. Even without China, it is the biggest economic deal in the last two decades since the U.S. formed the NAFTA alliance with Canada and Mexico in 1994. The extent to which Obama feels the competition with China was also clear during his brief opening speech, "95 percent of our potential customers live outside our country's borders," he said. That's why "we can't leave it to countries like China to write the rules of the global economy. *We* should write the rules. That's what today's agreement is for."

In addition to the geostrategic move, the advantages were obvious. U.S. corporations were to be able to conduct easier and, above all, more business with Asia. American consumers were to enjoy more inexpensive products from Asia and thus increase their purchasing power. More goods for less money. The World Bank expects the pact to significantly increase economic growth in the participating countries. Some Republicans and union representatives, however, oppose the trade agreement. They fear the loss of jobs in the USA. The fact that Republican presidential candidate Donald Trump is "totally against the free trade agreement" does not play much of a role, at the time. Obama's strategy is to use a threatening scenario to keep opponents in the country quiet. If the U.S. does not change the rules of the game for global trade, then China will do it with its own free trade agreements. The Senate finally votes in favor. On 4 February 2016, nine months before the U.S. election, TPP is signed.

Beijing is playing it cool. "China is too big to be restricted by a trade agreement. Beijing is the largest trading partner for many neighboring countries, such as Singapore, Japan, and Australia," argues the state-owned *Global Times* newspaper. Nevertheless, Beijing is working all the more intensively on its own agreement.In June 2016, China already signed a free trade agreement with South Korea and Australia. The Regional Comprehensive Economic Partnership (RCEP) is to be the next step. China, the 10 ASEAN countries, and Australia, India, Japan, New Zealand, and South Korea are negotiating for this. RCEP comprises over three billion people, or around 45 percent of the world's population, and accounts for 40 percent of global trade.

But then an unexpected turn of events plays into the hands of the Chinese. On 9 November 2016, Donald Trump is elected the 45th president of the United States. Trump acts faster than anyone could have imagined. As early as mid-November, he announces that he is in favor of "fair bilateral trade agreements, bringing jobs and industries back to America." That's why he wants to terminate the TPP agreement with Asia, as one of his first actions as president. On 21 January 2017, he signed an executive order to that effect. Even his Republican Party colleague Senator John McCain is appalled. Trump will "send the troubling message that America is less engaged in the Asia–Pacific region at a time when we can least afford it." This is a position shared by most experts and observers.

Asian heads of government are disappointed. Even the Japanese, the U.S.'s closest allies in Asia, are not holding back accusations. "TPP is meaningless without the U.S.," says Prime Minister Shinzō Abe resignedly. He immediately flies to Washington, however, he cannot change Trump's mind. Australia's Prime Minister Malcolm Turnbull, also a close ally of the United States, agrees with McCain's assessment. "This is a huge gift to the Chinese. They can now distinguish themselves as the pioneers of global trade liberalization." And that's exactly how it should turn out.

"If your opponent leaves a door open, rush in" is a phrase from Sunzi's famous *Art of War*. Since it was foreseeable what Trump would do, state and party leader Xi Jinping travels to Davos, Switzerland, three days before Trump's official inauguration in order to make his mark as a champion of free trade at the World Economic Forum.

Xi's advisors were uncertain for a long time as to whether this was wise. Xi will not have an easy time at this most informal of the world's major political and economic events. He may be carrying a fiery plea for free trade in his luggage, and he is regarded by his Western interlocutors as clever, quite ready to hit the ground running, and in any case more relaxed than his two stiff-upper-lipped predecessors Hu Jintao and Jiang Zemin. But Xi is subject to constraints that his Western counterparts do not have to contend with. The range of national expectations that Xi must serve is much greater than that of Merkel and all other European politicians. And even greater than for Trump, although he already has to balance between the Washington establishment and the farmers and factory workers in the Midwest.

Xi, on the one hand, needs to represent traditional Chinese people such as the new Mao, who still live in the past century in some way. On the other hand, he must appeal to Chinese city dwellers, who prefer a less pathetic political style and have long since made the leap into modernity. And then there are the expectations of the West, where people are eagerly anticipating the Chinese response between the outgoing charismatic President Obama and the new president.

Xi was not "witty and lively" in the Western sense, during his appearance, as the state news agency *Xinhua* claimed afterwards. But he manages something remarkable. He captivates the world for the first time with his speech in Davos. Xi says the now-famous phrase, "Protectionism is like locking yourself in a room. Although you are protected from rain and wind, at the same time you get no air and no light."

It was supposed to be a world-changing speech, although Xi said more or less what he always says. "Xi puts himself at the forefront of economic globalization," headlines the American *New York Times*. "Xi convincingly defends globalization," writes Britain's *Financial Times*. "Rarely has a speech on the state of the world economy elicited such enthusiastic praise," praises even *Der Spiegel*.

For a good hour, Xi defends globalization against it's enemies — especially against one whom he does not mention by name in the speech, future U.S. President Donald Trump.

It is forgotten that China itself seals off many areas and imposes tariffs on products so that its own economy can develop in peace. The Europeans are cheering for the president. The same president whom they accused of protectionism just a few weeks ago. He was responsible for the fact that state-subsidized Chinese steel was threatening to flood the Western markets. The same president whose country the EU denies the status of a market economy. A topsy-turvy world.

Not yet in office, Donald Trump has — unintentionally — caused a shift in the tectonic plates of world politics. Europe and the USA are drifting apart. Or to put it another way, Trump is giving Xi the leeway to create a wedge between Europe and the USA. To be sure, China and Europe are not moving toward each other to the same extent that Europe and the U.S. are drifting apart. But they have more overlap than they have had in centuries. Oddly enough, it's not just about interests, but also about values. This is a novelty in relations with China.

To the extent that Trump is interpreted in a partly exaggeratedly nega-tive, totally protectionist way, Xi is now allowed to play the champion of fair globalization in the media. But neither is Xi the Che Guevara of the free global economy nor is Trump the avenger of the disinheritance of globalization. The world looks different from the perspective of a rising world power like China and a declining one like the United States. Trump needs to see how he can minimize the annual U.S. trade deficit of about $560 billion, a budget deficit of a trillion, and create jobs at home. Xi must defend his trade surplus by selling as many products as possible to the world. In doing so, Xi's position is far more in line with the interests of Germany, for example, but also with the goals of the EU. This is not only political conviction but also coincidence.

It pleases Europe and especially Berlin when Xi emphasizes that pro-tectionism gets no one anywhere, that everyone is in the same boat, no one can win a trade war and that economic globalization is not to blame for the many refugees, terror and poverty. And when he concedes that "Nothing in the world is perfect, not even free trade," it only makes him more convincing. That the top communist in Davos would champion free trade against an American president would have been unthinkable five years ago.

"If you want to cross an ocean, you can't return to safe harbor every time there's a storm," Xi says to Trump in Davos. Yes, but, Trump may reply to him, if you feel the ship is in danger of sinking in the storm, is it stupid not to call at a protective harbor. And that's the feeling Donald Trump's voters have.

The respective dilemmas facing the rising world power China and the declining world power USA are more visible today than ever before. In a sense, neither can get out of its own skin. China must network more with the world if it wants to be successful, and at the same time must not become too dependent on the fluctuations of the global economy. America must produce more at home without making its products more expensive for domestic consumers.

For Beijing, this makes it easier to get into the game. The Davos speech is the preliminary culmination of China's new self-confidence and its new role in the world. In the weeks after Davos, Chinese diplomats have their backs. They are taking action. They signal to Donald Trump that if China and the U.S. are to cooperate, this will only be possible if Trump clearly commits to the one-China policy in his first telephone call with Xi. And he must do so publicly and without being asked.

Trump obviously knows pretty well who he can and can't mess with. He is cautious with China. He jumps over the little stick the Chinese hold out to him. The Oval Office describes the first phone conversation on 9 February 2017, between Xi and Trump as "very cordial." President Trump had "committed to the one-China policy at President Xi's request." Beijing would have liked to read this sentence without the addition of "at President Xi's request" and responded accordingly with reserve, "The two countries are fully capable of becoming good and cooperative partners."

In Beijing, it is clearer than in Europe that Trump is willing to compromise on issues that are not so much on the minds of his voters — if his opponent is powerful enough. Even during the election campaign, Beijing's ministries heard time and again that Chinese diplomats preferred Trump to Hillary Clinton if there were a choice. The surprising reasoning was that the former secretary of state is an ideologue; Trump is a businessman. "He's trained to make deals. Every deal is a compromise."

Beijing has made it clear to Trump that certain issues are non-negotiable when concerning others. "For Germany, it is not negotiable that Bavaria belongs to Germany, and for the U.S., it is not negotiable that Hawaii is American and for China, it is not negotiable that Taiwan is Chinese," a Chinese diplomat put it.

In their first telephone conversation, Trump and Xi agreed to meet as soon as possible. Two months later, the time had come. For less than 48 hours, China's President Xi Jinping travels to the Mar-a-Lago Hotel Resort in Florida at the beginning of April 2017 to exchange views with his counterpart in person, for the first time. This is also interesting: Trump does not receive Xi in Washington, but quite casually at his resort. Xi is not so important to the Americans that he would go to Washington, especially for this. And what's more, normally, the newly appointed president makes his inaugural visit to colleagues who have been in office for some time. The French president went to Angela Merkel after his election, not the other way around. In this respect, China is still the junior partner. But Xi is by no means traveling to America as a supplicant. Trump, on the other hand, wants "America first." The rhetorical warm-up before the meeting is correspondingly shrill, "We have been treated very unfairly and have concluded numerous trade agreements with China for many, many years." There it is, the grand motive of Trump's opera. And another pattern is already emerging: high-pitched tones in the run-up are followed by much milder ones as if nothing had happened. The meeting in Mar-a-Lago goes surprisingly well, with the big topics being bilateral trade and the problem child North Korea. It seems as if neither of the two wants to risk letting relations get out of hand. The reason for this is simple — if something goes wrong, the political costs are high. It is true that both serve the respective citizens of their countries with tight rhetoric. At the same time, however, they repeatedly make it clear through small but important gestures that not everything is as bad as it seems at the moment.

For example, Beijing has approved trademark protection for the Trump name in the Chinese construction business. Trump has been fighting for this for years. Trump, in turn, had sent his daughter Ivanka and his five-year-old granddaughter to the New Year's reception at the Chinese Embassy as recently as early February. Never before have members of the American president's family attended the New Year's reception. Afterwards, Ivanka posted a video on Instagram showing her daughter singing a Chinese song. The video was viewed 1.5 million times and received very good reviews. Even *The New York Times* called it a "diplomatic coup." And Trump's other daughter Tiffany not only sat in the front row at the fashion show of top Chinese designer Taoray Wang but also had her picture taken arm in arm with her. A revaluation of Chinese soft power was viewed with favor in Beijing.

For those who had a closer look at such side events, it is not at all surprising that the statements at the end of the summit were conciliatory. Which is not to say that tensions have been resolved. "I haven't gotten anything yet, *absolutely* nothing," Trump says during his speech that evening, looking toward Xi. People in the banquet hall hold their breath. The phrase hovers over the banquet until the first people start laughing. Trump's wife Melania leads the way, and as we all know, she doesn't laugh at everything her husband says. "But," Trump adds after an appropriately effective pause, "we've developed a friendship. We're going to have a great relationship together."

At dessert, however, the U.S. President reminds Xi where the old power still has more muscle than the upstart. Four hours after giving the order, Trump informs the Chinese President that he bombed a military base in Syria with a cruise missile. It was fired from the destroyer *USS Porter* in the Mediterranean Sea. It's a lesson Xi won't soon forget. In the end, he speaks only of a "good working relationship," while Trump announces with a proud chest that he has built up an "outstanding relationship" with Xi and that "many potentially bad problems can now disappear."

In the end, "there were no winners and no losers," summed up the Hong Kong newspaper *South China Morning Post*. That is true. But one could also say that a draw was good enough for the Chinese. Trump would have needed a clear victory, which he did not achieve. Even his rhetoric, as always exaggerated, could not distract from that. Nor could it conceal the extent to which the United States' room for maneuver is already limited by China. This, too, is nothing new: military aircraft collisions in the South China Sea or Chinese hackers who allegedly cracked the center of power in Washington would have been a good reason for war in the past. Today, the inhibition threshold is much higher; the two great powers are too closely intertwined. The hacking story in particular would have had the potential for a major crisis. In 2015, American data records and personnel files of the State Department were hacked by the Chinese. 18 million employees were placed in danger and not only those working in embassies. CIA Director James Clapper was forced to withdraw his people from Beijing immediately. "We do cyber espionage, too," he acknowledged, adding ironically, "And we're pretty good at it." Clapper called it unwise to punish other countries for things America was also doing. Among American hard-liners, that did not generate enthusiasm. Senator John McCain accused Clapper of allowing U.S. secrets to be stolen with impunity because the Americans were sitting in a glass house. Nothing further happened. It would have been too expensive politically.

It's a similar story with Trump. After the visit, he continues to rail loudly against the Chinese and yet one week after the meeting, he unexpectedly admits that China is "not a currency manipulator." During the election campaign and in the months before, he had repeatedly claimed the opposite.

One chance to get everyone around the table and further smooth the waters is the G20 Summit in Hamburg in early July 2017, which both Trump and China's leader Xi Jinping are attending. Chancellor Merkel will try to engage Trump and persuade him to rejoin the majority of the world. She knows the Chinese are on her side. It should remain a pious wish.

Even before the G20 Summit, it is clear that neither Washington nor Beijing will refrain from fighting for their interests and will only compromise when it seems useful to them. And we in Europe should have no illusions about this either; Beijing will, if it is useful to Beijing, also oppose those who are currently applauding China.

Where China's interests lie, Premier Li made very clear before the summit, "We take the state of employment today as our key indicator to judge how Chinas' economy is doing." Over the past four to five years, he said, Beijing has succeeded in creating 40 to 50 million new urban jobs nationwide. In 2017, however, 13 million graduates and school leavers alone would enter the job market. This requires "extreme efforts."

So when it comes to jobs for their own people, Li and Trump are in agreement. The balance of power can be seen very clearly in a large Chinese investment in the U.S. and a large American investment in China. Terry Gou, founder and head of the Taiwanese electronics manufacturer Foxconn, which employs more than one million workers in its factories on the Chinese mainland and produces most of the iPhones there, decides to invest ten billion US dollars in a new production facility in Wisconsin. At least seven billion of that is to be spent on a plant for the manufacture of displays. That's smart, because it benefits Gou as much as Trump and Xi. Gou is protected in case tariffs are levied against iPhones. Trump can say that new jobs are coming into the country, and Xi can emphasize that the trade deficit is being reduced.

The politicians are not interested in the fine print. Foxconn wants to reduce not only its dependence on China as a production location but also its dependence on human labor. To date, Foxconn has fully automated ten complete production lines. Further production lines with only a few human workers are to follow. The fact that Gou is foregoing this strategy in the USA, of all places, only makes sense if he receives government subsidies. In this case, it is 4.5 billion U.S. dollars. This enables Gou to become the largest private employer in Wisconsin. In short, Gou, who actually already relies on highly automated factories, is letting Trump finance a factory that operates like in the good old days. Thanks to the subsidies, this is cheaper for him than expensive fully automated production lines.

This brings a small smile to Beijing politicians. The U.S. will certainly not become more independent of China in this way. Nevertheless, Trump gave a flaming speech at the groundbreaking ceremony in June 2018. For him, the factory is the "eighth wonder of the world," which incidentally distracts from the fact that legendary motorcycle manufacturer Harley-Davidson, which has its headquarters just 25 miles to the north, is announcing that it will move part of its production to Europe.

The new American investment in China, in turn, comes from Tesla CEO Elon Musk. He cannot do without the Chinese market, and due to the trade war, he has no choice but to produce locally for the Chinese market. Musk, as mentioned earlier, wants to build a factory in Shanghai.

Beijing is even lifting the obligation for him to set up joint ventures in the automotive industry, which previously applied. A concession that makes a lot of difference, but doesn't cost much. Beijing has long had other, more efficient methods of keeping foreign investors in China on a short leash. What's more, a Chinese company is earning a share of the profits. In 2017, the Chinese IT group Tencent secured 5 percent of Tesla shares for around 1.8 billion U.S. dollars, making it one of the Californian company's largest shareholders. What's more, unlike Foxconn in the U.S., Tesla does not receive any subsidies. So there is no balance in this game.

All these skirmishes, these "tit-for-tat" games, naturally also take up space at the G20 Summit in Hamburg in July 2017. There, all the protagonists meet for the first time since Donald Trump became American president. Angela Merkel only just manages to prevent the hotheads from getting into a tiff. What she cannot prevent, not even in cooperation with the Chinese, is Trump's diplomats from integrating the following formula into the final declaration: The G20 recognizes "the role of legitimate defense instruments in trade." Trump has left the others no choice but to agree with this or nothing. History books may later say otherwise. Never before have China and Germany cooperated so closely against the United States as at this summit. Even if not entirely voluntarily. The Germans themselves will probably only realize in retrospect that their future was also decided here. Not the breaking of old alliances or the closing of ranks with a new partner but the riots of the summit adversaries that have shaped the memory of the G20 meeting in Hamburg.

The 2017 summer political recess in Germany has barely begun when the heated phase of the trade war begins. Trump is so keen on the prelude to this that on that Monday, the 14 August he returned to Washington, especially from his golf vacation in New Jersey. There he announces an investigation into China's trade practices. The accusation of intellectual property theft will also be investigated: "All options are on the table."

The U.S. should appreciate the current economic and trade relations, the Beijing Foreign Ministry coolly says, warning of a "trade war" that will only have losers.

Only a few days earlier, the U.S. Treasury Department, of all people, had once again made clear in a statement how the balance of power between China and the U.S. stands in another area that certainly has an influence on the U.S.'s negotiating leeway in trade matters. The U.S.

owes China a total of $1.15 trillion, making the People's Republic the largest creditor of the American state, ahead of Japan. Trump is often accused of running the USA like a family business. If that's the case, he should know that you can't behave in a hostile manner towards your benefactor.

With this in mind, President Xi was not too excited about Trump's first return visit to China. He knew that with the versed citizens he had a winning card in his hand. And that was not his only one, people in Beijing were already angered that Trump would only visit Beijing after Tokyo and Seoul.

Soberly, Beijing strategists looked at how to engage Trump. The man so many hate wants to be respected and liked. And he loves events that reveal how unique he is. Beijing therefore decides to calm Trump down with diplomatic caresses. There is even a term in Chinese for this kind of policy — *"Pai mapi,"* which means "patting the horse's behind." It goes back to a custom of the Yuan Dynasty. No matter what the horse actually looked like, the riders praised each other's animals when greeting them in order to create an agreeable situation for interaction. That's why Trump gets to experience what no foreign president has ever been granted before that is a dinner with the head of state and party, in the Forbidden City. It's cold and the fan heaters make the trouser legs flutter on that November day in 2017 — but no matter, it's a unique event. At the photo opportunity, Trump stands with his chest puffed out as if he himself were the emperor of China, while Xi, hands buried in the pockets of his gray coat, keeps a low profile. A picture for the history books. Not the calm host next to the excited upstart.

Trump is also effusive in his thanks for the "Impressive reception" in Beijing, which he will "never forget." And he speaks in an astonishingly moderate tone to the Chinese, who in many areas are outperforming the US world power on a daily basis. Not a word about the trade practices investigations, not a word about intellectual property theft. Nothing is negotiated. "The Chinese know our position," Trump succinctly lets his diplomats know, who have worked out their negotiating strategy to no avail. To Xi, the "friend," he conciliatively says, "We're going to do it fair and grand." What exactly Donald Trump is up to — at least that's what his diplomats say behind his back — neither they nor Trump, the most spontaneous among American presidents, know. And Xi? He announces at the end with a smile, "President Trump and I have set the tone for future development."

Back home, Trump now says that China cannot be held responsible for its trade deficit; rather, he says, his predecessor Obama is to blame. "It's a pity that the previous administrations pushed it so far," he shouted to his voters during an appearance, who immediately nodded. Still, in China, he declared that he could not be angry with a country that merely exploited others to help its own people. Trump's home country is also familiar with this. It goes under the slogan "America first."

Now, it is accepted that Trump will continue to annoy Beijing, but that outbursts and strategic appearances for his voters are more important to him than shaking China's economic statics and seriously endangering its further rise.

Such staging also takes place in March 2018, when Trump invites steelworkers to the Oval Office to sign a punitive tariff decree. "Today I'm defending national security," he says — wearing a striped light-dark blue-and-white tie — and puffs out his cheeks. White and black steelworkers in gray jackets stand around him as he signs the paper with a thick black pen in order for cameras to catch the signature from a distance. All signs seem to be pointing to a storm, but even as he signs, Trump shows a willingness to negotiate. "If they make sure their products no longer threaten our security, we can talk to individual nations about lowering or lifting tariffs."

Satisfied, he allows the steelworkers to approach his microphone console, and even challenges one of them to arm wrestle. Another tells him excitedly that he still remembers the moment when his father lost his job as a steelworker. Trump's sensitive response is, "Your father is very proud of you now. He looks down on you from above ..." — "But my father is still alive," the steelworker objects. "Well, then he's even prouder," Trump retorts and then laughs.

So it is with Trump's policy. He has delivered to his voters without counting on powerful China, too much. And that's how it should continue in the coming months, even if some of the reports on the subject sound dramatic and Beijing and Washington are just shouting tariffs around each other's ears. Trump's tactic of constantly surprising the world with new strategies and thus forcing it to react is annoying, but it can be managed by Beijing. Trump is a troublemaker, but he is also a deal maker. And he knows that if China really fights back, it will hurt the United States. For every Chinese company that Trump denies market access, an American company will have to suffer. For every American tariff, there will be a Chinese tariff. And in the end, China can hold its breath. The four largest trading partners of the USA, including China, have imposed tariffs of 6 percent on average. Conversely, the U.S. imposes only 3.5 percent tariffs on these partners. So, it's a matter of eliminating that 2.5 percent difference. The Chinese also know this — and unlike Europe, they have the latitude to give in.

Trump knows that he can get something out of this for his country. That he can succeed in getting the tariffs adjusted accordingly. Of course, he cannot stop the decline of the USA as a world power. And in some respects, he is even accelerating it, because he is drawing Beijing's attention, as no other president before him has done, to the areas in which China is still very dependent on the United States. Tactically, Trump would be wise to quietly increase this dependence, for example, by forcing China to buy even more high-tech in the USA. But the American president is only thinking in the short term. Since he realizes that China's politicians are comparatively insensitive to pain, he targets Chinese companies that will be hurt by his actions.

The first Chinese company to be hit by Trump's action is Huawei. The smartphone manufacturer and network supplier from southern China is one of the major global competitors of American companies such as Cisco and Apple. Since Huawei now sells as many smartphones as Apple, it is important for the Americans to stop Huawei. The intelligence community is coming to Trump's aid. In March 2018, no fewer than six American intelligence directors, including those of the FBI, CIA, and NSA warn against Huawei phones. Important data could fall into China's hands and result in espionage, they tell a U.S. congressional committee. Christopher Wray, the FBI's Director, says it most directly, "We are gravely concerned about the risks that come with allowing a company that is in thrall to a foreign government and doesn't share our values to have a powerful role within our telecommunications networks."

Neither the British nor the Germans have similar concerns. In the UK, the Chinese are cooperating on the technical side with intelligence services there and have even disclosed their source codes. In Germany, they are working with Deutsche Telekom, amongst others, to develop innovative data networks. So this American game is more about the power position of the USA than about security.

Apple is now trembling at the prospect of Beijing taking action against iPhone. Huawei only has a market share of around 1 percent in the U.S. — on the other hand, iPhones have a market share of almost 25 percent in China.

In March 2018, the next blow comes. Trump sabotages the largest takeover in the technology industry to date — citing national security. Singapore-based Broadcom wanted to buy U.S. chipmaker Qualcomm for $117 billion. Trump declared that Broadcom could act in a way that would "compromise the national security of the United States." It is about links of Broadcom subsidiaries to China, possibly about a resale of Qualcomm to the Chinese. The argument is that the takeover could delay the conversion of U.S. mobile networks to 5G data radio. Qualcomm is one of the most important technology developers in this area. After the takeover, the Broadcom management could significantly reduce Qualcomm's currently considerable research and development expenditure in the USA, and the company could fall behind and thus become dependent on China in a roundabout way. Even Broadcom CEO Hock E. Tan was unable to completely dispel doubts that this could happen when he had to appear before the Pentagon. However, Trump announced the toughest measure to date against a Chinese company in April 2018. The Department of Commerce banned U.S. companies from selling components to ZTE, China's second-largest network supplier, for the next seven years. Despite the embargo, ZTE has supplied network technology to Iran and North Korea via dummy companies, according to Washington. American intelligence agencies also accuse the company of using its phones to spy on U.S. citizens. "ZTE has not only violated export requirements but supplied hostile regimes with sensitive American technology. ZTE has also lied to inspectors and deceived internal investigators. The actions are egregious and warrant significant punishment," said Trump's Attorney General Jeff Sessions.

This is a major blow for the company, which employs 75,000 people in China. The company relies on components from the USA for its products, including Google licenses and processors, which are essential for Android phones. The company's existence is at risk, however, Beijing does not seem to want to follow the "tit-for-tat" principle. Neither Boeing nor Apple is made to deal with consequences. The Chinese are keeping their public opinion clean, but they are exerting pressure behind the scenes. And it's obviously massive because as early as 13 May, Trump backpedals via twitter, "President Xi of China and I are working together to give a major Chinese phone company, ZTE, a way to get back to business quickly." Three weeks later, Commerce Secretary Wilbur Ross announced ZTE would pay a $1 billion fine for supplying technology to Iran and North Korea. He also said the company would have to replace its top management within 30 days. The Americans would be allowed to install a compliance team of their choice at ZTE and ZTE would, in turn, have to deposit 400 million US dollars as insurance if the team discovers further misconduct. For Beijing, this is a political imposition that China will have to bow to this time. However, the USA cannot afford this arrogance for much longer. The Americans obviously believe they are "world police, world prosecutor and world judge all in one," a top diplomat rages. But Beijing is bending. The political cost of opposing it does not outweigh the penalty. But Beijing has remembered this impertinence well.

And it was to get even worse. Ten days later, the U.S. Senate votes against the deal by a large majority and wants to reimpose the sanctions. Trump now becomes — unbelievably — ZTE's chief lobbyist, so to speak, but he cannot prevent the share price from plummeting by a further 23 percent.

All in all, Trump's action is a wake-up call for Beijing, which will now do everything in its power to further reduce its technological dependence on the USA. Even the American magazine *Forbes* believes that this will be possible within the next five to seven years. Trump may have achieved short-term success, but in the long term, he has achieved the exact opposite. Beijing will ensure that chip manufacturers, such as Intel and Qualcomm, for example, can no longer sell anything to China. Currently both companies make 14 percent of their profits in the Middle Kingdom. In the future, it won't be about "China stealing our secrets, we have to protect them, they're our crown jewels," as Trump said. It will be about China making our crown jewels look like river pebbles. The 6 July 2018 measures won't change that. That Friday, 25 percent tariffs on $34 billion worth of Chinese imports go into effect. Semiconductors and other high-tech products are also at stake. Beijing is hitting back in kind: soybeans, fruits, fish, and cars are on the list. The media are talking about the biggest trade war in world history. That is certainly true, but the immediate economic consequences are manageable. Overall, tariffs on Chinese products will rise from 3.5 percent to 3.7 percent.

The fact that Trump is threatening further tariffs should not be ignored. For example, he told journalists on board Air Force One that he could increase tariffs on imports worth $550 billion. The North Korea crisis has shown how quickly such threats can become reality. Moreover, time is against Trump. Chinese tariffs are affecting American consumers faster than the other way around. But while Trump needs tangible deals to get re-elected, the impression of steadfastness is enough for Xi. For both countries, at least, it would be much better to work together. The idea that Trump can halt China's rise through bans and sanctions is naive. They may be able to slow it down temporarily. In the long run, the fact remains that the U.S. will lose influence and China will gain influence. A clear indication of the new balance of power. While the Europeans had to appear in Washington at the beginning of the trade war, the Chinese first held court. Two American ministers and other U.S. specialists traveled to Beijing at the beginning of May 2018. Only then did the Chinese send a delegation to Washington. In return, the Americans gave the negotiator, Liu He, a bad time. After an agreement was reached, the vice premier announced that there would be no trade war. The fact that Trump then let the deal fall through was an embarrassment that Beijing will remember for a long time.

However, the U.S.–China trade conflict continues, and whether it is rhetoric, showing off for the electorate, or serving populist reflexes, one consequence of Donald Trump's policies is already clear. In Asia, and also in Europe, the influence of the United States is diminishing. With his behavior, the U.S. President is virtually forcing the world's regions to reorient themselves. The Europeans, who have been accustomed to close cooperation with the United States for many decades, are finding it more difficult than the countries of Asia, which have long been fed up with the United States.

One milestone on the road to Asia's emancipation from the U.S. predates even the Trump era: the establishment of the Asian Infrastructure Investment Bank (AIIB) in June 2015, the first creation of a new World Bank global institution since World War II. And the first global institution is to originate in China. Beijing was angered by U.S. dominance of the IMF, which China sees as distorting the global balance of power. In addition to the 21 founding members, Germany, Italy, France, and the United Kingdom also declared that they would support the new development bank. This was despite the Americans exerting massive political pressure on the Europeans. But their motto is now: Better trouble with the USA than to miss the boat in Asia. Currently, 61 countries are members of the AIIB, and 23 more are listed as future members. Of the major countries, only Japan and the USA are missing. This is certainly not what U.S. President Barack Obama had in mind when he demanded that China take on more international responsibility and play by the global rules.

Since Donald Trump's termination of the TPP agreement, it has become clear to everyone in Asia that the Americans are no longer a reliable partner. The region is increasingly turning towards China, even if the dominance of the Chinese is a source of unease for many and brings back bad memories of "Middle Kingdom" ideologies. For a long time, China had seen itself as the center of the world and has given its neighbors the opportunity to appease Beijing with gestures of subservience.

Regarding the China skepticism of many Asian countries, the Americans would actually have had quite good cards to play if they had been cleverer. For a long time in Asia, the Americans were regarded as the guarantors of military security and economic prosperity. The myth of the "American Dream" has also long gripped Asia. Similarly, the Americans were a force for order and a role model in Europe after the Second World War. Not only did they defeat Hitler's Germany but as a Pacific military power they also put imperialist Japan in its place in 1945. They were so powerful that they could even deploy an atomic bomb without being punished by the world community.

As a self-proclaimed protecting power, the U.S. attempted to halt the advance of communism during the Cold War in Asia, including military intervention in Korea and Vietnam. American soldiers died in the fight for more influence of the USA in the world, but also in the fight for a free world order. Under U.S. protection, an unprecedented economic boom, an Americanized boom, unfolded in Japan, South Korea, Taiwan, Singapore, Hong Kong, Thailand, and the Philippines. Between 1967 and 1997, the tiger economies grew at an average annual rate of 6.7 percent. Even communist Vietnam, which had suffered from American bombs and another 20 years of U.S. sanctions, developed good relations with the Americans from the mid-1990s onwards. And Americans even helped Communist China along the way. U.S. President Richard Nixon traveled to Beijing in 1972 to shake hands with Mao Zedong and assure him that America would not stab the Chinese in the back. The common enemy was the Soviet Union.

Unlike in centuries before, it was not Europe that set the course in Asia in the second half of the 20th century, but America. Unlike the Europeans before them, the Americans did not see themselves as a colonial power, but only as a protective power — though often a self-appointed one. It was the United States and its American Dream that paved the way for Asia, as can still be felt today, in Singapore as well as in Manila. And for a long time, we Europeans benefited from this as part of the Atlantic alliance. We did good business in the slipstream of the Americans. As a rule, the U.S. opened doors for us.

The first major slump came with the Asian crisis of 1997, coincidentally the same year that the British Crown Colony of Hong Kong was returned to China and the British colonial period in Asia ended. The pride and satisfaction of the Chinese was clearly visible when Hong Kong was Chinese again. I was standing on the roof of the Hong Kong Cultural Center when, just 200 meters away, the last British colonial governor, Chris Patten, and the heir to the throne, Prince Charles, boarded the yacht *Britannia* at night in the pouring rain to head home.

It almost seemed like a curse from the Queen that only a few weeks later, the Asian economy collapsed. The crash was so severe that one got the impression that the affected countries would not recover for decades. They had revenues in their respective local currencies, however, their debts were denominated in US dollars. When their currencies plummeted because no one believed they could repay their international debts, they were bankrupt within days.

When the neoliberal managers of the U.S.-influenced International Monetary Fund entered countries like Thailand and South Korea, the people there expected saviors. However, bargain hunters came. They tried to secure the best cuts, forcing countries to open their markets thereby creating a longstanding dependence on the United States. In the two years or so after the crash, the Asians realized for the first time that they would be better off relying on themselves or, in case of doubt, on their neighbor China. Even if this was not always easy with Beijing.

During these years, Asia came of age. The countries began to cooperate more closely with the Europeans, and to their great surprise, the crisis passed more quickly than most had expected. The fact that Beijing fought the downward trend with all its might and did not devalue its currency prevented something worse from happening. No one in Asia has forgotten that. Since then, the ASEAN countries have not grown as rapidly as they did before the crisis, but the average growth rate is still just under 5 percent. And they have been moving away from the USA in small but steady steps ever since. A country that breaks its own rules of the game when it suits it and wants to keep other countries down. A country that believes its view of the world is the only correct one.

Meanwhile, the U.S. offers, at best, potential military security. But this plays a role in fewer and fewer Asian countries; in fact, only Japan and South Korea are affected. And even there, the skepticism of the population is growing. The Chinese may be a little scary at times, sometimes threateningly scary. However, they are incredibly successful and have a reputation among their neighbors for being reasonable. But above all, they offer their neighbors the chance for economic prosperity.

In addition, the Chinese under Xi Jinping are succeeding in scoring points on the political stage with issues that strike a chord with many countries in emerging markets. Incidentally, this was not only evident under Trump, as many believe. This was already clear at the UN General Assembly in September 2015. It was the last appearance of the outgoing U.S. President Barack Obama there. Those who had expected Sunday speeches were surprised to see how differently the three most powerful heads of state in the world — Barack Obama, Xi Jinping, and Vladimir Putin — presented their priorities on the state of the world in their speeches.

Obama stressed that the global community must work towards democracy in as many countries as possible. Intervention is therefore important to him. For him, strengths of democracy are non-negotiable in that everyone should be able to practice their religion peacefully, be able to live in dignity, be able to criticize the powerful peacefully without being exposed to their arbitrariness. "The more democracies there are in the world," Obama said, "the more stable and peaceful the world is." With that, he succinctly summarized the value system of the West.

China's President Xi Jinping, surprisingly, also spoke of democracy. But not so much about democracy within countries but rather *between* countries, "The big, the strong, and the rich should not bully the small, the poor, and the weak." Every country should have the freedom to discover its own path of development, he said. Whoever tries to enforce good things in other countries by force, even if it is with the best of intentions, "the stone he picked up will fall on his feet." Xi sounded almost like a sixty-eight-year-old, "Nobody has to tell me how to live."

Xi thus touched on a point over which the West is already torn today. For the Europeans, and especially the Germans, on the one hand, have for some time stopped backing the policy of U.S. military interventions. On the other hand, we find it difficult to grant authoritarian systems or even dictatorships self-determination. Turkey under Erdoğan is a good example of this. Didn't we learn *"Wehret den Anfängen!"* in school? Aren't our values universal after all?

Vladimir Putin, on the other hand, focused on a different point, for good reason. He believes that strong global institutions are indispensable. Institutions whose rules of the game must be respected by all. And, but of course, he didn't say that out loud, in which the Russians play a major role and, together with the Chinese, can assert themselves against everyone else. Political actions "that undermine the UN" are "very dangerous," he said, because in the end only the law of the strongest remains. Putin emphasized the adherence to international law that all must abide by. An important point, of course, even if one exposes the weakness of his argument: Rule of law in the world, yes, but not necessarily in his country.

It is interesting to note that the phrase "rule of law" exists, but "legal worldliness" does not yet. The legal vacuum that globalization has created is obvious. The USA in particular has been happy to use it for its own purposes over the past two decades. It was and is the law of the strongest. So, Putin not only disguised his own weaknesses but he also is also right. We must expand the *world of law.*

Ultimately, all three make a point. But only when the positions are brought together does a reasonable blueprint for a new world order emerge; Obama sees national democracies as the key, Xi wants international equality for all states, and Putin is focused on strong global institutions and international law. Individually, each of these demands remains incomplete. A world in which there should be as many democracies as possible without countries being forced to become a democracy than its level of development allows. Or a world in which all nations are treated equally, without their economic or military strength playing a role. And finally, a world with strong global institutions and a legal system to which all must submit as naturally as to national legal systems. Such a world cannot function if all countries are not equal, but there are world powers that do not feel bound by it.

But without all three world powers having to make drastic compromises, a common new world order will not emerge. This will be the hardest for the U.S. because it will have to give up the most power. And that is why Trump is ranting the loudest against it. The Chinese will find it the easiest because Beijing is only just establishing itself in the global community. That must never be forgotten in the current trade dispute.

Of the representatives of the 193 member states, at any rate, the rather stiff Xi Jinping received the most applause, followed by Vladimir Putin. The charismatic Obama had to settle for third place. Logical, the quick analysis might be, the Chinese have won over many states economically, so it's no wonder that the applause from their ranks is great. But a closer look makes it clear that it is, of course, important to the governments of emerging countries to be recognized as equal states in the global community and to be allowed to play a role. Second, most important to them are stable global institutions, and naturally cleaning up one's own house comes third, especially if the old guard tells one what to do and what not to do in the process. At the same time, their skepticism about democracy is growing. One need only compare the development path of democracy in India with China's authoritarian system. In India, people can vote freely, but they are much poorer and have fewer opportunities for advancement. In China, they are not allowed to vote in the Western sense, but their chances of advancement are much greater. Some have more collective human rights, others more individual.

From this perspective, democracy has long since ceased to be the panacea when it comes to rapidly developing a country and creating prosperity for its citizens. The development dictatorship is much more popular with the people in the emerging countries than we think. In addition, Beijing is negotiating new global rules of the game with its partners. These are tough negotiations, but they are negotiations nonetheless. The West, and Washington in particular, would prefer that the upstarts, including China, join the global rules network that the West has devised and that it considers tried and true. As a result, Washington and also Brussels and sometimes even Berlin behave condescendingly to politicians of emerging states, while Beijing tends to be more obliging and cooperative.

Exceptions prove the rule: Germany and China have succeeded in convincing Obama to lift sanctions on Iran. And Obama has re-established relations with Cuba. But that is little compared to the fresh trust Beijing has been able to build in Southeast Asia, Africa, South America, and Eastern Europe in the same period. Whether Hungary, Poland, Australia, the Philippines, South Korea, Brazil, Myanmar, or Thailand, all these countries are much closer to China today than they were 10 years ago. In fact, there is hardly a country in the world — with the exception of Japan and the USA — that is as distanced from China today than it was 10 years ago.

Historical coincidence also plays a role here. Just at the moment when it became clear to everyone, including the Americans, that military interventions do not work, the new world power China entered the scene.

It has long been clear that the gain in power through armies is redundant. The Korean War in the 1950s ended with the division of Korea. The Vietnam War was lost. The Iraq War in the early 1990s liberated Kuwait and otherwise achieved comparatively little because U.S. President George Bush turned back before Baghdad. The second Iraq War brought only instability, as did the Afghanistan War. That is why Obama wisely began the military withdrawal — even if this was difficult, since the best army in the world was long regarded by the U.S. as an indispensable means of gaining and securing power. Today, it is a different field on which battles are being fought. And it seems that the Asians have adjusted well to this.

A little over a year after Trump's cancellation, the Asians have produced a trade agreement ready to be signed, in which neither China nor the USA is represented. As far as the U.S. is concerned, the agreement doesn't include the U.S. demands, only ignores them, so it would be possible to reintegrate the Americans very quickly under a new president. So the invitation to Washington stands — no hard feelings. Trump, unlike Xi, will not stay forever, after all.

The Comprehensive and Progressive Agreement for Trans-Pacific Partnership (CPTPP) was signed in Santiago de Chile in early March 2018. The roughly 500 million people living in the member countries still account for 13.5 percent of global GDP. That's not even half of the U.S. market, but it still opens up enormous opportunities for the new Trans-Pacific economic area, which is still two-thirds the volume of the EU. It is a trade agreement that now operates in the slipstream of the three big players — without China, Europe, and, for the time being, the USA. The newcomers are standing on their own two feet. It is an event in which the historical impact has yet to unfold.

Of course, Trump did not begrudge the TPP supporters this success. On March 8, the day that CPTPP members in Chile held their celebrations to mark their success, Donald Trump announces punitive tariffs on aluminum and steel. Of course, this is no coincidence. The news of trade restrictions also has air supremacy in Beijing on this day. Trump even manages to kill two birds with one stone. For at the same time, the National People's Congress, the Chinese parliament with 3,000 members, is meeting in Beijing for its annual assembly. Three days earlier, Premier Li Keqiang had delivered his annual report. It is always the most sensitive time of the political year in Beijing. Perhaps for this reason, the Chinese government is conspicuously reticent about criticizing Washington. The Ministry of Commerce wrote in a statement that the tariffs were a "serious attack" on the international trade order. China will take "effective measures" and defend its legitimate rights and interests. The U.S. would harm not only other countries but also its own interests through the tariffs, it said. However, there are no comments from leading Chinese politicians.

Similar to CPTTP members, Beijing is trying to look ahead and find a solution that costs less power. China wants to open its markets. In any case, Premier Li Keqiang speaks of this before parliament with forceful-ness never before heard from a premier. Li says that the Chinese market for manufacturing should be "completely opened up." Access to sectors such as telecommunications, medicine, care for the elderly and education should also be improved. Banks and other financial institutes that want to open a business in China should also have it as easy as domestic institu-tions in the future. "China is committed to promoting economic globaliza-tion and protecting free trade," Li said, assuring that he also intends to further reduce overcapacity in the coal and steel industries. Highly indebted state-owned enterprises would be wound up.

One thing is clear and that is that China will only open up if it benefits the Chinese. Nevertheless, his speech reads like a counter-draft to Donald Trump's policy.

At the same time, Beijing is negotiating a free trade agreement with the ASEAN countries. It is to be signed before the end of 2018, even if Beijing is still wavering over whether bilateral agreements should be given preference over a joint trade agreement. China is already ASEAN's second-largest trading partner, with a trade volume of $500 billion and a growth of 13 percent last year. The U.S. currently accounts for 630 billion, but new agreements between Beijing and the ASEAN countries will drastically change the relationship.

While the USA is driving its chariot and trying to turn back the clock, the Chinese are persistently staying on course and using every vacuum, every gap that Donald Trump creates to increase their influence and estab-lish themselves as the new number one in the world. The remaining Asian states are moving toward Beijing, partly out of sheer necessity. Europe is acting indecisively and hesitantly and does not yet have a clear strategy. Not in dealing with Trump, not in dealing with China and certainly not with Asia in general.

The EU is too weak to play referee in the countless major and minor conflicts between China and the United States. It can do no more than intervene now and then to soothe or encourage. As for the rest of Asia, the new center of the world, the Europeans do not play an important role. This should not be surprising, since Europe has also failed to position itself and to advance its own interests. Yet great opportunities could have opened up for Europe precisely because of its disappointment with the Americans and its skepticism about China. But Europe is acting hesitantly or even indifferently. At best, one or two companies have seized the opportunity, including many German SMEs. This was not politically coordinated or even forced by Brussels or Berlin. Here, too, the European aversion to industrial policy is now taking its toll.

There would certainly have been time to change course. When Obama negotiated the TPP free trade agreement and the Chinese followed suit with the RCEP program, the EU should have felt the competitive pressure and accelerated negotiations with China and its neighbors to avoid falling behind. Instead, little happened. In December 2017, the EU signed a free trade agreement with Japan. There is already an agreement with Singapore, negotiations are still underway with Vietnam and the EU has at least reached an agreement with Thailand. But Brussels will not sign it until democratic elections have taken place in Thailand. That can take time and does not bother the Thais very much. After all, there is China.

The negotiations between the EU and Asia as a whole have practically gone to sleep. Political skepticism in Europe is high. Brussels has the blues. While China seizes every opportunity to expand its position in Asia, we let one after the other slip away. And this despite the fact that it is becoming increasingly clear that we have few alternatives to rapprochement with Asia and especially with China. The EU's internal market itself is large, but it is growing only moderately and Germany's position in Europe is weakening. The USA is isolating itself, also from Europe. We are at odds with Russia.

At the same time, the countries of Asia are being better and better served by their neighbor China, because they are increasingly able to manufacture products of European quality themselves. The Chinese are thus benefiting not only from their own huge domestic market but also from the ASEAN countries, the world's largest growth market, right on their doorstep. And Africa, the next big growth market, is likewise already firmly in their hands. Here, too, Europe has missed its opportunities (see Chapter 9).

This inertia is particularly risky for Germany. In 2016, China replaced the USA as our most important foreign trade partner for the first time. In 2017, Germany and China increased trade by another 10 percent to a volume of almost 187 billion euros. The USA even slipped behind the Netherlands into third place that year. And Germany imports twice as much from China as from the USA, with a value of 100 billion euros.

The trade war between China and the U.S. can cause enormous damage for Europe and especially for Germany. Trump is accidentally showing us our limits in terms of our dependence and lack of alternatives in other markets. Whatever the outcome of this power struggle, it is already clear that it is a power struggle that America cannot win and one that will directly affect Germany. So, we should be very vigilant when the U.S. and China are at odds.

German Chancellor Angela Merkel is acting cautiously in this conflict. She is not inclined to make a brilliant plea for free trade like Xi did in Davos. And she is certainly not inclined to fan the populist flames with hype speeches like Donald Trump. Her behavior is partly in keeping with her character, but it is also shaped, to no small extent, by political circumstances. In Germany, Merkel is dealing with voters who want to profit from global trade, but for whom globalization always remains a bit suspect. Within this framework, she has set a cautious tone that nevertheless will make history books, "The times when we could rely on others are somewhat over. That's what I've experienced in the last few days." She said this at the end of May 2017 after the disappointing G7 Summit in Italy. And, "We Europeans really have to take our chisel into our own hands." She didn't say this remarkable sentence in a government statement, but, and it couldn't be more casual, in a beer tent in München-Trudering. It is an expression of their annoyance and disappointment with the then new U.S. administration under Trump.

Does turning away from the U.S. imply turning toward China? It is not that simple. In any case, the dispute between China and the U.S. offers room for maneuver, especially in political terms. It could not only lead to closer economic ties but also to an understanding of opinions that Beijing is otherwise cagey about. Human rights issues, for example, or environmental protection.

The extent of the room for maneuver was demonstrated in April 2018 during Foreign Minister Wang Yi's visit to Berlin. At the same time as Wang's trip, Beijing resolved an issue that had been increasingly straining relations with Berlin. A new law for non-governmental organizations (NGOs) in China would soon have made it impossible for several German foundations to operate. Completely unexpectedly, the Beijing Ministry of Security announced that new partners had been found for the Konrad Adenauer, Heinrich Böll, and Rosa Luxemburg Foundations in an exemption for Germany and that they could continue their work. The Friedrich Ebert and Hanns Seidel Foundations may even continue to cooperate with their old partners. A step that was received with goodwill in Berlin, even though one must, of course, read the fine print carefully here as well. It is still to be decided whether the heads of the foundations are to be evaluated according to a points system and that, too, will be open to discussion. It is the time of new leeway, which intuitive politicians like former Foreign Minister Sigmar Gabriel immediately recognized. He used the visit of his Chinese counterpart to send a message to the world that will have been understood both in Beijing and in Washington, "We see that part of the world is beginning to isolate itself, to take protectionist measures, following that it is clear that we are looking for new and more intensive partnerships."

A good 70 years of the transatlantic alliance seems to be coming to an end — but without anything else taking its place that would be available, for example, a closer partnership with China, not to mention an alliance. But perhaps such solid alliances have served their purpose in times of globalization, and changing coalitions are more appropriate.

In addition, when it comes to reaching out to the Asians in the course of the great battle between the U.S. and China, Merkel is in a dilemma, she must ensure that the Germans can sell as much as possible to China, which is currently their largest trading partner. At the same time, she must avoid becoming politically and economically dependent on China. After all, there is still a great deal of skepticism about the Chinese. There are the concerns about the human rights situation, which have a high priority due to our own history, and the Chinese takeovers of German companies, which continue to cause unease. What applies to Germans and world trade in general applies to Germans and China in particular. Profit, yes, but not truly from the heart. So, it does Merkel little good to take a clear side in the power struggle between China and the United States. In the eyes of the voters, she has only the choice between plague and cholera. Merkel cannot embrace Xi Jinping or Donald Trump as warmly as she did Barack Obama.

# Chapter 9

# Africa: Alternative-Free Departure

## How We Are Missing Out on the Last Big Growth Market and Beijing Partners With a Continent

*Europe is just missing Africa as an opportunity of the century.*

Gerd Müller, German Development Minister

How proudly they laugh, the two young women. 23-year-old Concilla Owire and 27-year-old Alice Mugure are aspiring train drivers. Today, the two are driving the first train on the new line from Nairobi to Mombasa. Wearing bright blue uniforms and red ties, they are sitting in their driver's cab. Behind them stands a Chinese man, also wearing a red tie, but only a vest, no jacket, and the top button of his shirt is undone. He does not behave like a colonial lord and seems almost embarrassed. He is the representative of those who built and financed the train line and who will assist the Kenyans over the next five years to one day be able to operate it themselves. He is a service provider, a business partner, not a governor of the new "conquerors" from the Middle Kingdom, as people in the West like to believe when it comes to China's activities in Africa.

The route that the train is following is not the first railroad track that the Chinese have built in Africa. The first one was built more than 40 years ago: it was the Tanzania–Zambia line. Many people in Africa still remember this. While we in the West like to think that the Chinese have only been involved for a few years and that it's the longest route that

213

Africa has had built by China. The longest route stretches across 750 kilometers and runs between Addis Ababa, the capital of Ethiopia, and the Port of Djibouti, the capital of the republic of the same name on the Horn of Africa. It was opened last year and is Africa's first electrified rail line. Other even more massive projects are in the pipeline. The 1,400-kilometer rail line between Lagos and Calabar along the coast of Nigeria is to be built for $13 billion. And then in May 2018, a $6.68 billion project was awarded to the Chinese: a rail line between Lagos in the south and Kano in the north of Nigeria. All of these rail lines are costly to build and open up regions that were previously inaccessible by rail. Nevertheless, the Nairobi–Mombasa rail line, which the trainee train drivers Owire and Mugure now run regularly, is *the* symbol of the African boom, the progress spurred on by China on a continent that was long considered hopeless in the West. A symbol of which both the Chinese and Kenyans are proud. A symbol that the colonial era in Kenya has finally come to an end — a good half century after the country's independence in 1963. Yes, even more, it is a symbol that Africa is now standing on its own two feet. And it will probably also mean that we Europeans are losing our connection in Africa.

It's about the new route of the once colonial "Madaraka Express," which became famous recently through Sydney Pollack's Hollywood film *Beyond Africa* with Robert Redford, Meryl Streep, and Klaus Maria Brandauer in the mid-1980s. A train so run-down that it was popularly called the "Lunatic Express." The new line is 472 kilometers long and runs between Nairobi and Mombasa. It opened at the end of May 2017 — 18 months ahead of schedule. However, this train also represents the fact that Africa is now, for the first time, freely joining the globalization process. It's a fact that, for the first time in the continent's history, African politicians have the choice of what they want to do with their countries and, above all, with whom they want to cooperate. Will these co-operations create new dependencies? Counter-question: If you become massively dependent on your bank in order to be able to afford a house, will that ultimately increase your family's wealth? As a rule, yes. Only in exceptional cases does it lead to bankruptcy. And does the bank profit from this? Yes, of course, otherwise it wouldn't do the business.

The same is true of African countries. They've been offered undreamed-of opportunities to become even more independent, even stronger. That is why the label "neo-colonialism" that some critics of China's involvement attach to this and many other projects is inappropriate. After all, colonialism means that the colonized have no choice. In fact, the room for maneuver of African governments has never been greater. And never has what they do, or don't do, been more important for the world, for Europe, for Germany. More than 1.2 billion people live in Africa. The population is extremely young. This is a huge opportunity. They can work and they have great talents. But until they can develop, until enough jobs are created, they first need electricity, Internet, roads, and railroads. The Africans are learning how to create this important infrastructure — not from Europe but from China. The most common criticism that comes from Europe is that too many Africans take the route across the Mediterranean to participate in our prosperity. At the same time, many African politicians are dumbfounded by the criticism that China is helping to generate prosperity in Africa.

Together, Chinese and Africans make up one-third of the world's population. The path that they take together matters. In 2050, Africa will have twice as many people as it does today, estimates the World Bank. There will be as many people as China has today. That is more than half of the world's population growth in this period. Nigeria, for example, will then have more people than the USA.

This is an enormous challenge that will have an impact on the statics of the countries of the world. Therefore, it is crucial for Europe to finally understand how important this last undeveloped continent is for our future. However, it seems as if Europe has hardly a clue. Yet it would be an opportunity for us to ensure that the living standards of Africans improve. After all, Africa's prosperity also means growth in our economy and thus prosperity for ourselves, when we otherwise don't care about Africa. Beijing has understood this, while Berlin and Brussels have not yet — Washington even less so. "Beijing is investing. They don't have to worry about hundreds of thousands of refugees arriving at their doorstep," says former Foreign Minister Sigmar Gabriel self-critically.

No country invests more in African infrastructure than China — 80 sports stadiums and more than 200 schools. The Chinese have to date built around 6,500 kilometers of railroad tracks, 6,000 kilometers of roads, 70 power plants, and dozens of airports and seaports in Africa. "Africa has benefited from China for the most part," even the long skeptical London *Financial Times* now writes.

For Kenya, the new train line between Nairobi and Mombasa is a sensation — a leap into the present. It is the first new railroad line in 116 years; at that time, the British colonial rulers had built a very modern narrow-gauge railroad. By the way, this was not done altruistically. At that time, they wanted to protect their power-political interests in neighboring Uganda from the Germans. Today, the new railroad is the first section of a network that will connect Kenya with six other East African countries in the future. Kenya plays a central role in this. The New Silk Road, which China is building as part of the "One Belt, One Road" initiative to Europe and Africa, is the largest infrastructure project in human history. The following map shows what the network will look like:

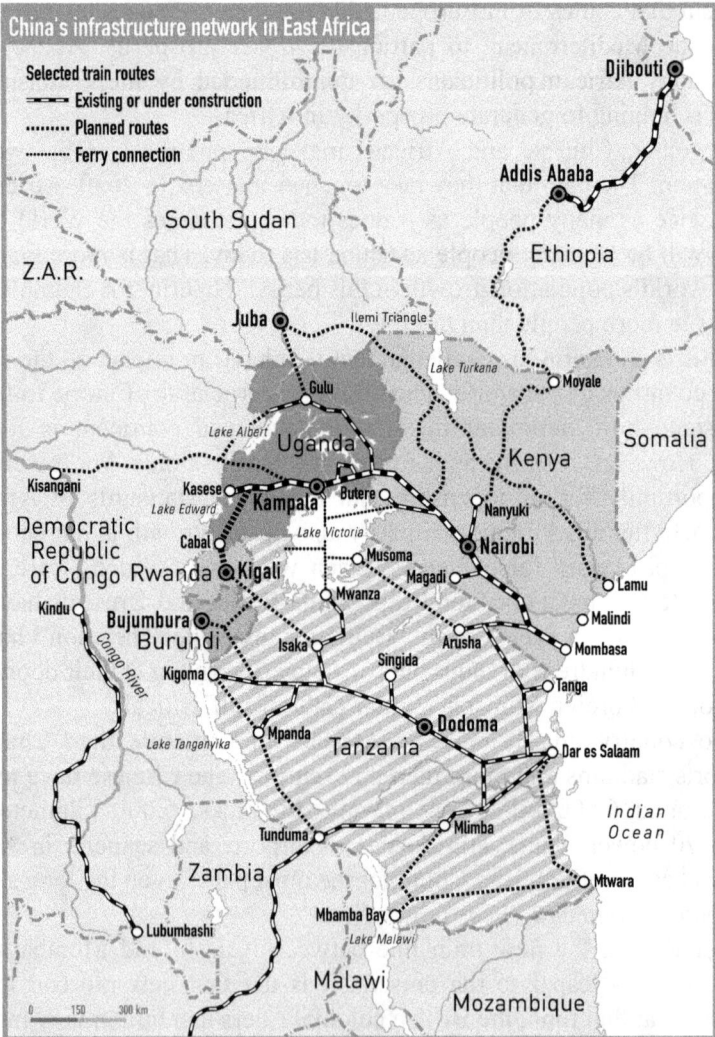

Mombasa's new train station was designed by local architects. With its rounded glass fronts and the high tower in the middle, it is somewhat reminiscent of an airport terminal. On one of the large columns, I find the small bust of the seafarer Zheng He. He was the first Chinese in Africa. He came to Mombasa four times at the beginning of the 15th century. Not as a conqueror but as a friend and partner. No one was massacred by him and his fellow travelers. No land was taken from the natives although the Chinese would have been able to do so. Instead, he traded gold, silver, and porcelain with the Swahili for zebras, camels, ostriches, and ivory. He even brought a giraffe back to China. It was revered at the imperial court as a lucky animal.

80 years later, the first Europeans, the Portuguese, landed on the coast and did not come as friends. Fort Jesus in Mombasa, completed in 1596, still tells the story today. A massive foreign body on the beach, it is still fearsome with its heavy cannons. How must the fort have looked to the Africans of that time, who knew only mud huts?

For centuries, the respective colonial powers fought over the rule of the fort — over the heads of the Africans. For even the Arabs did not come peacefully to Africa later or did the Germans at the end of the 19th century, and certainly not the British, whose world domination was based on the colonies in Africa. Those who rebelled against them often paid for it with their lives. And those who had to work for them did so under inhumane conditions. During the construction of the first train line, 4,000 forced laborers, mostly Indians, died. No one cared at the time. For the new Chinese line, only a few elephants sacrificed their lives, underestimating the power and speed of the new locomotives.

Of course, the fact that the Chinese are more civilized in Africa than their colonial predecessors does not mean that they do not sometimes go overboard. They are interested in African mineral resources, in rare earths, as well as in copper and other ores. They want to import as many tons as possible to China for as low a price as possible in order to further fuel the boom in their own country. Raw materials, by the way, that we could one day lack. Of course, they also want to open up the African market for their products. Consumers who are lost to us. And last but not least, they are looking for political allies in the global power struggle. Allies that we will soon lack when it comes to integrating our values and ideas into the rules of the game of the global community. That is, when it comes to ensuring that the majority of the population calls the shots.

In the French and German election campaigns in 2017, hectic trips to Africa did play a role. The signal to voters was clear — we will make sure that Africans stay at home. But there is still no grand plan. Minister Gerd Müller (CSU) is pushing for just such a plan in the Summer of 2018, and elections will be held in Bavaria in the fall. What's more, when you hear that Müller wants to provide refugees with more information in transit centers near their countries of origin about the dangers of fleeing towards northern Europe "and wants to warn them against illusions about Europe," you already know where the journey is headed. A sustainable plan looks different.

After all, Müller is one of the few to say clearly, "Europe is in the process of missing Africa as an opportunity of the century." And, he said, migration from Africa is "a question of fate for Europe." The EU and its member states pump billions in development aid into Africa every year, he said. "These are basically all lost grants. China, on the other hand, is giving loans. I think we as the EU are not engaged enough in Africa and, above all, we're not efficient." He's right about that. And Günter Nooke (CDU), the German government's Africa Commissioner, adds, "For me, it would already have achieved a lot if we coordinated better within the federal government."

The EU still does not have an Africa Commissioner. From 2021 to 2027, 39 billion euros are earmarked for the continent — a 10th of what is spent on EU agricultural policy. It's a conundrum: People in Europe are worried about refugees, and yet hardly anything happens. Instead, the EU delights in playing the moralizer. Antonio Tajani, Martin Schulz's successor as president of the European Parliament, warns of the danger of "Africa becoming a Chinese colony." The Chinese, he says, are only interested in mineral resources, "but not in stability." This is, of course, nonsense and a statement that sounds just as narrow-minded in Africa and China as it does here. Anyone who invests billions in a foreign continent is interested in stability. And the most important characteristic of a colony that the colonized have no choice. To reiterate, because the talk of neo-colonialism is not dying down: Never in history have African governments had greater latitude to pick and choose who they work with around the world. Never before have they and the people in their countries been freer and never before more optimistic about the future. We would best increase Africa's latitude if we too sought cooperation. Then, the African countries would have the opportunity to choose between different providers and would not automatically have to fall back on the Chinese. To date, there is no adequate European investment program that would make it easier for Africans to cooperate with Europe instead of China. Meanwhile, even the Indians are waking up: "Africa will be our top priority," Indian Prime Minister Narendra Modi announced in Uganda's capital Kampala in July 2018. "We will keep our markets open to Africa. We will support our industries to invest in Africa." Modi promised, among other things, 18 new embassies to open on the continent. This is good for Africans because it reduces their dependence on China. It is not good for us because we continue to lose influence.

The idea that without economic engagement in Africa we will retain our sovereignty over values that are dear to us is naïve. It is also naïve to think that we will automatically participate economically in Africa's rise. It is already becoming apparent that the next generation in Europe will no longer be able to solve the world's major political issues without Africa. Beijing, on the other hand, considers the continent more important than ever. In the past decade, the Chinese president, premier, and foreign minister have traveled to Africa a total of 79 times, to 43 countries. "Nowhere is there more potential for development than in Africa," President Xi Jinping said on his most recent trip in July 2018. This is when he integrated Senegal, the first West African country, into the Silk Road Initiative and pledged to invest another $15 billion in the continent. At the next stop, Rwanda, President Paul Kagame gushed in Xi's presence that China treats Africa "as an equal," a "revolutionary attitude" that is "more valuable than money." Clearly, he has had different experiences with other countries.

The Chinese plan to stay in Africa for a long time. We are not even there yet. Beijing is convinced that their investments will pay off economically and politically. Even the New York-based management and strategy consultancy McKinsey now agrees, "Overall, we are convinced that China's growing involvement in Africa is very positive for Africa's economies, governments, and workforce," they summarize in a study. And Jeffrey Sachs, director of the Earth Institute at New York's Columbia University, notes that Chinese involvement is the "most important positive event for Africa of our generation."

Of course, the Chinese are not Samaritans. Of course, they are brutal investors who dig deep under the skin of Africa to harness its mineral resources. There are investors who don't care about labor laws and environmental protection. And of course, there are the farmland buyers, the traders who flog cheap made-in-China products to Africans for inflated amounts and then make off with the profits. But they are the exception rather than the rule.

Perhaps that is why Africans have been comparatively quick to shed their skepticism. Some wonder about the Chinese, who prefer to stay in their camps, quarters, and Chinatowns. And "Made-in-China" still does not enjoy a good reputation, as traders continue to flood the markets with cheap products. But the bottom line is that most Africans are positive about the Chinese. And they are proud of the roads, rail networks, and power plants built with Beijing's help. We Europeans have contributed nothing to this indescribable sense of awakening.

In Kenya, the journey from Nairobi to Mombasa no longer takes 10 to 12 hours but only four and a half. Seven new stations have been built. Tens of thousands of people, whom the old train used to pass by, can now travel effortlessly to the Kenyan metropolises of Mombasa and Nairobi. All this has become possible because the Chinese have taken a risk that Americans, Germans, Englishmen, or Frenchmen have shied away from for years. The route cost 20 percent of an annual budget. Kenya had to borrow 90 percent of the money from the Chinese. The question is as follows: Can it pay off? President Uhuru Kenyatta is probably being a little too optimistic when he says that he wants to pay back the loan in four years. But even if it took eight or 10 years, it would still be a success. Perhaps it is also too optimistic to believe that this development alone will grow GDP by 1.5 percent, as the president hopes. But it helps the economic upswing in any case. After just four weeks, the frequency of trains had to be increased from two to six per day. And since the beginning of 2018, the freight trains have also been rolling along the line. The rail line is currently being connected to 10 berths in the port of Mombasa so that bulky and heavy goods can be loaded directly from ships onto freight trains in the future.

What rail lines mean for the upswing of a country, we experienced in Germany after December 1835. That was when the first German train, the Ludwigseisenbahn from Nuremberg to Fürth, got underway — still with a locomotive built by the British in Newcastle, the "Adler," which was driven by British engineers. Soon after, Germany was playing a leading role economically. It was at least as spectacular when the British built Africa's first railroad in Egypt 20 years later and then the Kenyan railroad to Lake Victoria in 1901. But after Kenya's independence in 1963, the West lost interest in Africa, and the Africans were not yet in a position to modernize the line on their own. It was to take a good 50 years before the Chinese considered it worthwhile to invest in this railroad line.

Why the former British colonial rulers let this opportunity pass is a good question. No money? Or perhaps they had no political interest in Kenya's real independence? Of course, there are always several reasons. One might be the unspoken but deep-seated desire that these countries will fail because of their quasi-forced freedom. As recently as 2000, *The Economist* headlined Africa as "The hopeless continent." An opinion that was as gloating as it was short-sighted, as has since become clear. At the time, other investment projects seemed more lucrative, and Europeans were convinced that the world would turn without Africa — just put a lid on it and ignore it.

The Chinese also realized much more quickly than the Europeans, the value of African raw materials and Africa's potential as a sales market. Fifteen years of Chinese involvement have left far more positive traces in Africa than half a century of mostly honest, sometimes thoughtless, sometimes cynical development aid from the West. It is not that the Europeans have not recognized the problem. In Spring 2018, Chancellor Merkel once again emphasized Germany's and Europe's responsibility for Africa. She said it was not just a matter of preventing future refugees. Europeans also have a moral responsibility, she said, "because we have done a lot of damage there with colonialism over decades and centuries." In Africa, she said, whole generations were unable to take responsibility for their countries. "After centuries of foreign rule, all of a sudden, as if at the push of a button, everyone is supposed to become entrepreneurs and govern superbly and do everything really great," Merkel said. "That's where long-term damage has been done." Merkel had already made similar remarks in her speech in Davos in January 2018. Acknowledging Germany's historical responsibility honors Merkel. Nevertheless, in these times, it may be the wrong text for Germans to use. No one likes to act out of guilt. It would be much better to argue as the Chinese do: These are investments. They help the Africans and benefit our economy, in equal measure. And for Europe, there is another very important factor: Such a policy can help prevent more and more Africans from migrating to Europe. But so far, Europe has not been able to get its act together.

The Chinese do have their act together. Not only through their infrastructural projects but also those of the Japanese, Indians, and South Koreans, who ignited the African boom. What was once North–South aid has been replaced by a South–South business partnership that has catapulted the African continent to incredible heights of growth. Africa's GDP grew by 3.6 percent in 2017 and in 2018, the figure will be as high as 4.1 percent, estimates the African Development Bank (AfDB). This means that Africa is recovering from the resource price crisis that occurred in 2015 and 2016 "faster than expected," according to AfDB analysts.

Of course, it is not easy to invest in Africa. The administration is imperfect and the elites are still corrupt, even if things are slowly improving. Sub-Saharan Africa is still at the bottom of Transparency International's ranking of continents. The infrastructure is steadily improving, but it is still nowhere near what it should be to make any German middle-class person feel comfortable. There is no continuous road from Johannesburg to Cairo, at least not one worthy of the name. Not yet. Famine has decreased significantly, but it is still a major problem. The same applies to infant mortality and disease control. Wars or local uprisings can destroy a delicate economic upswing at any time. And Africa is far from being satisfactorily integrated into the global economy. It contributes only around 3 percent to world trade. Also because Africa is still heavily dependent on mineral resources, the boom is vulnerable to the vicissitudes of the world market.

In fact, prices that have fallen on the raw materials market has even caused some African countries to slip into recession. These include Egypt, the largest economic power north of the Sahara, and Nigeria, the counterpart south of the Sahara. South Africa, which still claims a leadership role on the continent, also experienced a recession in mid-2017 — it's second in eight years. The economic situation became so difficult that President Jacob Zuma was forced to resign in February 2018. Most recently, even Beijing could no longer be patient with the stubborn old man, once one of Africa's great freedom fighters, however as president he'd become increasingly entrenched in his own political tug-of-war. Angola is also in trouble. Despite an economic boom, the government has not managed to get poverty under control. The country is now something like a "fallen star."

While we in the West tend to register such crises and see problems and risks, the credo in Beijing is that Africa may have difficulties, but the continent is still on course. The big surprise is that countries that are not so dependent on raw material exports are now growing stably, for example, Ethiopia (up 8.3 percent in 2017, according to the World Bank), which we will cover more closely later, or Tanzania (7.2 percent), Côte d'Ivoire (6.8 percent), and Senegal (6.7 percent). And now that prices for mineral resources have picked up again, the crisis countries are also getting back into the groove.

Chinese companies are demonstrating how to deal with this. Transsion Holdings from Shenzhen in southern China has achieved a market share of almost 30 percent in sub-Saharan Africa in just 10 years with its inexpensive smartphones, followed by Huawei, which also comes from China and offers high-quality smartphones. No matter how well, or how badly Africa is doing, both are earning money in any case.

The secret of Transsion's success is that the cameras on its phones take better pictures of black faces. The Tecno and Itel models also have space for two SIM cards. This gives customers the option of choosing the mobile phone company that offers them the best and cheapest reception at any given time. This is important in Africa, where not all network providers are equally strong in all locations and customers are price-conscious. The company has also built up a dealer network in 30 African countries and launched a marketing campaign that Africa has yet to experience in its opulence. Surprisingly, in China, the brand is virtually unknown, but it is scheduled to be listed on the Shenzhen Stock Exchange before the end of 2018. Following its success in Africa, Transsion is now also conquering the Indian market.

Africa now has an astonishing 12 percent share of the global cell phone market — an increase of 70 percent in the past five years. Everywhere, improvements are being made on network stability, while at the same time, the fiber-optic network is being expanded for faster Internet. China Telecom Global has been cooperating with the Djibouti Data Center since the end of 2016 to expand the network in East Africa. Where is Deutsche Telekom?

In the meantime, the average mobile Internet and download speed in Kenya is higher than that of the USA. The network was built by the Chinese, even though there is still a lot of room for improvement. The continent is home to 17 percent of the world's population but only 6.2 percent of Internet users. You can imagine the economic potential that would unfold if the number of users was to increase to just 10 percent. So, there would still be opportunities for us to invest. But no one is warming up.

In the Summer of 2017, a joint Chinese–African project was initiated to guarantee the construction of a broadband cable network to which over a hundred large cities could be connected. Here, too, one has to ask the following question: Where is Europe? Germany is obviously only concerned with itself in this area. It is no longer absurd to imagine that broadband coverage in parts of Africa will be better than on the outskirts of Germany's major cities.

In Europe, Sweden should be our role model. Their high broadband density has made a large number of start-ups possible. Digital business models can be implemented much more easily there. This is also precisely where an enormous opportunity lies for Africa, which would give the economy another big boost. Once again, the Chinese have understood this. While we Europeans still think of Africa in terms of drilling wells and the Asians in South Africa, Kenya and Nigeria have long been investing in tech start-ups. Around 160 such dynamic young companies were founded in Africa in 2017 and have already raised almost 414 million U.S. dollars. In 2018, this figure is expected to rise to over 600 million. That's still low by international standards, but it's a creative explosion for Africa.

And who in this country knows that the South African company Naspers holds 31 percent of the Chinese tech giant Tencent, which is now worth more than Facebook? It is also largely unknown that this shareholding is worth 114 million U.S. dollars. An exception to be sure but it will soon be just one of many milestones on Africa's path to the future.

"There can be no clearer sign of the quality of innovation from African start-ups. We are very proud of that," says Gabriella Mulligan, a white African and co-founder of Disrupt Africa, the continent's leading start-up portal. Many start-ups are emerging in FinTech, the most attractive financial sector, and agritech. On a continent that is constantly struggling with supply shortages, the agritech sector is particularly important. And who would be surprised to hear that the Chinese are also playing a central role here?

The extent to which Beijing is looking to the future can also be seen in the fact that China has been the most important port of call for English-speaking African students since 2017, ahead of the USA. Over 100,000 are now studying in China. In 2003, there were just 2,000. Beijing lures students with attractive scholarships. However, visas are not extended after graduation. The young people are supposed to return to their countries and help build Africa. It is true that students from French-speaking countries still tend to go to France rather than China. But what does that mean for us if the new elites give our universities a wide berth? They will do business with China later. They will get used to the fact that Europe and the USA symbolize the past and China the future. Our companies will then go away empty-handed, on a continent that lies in the same time zone as Europe, of all places, and with which Europe also has close linguistic ties. And trust between the Chinese and Africans continues to grow. The brief economic slump caused by the price crisis on the commodities market has made it clear to Africans that some of the most persistent clichés about China's commitment to the continent have been proven wrong: The suspicion, for example, that China is only there for Africa in good times and gets cold feet as soon as things get tough. In fact, China increased its commitment to Africa by at least a third during the two years of the crisis. In the Fall of 2015 alone, just when the whole world was also speculating about China's slump, President Xi Jinping pledged $60 billion in new loans. Domestically, this was not at all easy for Xi to convey. Wouldn't it be better to invest the money in his own country? Despite critical voices, Xi got his way.

Xi's commitment to Africa is not a foregone conclusion. This became apparent when, in 2018 at the New Year's gala of the state television station CCTV, an unexpected "natural superiority" became visible to millions. The TV event, which has been broadcast since 1983 and, with 700 million viewers, is the most-watched TV program in the world, is said to be a mirror of Chinese society. A distorted mirror is more accurate. Somewhere between the coziness that once emanated from the ZDF show *Wetten, dass...?* and the pomp of the Chinese National Circus, singing, dancing, acrobatics, and comedy interludes, there is something for everyone.

But it's not just pop stars, Beijing opera singers and simple heroes of the people who are featured in close succession. Political self-praise is also traditionally part of the program. In 2018, China's economic engagement in Africa could not go unmentioned. A 10-minute show was dedicated to the figurative cooperation with Kenya in the construction of the railroad. To the sounds of Shakira's Africa World Cup anthem *Waka Waka (This Time for Africa)*, drumming bushmen hopped across the stage, dancers flown in from Africa were dressed in gazelle and zebra costumes and a black performer dressed as a monkey was even given a leading role. The crowning glory, however, was the performance of the black-painted Chinese actress Lou Naiming. With padded buttocks and a fruit basket on her head, she performed as "Mama Africa," saying with gratitude, "how much China has already done for Africa, I love China! I love the Chinese!"

The backlash was not long in coming. On Chinese social media channels, the show was called "highly racist" and "repulsive." One user proclaimed he was "ashamed" of his country and its people. The ill-fated sketch is a testament to how backward and not very diplomatic China can still be. So backward, in fact, that no one in charge of television had thought that Africans might feel snubbed. And this episode also shows that the Chinese government's commitment to Africa is not a foregone conclusion. It has to push through against the will of the majority.

The TV derailment on Chinese New Year was not the only example in the recent past from which lessons should have been learned. In a Chinese detergent commercial in the Summer of 2016, a black man was put in the washing machine and washed white to a light-skinned Chinese man. And in the Fall of 2017, an exhibition in Wuhan, central China, had to be closed because the creators had selected portraits of African animals and people based on similarity and hung them next to each other. To date, CCTV has not apologized. Instead, Beijing announced that the international public wanted to see China's involvement in Africa.

Cosmopolitanism and sovereignty are different. But it is also astonishing that no African country expressed indignation. Are people simply more considerate of their friends? Donald Trump, at any rate, did not let them get away with anything. In early 2017, he referred to Africa's states as "s***h****," among other things. The African Union demanded an official apology. "We are shocked, dismayed, and outraged. There is great misperception in the U.S. government about the African continent and its people."

With Xi, Africans know what they have in him.

Trump's first foreign trip was to Saudi Arabia, Israel, Brussels, and Italy for the G7 Summit. State and party leader Xi Jinping's first foreign trip was to Africa in 2013. So times are changing. While the Chinese are becoming more and more credible and investing more, the Americans are becoming less and less involved in Africa and more and more untrustworthy. Although they are still the largest investor in Africa because of their involvement in the oil and gas industry, in 2016 alone they invested a good 5 percent less than the year before. China now trades twice as much with Africa as the United States. And three times as much as the next largest trading partner, which is not Europe but India. If trade, investment, and the presence of Chinese companies on the ground are combined, China is by far Africa's largest economic partner.

And in yet another area, Beijing is getting ready to to drive out the previous top dogs. For a long time, China scored points in its foreign policy by focusing solely on economic relations. In June 2015, the government's new security law indicated that they at least wanted to secure economic success militarily. At a military meeting in late November 2015, President Xi Jinping virtually announced a general reform of the People's Liberation Army. Instead of rigid land and naval units, the aim is to now form flexible and cooperating forces under a unified command. A major priority is the security of international waters and defense of territorial claims — a small nod to the island dispute in the South China Sea. At the People's Congress in March 2018, Premier Li Keqiang announced an 8.1 percent increase in the military budget. These are unmistakable signs of a new self-confidence on the world stage.

So far, China has acted in Africa only within the framework of the United Nations and not on its own. Of the five permanent members of the UN Security Council, China has the most peacekeepers in Africa, with over 2,000 troops. Since 2008, some 60 Chinese naval vessels have helped with escort missions as part of a UN mission in the Gulf of Aden and off Somalia. In July 2017, however, Beijing came of age in this regard as well. Chinese warships were dispatched to the first Chinese military base abroad. The small state of Djibouti is located at a strategically important point, the Bab al-Mandab Strait. It separates the Red Sea and the Gulf of Aden. Crisis areas such as Yemen and Somalia are in the vicinity, and the strait is also a gathering place for pirates. The new base is a big step. For the first time in history, Chinese soldiers are permanently stationed on another continent. Beijing says it wants to protect its own countrymen from pirates and be present at UN missions. But of course, the stationing is also a symbol of China's new global power and one of the landmarks in China's rise that will be recorded in history books. Nevertheless, the propaganda department in Beijing has given instructions not to use the term "military base." It is simply a "base to support the troops of the DPRK (Democratic People's Republic of Korea)." Beijing cannot make it any clearer than it is well aware of the explosive nature of this step.

Compared to what the U.S. offers, however, that is still not much. Washington operates 800 military bases in 70 countries. At Camp Lemonnier in Djibouti alone, just a few kilometers from the Chinese base, 4,000 American soldiers are stationed. In this case, neither the Chinese nor the Americans are interested in the fact that, according to Amnesty International, the country is one of the most repressive in Africa. And they are not the only ones who feel this way. Japan and Italy are represented, as is France, which has about 1,500 armed soldiers in Djibouti alone.

Russia actually wanted to position itself there as well but was turned away because of conflicts of interest with the United States. China, however, was not turned away. On the contrary, at the end of February 2018, Djibouti's President Ismail Omar Guelleh terminated the port's management contract with DP World, a Dubai-based port operator. The contract had been signed in 2006 for 30 years. The port, which is located directly next to the new military facility, will now be given to the Chinese. Beijing showed its appreciation. In July, the first construction phase of the Djibouti International Free Trade Zone (DIFTZ) was inaugurated. It is the largest free trade zone in Africa. A total of 3.5 billion US dollars is being invested there. Djibouti is now one of the countries in Africa that is most indebted to China. Nevertheless, investments are continuing. There is already talk of a new highway to Addis Ababa.

Beijing is enjoying its new role. Chinese diplomats also mediating in the peace negotiations between North and South Sudan. This is a role that the Americans would also have liked to play. They, in turn, are now trying to stay in the game via UN sanctions. China and Russia abstained from voting in the UN Security Council at the end of May 2018, considering the renewal of sanctions against South Sudan during the peace talks counterproductive. France and England, on the other hand, supported the Americans. So, the new balance of power is also emerging at the UN.

In July 2018, Beijing hosted the first China–Africa Forum on Defense and Security. Beijing has provided 100 million euros to the African Union for a rapid reaction force. 8,000 Chinese troops are to be on standby for a UN peacekeeping force.

The new base in Djibouti is important for China for another reason. It is an important link in the so-called string of pearls that China is creating along the Indian Ocean coast. Chinese ports are under construction or in the planning stage at several locations. With them, the Chinese navy would have ports of call to replenish fuel and supplies without having to return to China. The chain could start in Southeast Asia — in Cambodia, for example — and then extend into the Indian Ocean through the planned Kra Canal in Thailand. From there, it would continue through a port in Myanmar to Bangladesh and Sri Lanka to Gwadar in Pakistan. The Americans don't like that at all. Militarily, they are still much more present in Africa. Moreover, Washington claims that the West must be united in preventing the Chinese from expanding militarily even more in Africa are hypocritical. Why should what we have allowed ourselves to do there for decades be forbidden to China?

The tough stance of Washington, and also of parts of Europe, is not only aimed at the military sphere. The club is wielded against China whenever an opportunity presents itself. The criticism is often backed up with alleged facts that, on closer inspection, turn out to be unsubstantiated. Let's take a closer look at some of these "arguments."

One of the most popular misconceptions is that only Chinese state-owned enterprises invest in China. They are forced by the state to go to Africa, whether it pays off or not. The fact is that of the more than 10,000 Chinese companies now based in Africa, over 95 percent are private. This is not a claim made by the government in Beijing but by the American management consultancy McKinsey. The analysts are also able to prove that the number of Chinese companies producing product in Africa is now significantly higher than the number of construction companies, at 30 percent. They have always been criticized for employing mainly Chinese workers, however Chinese companies have long relied on local labor. Not only because it is cheaper than flying in Chinese but also because the companies want to develop over a long period and it is therefore worthwhile to train Africans. The Chinese cell phone manufacturer and network provider Huawei trains 12,000 people alone in Africa every year. Today, almost 90 percent of the employees of Chinese companies are Africans, and over 40 percent already work at management level. African governments have also learned their lesson and insist on a local quota in contract negotiations.

As already mentioned, the vast majority of Chinese companies in Africa are private enterprises. Although the Chinese state supports them with favorable loans, they bear most of the entrepreneurial risk themselves. Tens of thousands of small traders have set off for Africa in the hope of earning more there than at home. Just as the Irish, Italians, or Germans once set out for the USA.

Africa's financial dependence on China also repeatedly invites excessive exaggerations. First of all, no one has forced African countries to accept money from China, and the interest rates are quite reasonable. In most cases, the investments have a positive effect on economic growth, so governments can usually service their debts. Moreover, they are not as high as one would assume at first glance. Africans owe only about 14 percent of their debt to the Chinese. "The ratio of Africa's foreign debt to

GDP is moderate," says the United Nations Conference on Trade and Development (UNCTAD).

However, the strong growth in debt in some countries — including South Africa, Kenya, and also Angola — is a cause for concern. "Every Angolan owes China 745 U.S. dollars," the Angolan newspaper *Expansão* headlined in May 2018. With regard to Angola, it is important to know that when the oil price is high, it doesn't matter, however when it is low, Angola has a problem.

However, the International Monetary Fund sees the greatest dependence on Chinese loans not in Angola but in Zambia, a country with a population of around 17 million. Here, external debt alone amounts to around 300 percent of GDP. That's a lot. However, Zambia owes only half of that to China; the other half, surprisingly, is invested in Eurobonds. At least Zambia has copper deposits; prices for this raw material have already risen by 30 percent in 2017 after the slump. The situation should therefore ease again soon. Kenya pays just under 50 percent of the interest on foreign credits to China. The other 50 percent is shared by Japan, France, and the World Bank. The debt burden is still moderate at one-third of GDP. South Africa is already worse off at 70 percent and Mozambique is also one of the front-runners at 300 percent. However, there can only be a debt crisis if Beijing reclaims its debt. However, Beijing has no interest in seeing the countries in which they invest fall to their knees and inevitable social unrest. For this reason, China's creditors are usually patient and willing to negotiate in case of doubt. In return, however, they expect political cohesion on the international stage.

Criticism, however, comes not only because of the level of indebtedness in some African countries. One of the critics' most important arguments is that the Chinese, together with corrupt African governments, are undermining international transparency standards. This was indeed the case in the past, but it has long since changed, more and more projects are now being financed by international consortia.

Ironically, the big time for the Chinese come after the OECD countries enforced that the bidding process must be transparent. They had hoped that this would enable them to pinpoint the Chinese weaknesses and put their finger on the problem. The opposite was the case; hardly any weaknesses could be found. However, the Chinese now knew the prices and were able to systematically undercut the Western suppliers for the same quality. And even when the World Bank is not on board, African governments have now found ways to ensure that they are not ripped off.

They hire European engineering firms like GAUFF Engineering in Nuremberg. They control and coordinate the work of Chinese construction companies in Africa — and, by the way, have been doing so for decades.

Regarding the allegedly poor quality of Chinese infrastructure projects, "Such problems have been widely reported in major media outlets, including *The Economist*, for example. But they are very big exceptions," notes Jamie Farrell of Johns Hopkins University. The quality of World Bank projects in which the Chinese are involved can be measured very well. The result is clear: "On average, there is no difference in the quality of construction between the highly developed OECD countries and China," says Farrell. "We were very surprised by that. The Chinese had a few projects that didn't work," he said. "However, China now offers the same quality at a lower price. That's why no other country gets as many contracts in Africa from the World Bank. One-third of World Bank projects worldwide go to China — and the trend is rising."

And what about the cliché that China is only interested in land and mineral resources? The fact is that the Chinese do not even put 30 percent of their investments into mineral resources. As American researchers have found out, the USA's share is twice as high. Critics also criticize China's actions in the area of agriculture. Again and again, one reads that the Chinese have allegedly bought many hundreds of thousands of hectares of farmland in Africa. Some media even speak of six million hectares. Others speak of 1 percent of African farmland. Thousands of Chinese farmers are supposed to grow grain there, which is then exported to China. This is a large-scale strategy of the Chinese state, which is buying into African agriculture through state-owned enterprises and funds.

According to Deborah Bräutigam, one of America's leading China–Africa specialists, none of this is true. She is a professor at Johns Hopkins University in Baltimore, near Washington. In her book, *Will Africa Feed China?* published by Oxford University Press, one of the world's most prestigious scientific publishers, she has published the results of three years of research. According to the findings, she was able to identify only 240,000 hectares on the entire African continent owned by the Chinese — twice the size of New York. "That's vanishingly small," Bräutigam says. Most reports of Chinese "land grabbing" have turned out to be rumors, she says. "There's also been very little Chinese investment in African agriculture so far." And what little they do produce, they produce for the local market. Nevertheless, American professors who then claim in "Voice of America," the official U.S. government foreign broadcaster, were quoted as saying that the Chinese were growing grain in Zimbabwe, for example, and then exporting it, while at the same time local people were starving. "None of that is true," Bräutigam says. "But the rumor is out in the world and spreading furiously."

And what about the rumor that countless Chinese farmers have already settled in Africa to cultivate the land? The largest "cluster" that Bräutigam and her team have been able to identify is a group of 134 agricultural specialists in Uganda. The renowned Center for International Forestry Research comes to the same conclusion: "China is not a dominant investor in Africa's agriculture, although it is repeatedly described as such."

Bräutigam was also unable to verify any grain or rice exports to China. On the contrary, Africa imports about ten million tons of rice annually from Asia and also from the USA. Exported produce includes sesame seeds, coffee, cocoa, and cotton, but hardly from Chinese cultivation. So if anyone is feeding here, it is China, which is supplying the new middle class — in South Africa, for example — primarily with processed foods. The current imbalance between imports and exports in the African agricultural and food sector means that there is still a lot of catching up to do in terms of efficient and sustainable agriculture. To get to grips with this, China has established small agricultural development centers in 30 African countries, but they have not developed well. That's why in 2016 the Chinese teamed up with the Bill & Melinda Gates Foundation, that has, for decades, been one of the most important donor institutions in Africa. The cooperation includes pilot projects in Mozambique, Zambia, and Ethiopia and even a joint fund for health and agricultural development has been set up. "We are cautiously optimistic that these collaborations are now beginning to show results," says Mark Suzman, President of Global Policy and Advocacy at the Gates Foundation. A partnership, in which, by the way, the rules of the game are also being played out according to Western standards.

The cooperation is taking place within the framework of the China–Africa Development Fund, which has a volume of US$4.5 billion. At the end of 2017, 3.2 billion U.S. dollars had already been invested. The fund's goal is to increase Africa's exports by two billion U.S. dollars annually. The fund also cooperates with the World Bank, the United Nations Organization for Economic Cooperation and Development, the World Bank, and the African Development Bank.

It is a strange phenomenon that all the clichés outlined here are so persistent. While it is not a deliberate disinformation campaign that we in the West are waging against China and on the backs of Africa, it is a cluster of rumors fueled by our guilty consciences and arrogance. But who are we to dictate to the Chinese and Africans how they should cooperate? We can make appeals, but they are less and less likely to be heard. We can set a good example. Whether the Africans want to follow this example is, however, their decision.

The fact that Africa is one of the fastest growing regions in the world — not least thanks to Chinese investment — is primarily due to the continent's newcomers. Tanzania, for example, is close on the heels of Nigeria and South Africa with a growth of 7 percent. The country's economic power has doubled in the past 10 years. And with an increase of a good 11 percent, Africa is now the second largest recipient of foreign direct investment after Asia, unfortunately only a small proportion of which comes from the EU.

East Africa in particular is developing well. And so the rail line between Mombasa and Nairobi will remain. The government of Uganda, a country without its own coastal access, wants to connect to the Kenyan line. The Chinese are also financing this project with 2.3 billion U.S. dollars. The 270 kilometer long line is scheduled for completion in just three and a half years. For the first five to 10 years, it will be operated by John Holland, an Australian company. The China Communications Construction Company, the fourth largest construction company in the world, acquired John Holland in 2014 for just under one billion US dollars.

In total, the East African rail network will reach Kigali in booming Rwanda and continue on to Africa's largest country, the long-stumbling Democratic Republic of Congo. By 2018, it will have the world's fastest-growing domestic market.

It is no coincidence, then, that East Africa has increasingly pushed itself to the forefront of the Africa boom, relegating South and West Africa to their places, especially since the current wonderland of African awakening is also located in the east of the continent. Since 2000, Ethiopia has been supplied with Chinese loans for dams, railroad lines, and production facilities. In total, this amounts to more than 12 billion U.S. dollars, twice as much money as oil-rich Sudan or Congo, which have abundant natural resources.

So why Ethiopia of all countries? The country is unique in terms of its mix — it has oil and gas reserves, is geostrategically located on the Horn of Africa, and its level of development makes it easier than elsewhere to advance light industry. In Europe, on the other hand, Ethiopia is remembered as a famine-stricken country. The images from the 1980s, when eight million people starved due to a drought and up to one million people died, are burned into our memories. The difference today could not be greater. In just 15 years, Ethiopia's GDP has tripled. "More than any other country in Africa, Ethiopia is following the Chinese model," writes *Time*. "Ethiopia is the new China," summarizes the *Financial Times* even more succinctly.

I want to get a personal impression of this country, which I have so far only known from transferring from one Ethiopian Airlines flight to another. Ethiopian Airlines is now the largest airline in Africa and the first African airline to order the newly developed Dreamliner from Boeing in Seattle. Unfortunately, I arrive at an inopportune time in January 2018. A government crisis is shaking the country, so unfortunately some of my interlocutors have more important things to do than receive me.

The capital Addis Ababa appears surprisingly modern and at the same time still very backward. However, the impression of modernity is more intense, a surprise effect, so to speak. Large LED screens at the Edna Mall, one of the city's chicest shopping centers, high-rise buildings with glittering facades, and clubs and restaurants not unlike those in Shanghai or New York. But of course, you also come across run-down corners, for example, around the Mercato, Africa's largest open-air market.

The driver who will accompany me during my trip through Ethiopia suddenly stops at the gate of the Ethiopian Orthodox St. George's Cathedral. Bulcha, my driver, has that open laugh that one encounters so often here, speaks a little English, and is dressed in such a modern way that he would not be singled out New York or Berlin. He has a mid-size Toyota car that he uses to drive his customers around. "I want to show you something," he says meaningfully. We get out and don't enter the cathedral but take the escalator down into a suburban train shaft. At the bottom, a long line of people are waiting, held in check by a uniformed attendant with a cane. No one is allowed to jump the queue. Bulcha talks to her briefly and then nods to me. We are allowed to go past the queue to the platform. The concrete wall that separates the two tracks is painted with modern silhouettes of pale-green buildings. As the train pulls in, a glow crosses Bulcha's face. "Our light rail," he says proudly. "Built by the Chinese."

A strange coincidence since Bulcha does not yet know why I am here or what I am interested in or that I live in China. It would have been more appropriate if he had shown me, the European, around the cathedral. The cathedral was built in 1896 after the victory of the Abbessinians against the Italians. But while the church bears witness to a glorious past, the new suburban railroad across the street symbolizes the future.

The 34-kilometer line, 85 percent of which was financed and built by the Chinese, cost 475 million euros, I later read. It is a pioneer on the continent. Only in July 2018, a similar railroad was inaugurated in the Nigerian capital Abuja. That, too, was built by the Chinese.

The biggest problem with Addis Ababa's commuter rail system is that with its route length and only two lines, it is inadequate to cater to the city's four million people such that the queues at the old minibusses are often still over 100 meters long. "Dented donkeys" are what commuters call the buses. Since February 2015, the light rail has already transported 50 million passengers. Bulcha reflects on how he can sum up the development the capital and country have taken. "China makes Ethiopia strong," he says with a laugh.

As in Berlin and other cities, Addis Ababa's commuter rail system cannot be financed from the revenue generated by ticket sales. Berlin's BVG, for example, has debts of almost 680 million euros. And even the subway network in Shanghai, now the largest in the world, is far from breaking even. The situation is different, at least in China, with some high-speed lines. The Beijing–Shanghai rail line is now the most profitable in the world, with a profit of one billion U.S. dollars.

But the new rail line, Africa's longest electrified rail line at 750 kilometers, also has what it takes to make a quick profit. It runs between the capital Addis Ababa and Djibouti and gives Ethiopia access to the sea. The train station in Addis Ababa, the Furi-Lebu Railway Station, already exists, but you have to look for it. It is located 40 minutes outside the city in no man's land, an orange-painted building with many towers in the African confectioner's style. But it won't be long before the unused land is developed, as the Ethiopian capital is growing so rapidly.

The line is China's largest project in Ethiopia to date. Both countries have an interest in ensuring that the railroad quickly turns a profit. After all, Ethiopia is in Beijing's debt, and not just because of this project. As already mentioned, the Chinese built the headquarters of the African Union in Addis Ababa for around 200 million U.S. dollars. Beijing is involved in the construction of the Renaissance Dam, Africa's largest, which cost around 4.7 billion U.S. dollars. In addition, there are numerous smaller investments. At the latest, the Chinese will receive gas in large quantities from Ethiopia. The gas field, one of Africa's largest, is operated by a joint venture of the Chinese state-owned company Poly Group. The group pumped the first oil to the surface in the summer of 2018. Gas production tests followed shortly thereafter. At full production, the gas alone will bring in seven billion U.S. dollars a year, for decades.

This is a milestone for Ethiopia. For the first time in its history, the country is becoming a supplier of raw materials. Construction of a 700-kilometer pipeline began in 2018. Including the technical facilities, investments of four billion U.S. dollars are needed before gas can flow. To prevent Addis Ababa from becoming too dependent on China, the refinery is to be financed by Japanese, Indian, and South Korean investors. Incidentally, the gas reserves were discovered as early as 1972, by the U.S. company Tenneco. However, in the 45 years that have passed since then, no Western company has been able to come to an agreement with Addis Ababa. The Chinese succeeded in doing so in 2013.

The Ethiopian Government can be criticized for a number of things, for example, the development of democracy has been slow. However, it can be mightily proud of the fact that it has ignited an economic boom in this poor country and kept up the momentum for over a decade. President Mulatu Teshome has a plan, and he consistently follows through with it — even when things are boiling around him. However, the boom has come at a price. In 2017, Ethiopia exported goods worth three billion, but imports were worth 17 billion U.S. dollars. That's dangerous. China did something similar in the 1980s. In the end, inflation stood at 30 percent, the population became restless, and in 1989, there was an uprising in Tiananmen Square.

In Addis Ababa, inflation is already at 10 percent. In February 2018, shortly after my departure, unrest broke out, forcing Prime Minister Hailemariam Desalegn to resign. A state of emergency was declared, for the second time in three years. Nevertheless, Beijing continues to invest. These are the risks in Africa that you have to be prepared for if you want to be successful there. The Chinese know — only those who persevere win. Desalegn's successor is 42-year-old Abiy Ahmed. He wants to push ahead with the "dramatic reform course at all costs" and received a World Bank loan of one billion USD in August 2018.

"Such success stories, of which Ethiopia is just one of many, hardly reach Germany," marvels Alexander Demissie, an Ethiopian who grew up in Germany and established the Cologne-based consulting firm The China Africa Advisory. "Africa is the last continent to develop." Almost every German manager or entrepreneur that Demissie has driven through Addis Ababa has been dumbfounded by the booming city. "Most still have the old clichés in their heads. That's a shame."

In Ethiopia in particular, the Chinese are particularly far-reaching when it comes to creating permanent industrial jobs and thus prosperity. The Huajian International Group, one of the largest women's shoe manufacturers in the world, is expanding its production of shoes and leather goods in Ethiopia for a good two billion US dollars. They also intend to export duty-free to the USA. The company, which produces for Tommy Hilfiger and Guess, among others, will create 100,000 jobs for Ethiopians.

Huajian has been active in Ethiopia for six years and currently employs 4,000 workers in a factory 40 kilometers south of Addis Ababa. Here, in the "Oriental Industrial Park," more than 20 Chinese companies have already settled. This factory alone, which produces 2.4 million shoes per year, earns the Ethiopian state $20 million in taxes per year. It is not very different from factories in China, except that Ethiopian women sit behind the machines. Particularly talented workers are now even sent to China for training. They become foremen and later even managers.

One of them is Demis Degef, Assistant Manager and only 25 years old. Currently, the tall, slim man earns 10 times as much as he did on his first day of work at Huajian. It may sound a little corny, but it's true. Demis will never forget what the Chinese have done for him.

Now and then, he says, there are protests against Chinese investors but also against Indian or Turkish ones. Since land has become very valuable during the boom, the companies compete with agricultural businesses for the land. The fact that sometimes the government in Addis Ababa has entire villages forcibly relocated is causing resentment among the farmers. Overall, however, China enjoys a good reputation in Ethiopia. It's no great surprise; people in Africa want to earn money, just like people in the rest of the world. They don't want to be charity recipients; they want to be able to provide for themselves and their families. Above all, Chinese investors are making exactly that possible.

In addition to the leather industry, whose production has increased fivefold in the past five years, the textile industry is now being developed. "The Chinese are simply focusing on their job," says Fasil Tadesse, President of the Ethiopian Textile Association, "no matter how difficult the conditions are."

Ethiopia wants to become the hub of light industry by 2025. To achieve this goal, the country must be the most favorable in global market comparison. No one produces in Ethiopia just like that. Therefore, the country needs inexpensive electricity generated by hydropower. In this respect, Ethiopia is already in a better position than Cambodia and Bangladesh, says Juan Pérez Carpena, who buys shoes for the American chains Sears and Kmart. But much more important, he says, is the low cost of labor. "In China, workers earn between $400 and $500, in Kenya it's already $140 to $160, in Bangladesh it's $70 to $90, in Vietnam $140 to $150, and in Ethiopia only $50." The combination of low price and good quality is now also winning over the really big buyers. H&M buys in Ethiopia, as does the British supermarket chain Tesco and Walmart from the USA. "Asian investments are turning Ethiopia into a textile center," writes the Japanese *Nikkei Asian Review*.

Industrial parks are springing up everywhere. For example, Hawassa Industrial Park situated 300 kilometers south of Addis Ababa, and covers 140 hectares, is now considered the largest in Africa. It has been open since mid-2017. 10,000 people already work here, and 60,000 are expected to do so in the future. The Chinese company JP Textile alone is investing 260 million US dollars there. Calvin Klein underwear produced there will then be labeled "Made in Ethiopia." We will have to get used to this, just as the "Made in Hong Kong" label was first replaced by "Made in China" and then by "Made in Bangladesh".

The Ethiopians have copied the industrial parks from the Chinese. "We want to have world-class industrial parks, after all," says Arkebe Oqubay, the architect of Ethiopia's industrial revolution. He studied in London at the School of Oriental and African Studies (SOAS). "We need to create jobs, jobs, and more jobs and we must not forget environmental protection in the process," says Oqubay. "For that, we need foreign investment." And again, I hear the complaint about how reluctant Europeans are. On the one hand, Oqubay finds that regrettable. On the other hand, he says Asian investors can make it possible for Ethiopia to be the leading textile-processing country in Africa by 2025. "Vietnam has done it, Bangladesh has done it, and we will do even better."

The population is growing by 5 percent a year, he says. "That's why we need a million new jobs a year," explains Oqubay, who has been promoting Africa on the international stage for years with great patience and persuasiveness. Ethiopians have learned from the Chinese, he says, "how important long-term investments in infrastructure are. We've seen China go from a low level of development to being the factory of the world." In fact, China is considered the most relevant model for development on the continent. The Chinese know from their own experience the problems with which African countries are now also struggling.

And what are we Germans doing in Ethiopia?

We are the largest importer of coffee, do a little urban planning, and invest a little in dual education and vegetable cultivation. Germany does not yet have a chamber of commerce in Ethiopia. The chamber in Nairobi, Kenya, helps us to take care of the needs in Ethiopia. The embassy building in which Ambassador Brita Wagener resides is located on beautiful park-like grounds; her predecessors first occupied it in 1905. At that time, Ethiopia had such good relations with Germany that no other great power came close. The German school in Addis Ababa is one of the oldest in Africa. But it is no longer enough to rest on our old laurels if we want to stay in the game.

Five ministers of the current government in Addis Ababa have been trained in Germany. They would like to engage more with us. But we are too expensive, too weak, and too inflexible. VW, for example, leaves the Ethiopian car market to Toyota. When Volkswagen and General Motors started investing in China, the level of motorization in China was lower than in Ethiopia. Today, it's one of the world's largest business consultancies. Nevertheless, Americans and Germans took a risk. At the time, no one could have foreseen that the Chinese market would grow so quickly. You have to ask yourself why you are treating Africa differently. And why the positive development of investment in China does not serve as a model for a market that perhaps has even greater potential. It looks like the generation of managers back then was more farsighted and more willing to take risks than today's generation. However, this may also be due to the increased influence of shareholders, who are looking for faster and more lavish profits.

The fact that some African countries are on the road to success and are taking a shortcut to modernity with the help of the Chinese should actually be more than fine with us. If Africa succeeds in standing on its own two feet and there are opportunities for young people in their own countries, fewer people will flee to Europe. So, we should stop pointing a finger at China. Beijing has understood that it is a question of balance, an attitude that we in the West, with our colonial past, find more difficult than politicians and investors from countries that were themselves once victims of the colonial era.

By the way, we are in good company with our lack of foresight. As in many regions of the world, the United States is withdrawing more and more from Africa. Since Donald Trump took office, Washington has had an even harder time dealing with the continent than before. His predecessor Barack Obama, for example, arrived late at the party.

In the Summer of 2015, he traveled to East Africa with a large business delegation, mainly to Kenya and Ethiopia.

Obama, whose father comes from Kenya and who still has family there, has failed to convince his country of the boom in Africa and the boom in Africa and its potential benefit for the United States. As the first black president of the United States, as a Nobel Peace Prize laureate, and as a bearer of hope, Obama should have addressed the issue of Africa earlier and with greater commitment. Obviously, however, he shied away from the opposition's absurd accusation of nepotism. Obama rhetorically announced brilliant initiatives, such as "Power Africa," which was supposed to supply the continent with electricity; however, it came to nothing. As much as Obama achieved in the causes of Iran and Cuba, little came of his endeavors to benefit Africa. In 50 years time, when African countries will play a central role as the world's factory and have a huge middle class eager to consume, historians will marvel that Barack Obama, of all people, has not been able to cooperate with the last "Emerging Continent."

Microsoft founder Bill Gates, who is very active in Africa with his foundation, warned very forcefully at the World Economic Forum in Davos back in 2018 that Trump's policies will drive Africa into the arms of the Chinese even faster, not only because Trump reduced aid to Africa by 30 percent in the Fall of 2017. Moreover, pronouncements such as those of former Secretary of State Rex Tillerson, who in 2018 accused China of rising to become a "new imperialist power" in Africa "whose posturing is reminiscent of European colonialism," are of little help. The people on the ground are likely to see things somewhat differently, and Tillerson has long been history.

Beijing, on the other hand, continues to court the favor of the Africans despite continuing economic fluctuations. And is certainly not influenced by our criticism from the sidelines. In many instances, we are only entitled to judge from the sidelines. The development of the automotive industry in Africa is a good example of this. A field in which one might expect us Germans to play a leading role. The continent is nothing less than the world's last untapped car market. On average, there are 42 cars per 1,000 people here. The global average is 182, and in the USA, there are even more than 800 cars per 1,000 inhabitants. That's why it is important to take a closer look at this industry, which also determines Germany's future.

Various international automakers are fighting for their market share in Africa. Volkswagen (VW), after all, has a strong position in South Africa. Peugeot has a plant in Kenya, as do Nissan, Mitsubishi, and Toyota, but currently mainly in the bus and truck sectors. And, believe it or not, VW is again manufacturing in Kenya, since 2016 after a break of four decades. In Thika near the capital Nairobi, the Polo Vivo rolls off the production line. The individual parts arrive by rail from the VW plant in South Africa and are assembled on site. VW is also the first automaker to open a plant in Rwanda. It is the fourth VW plant on the continent after South Africa, Nigeria, and Kenya. The first car produced in Kigali is a white Polo. In addition to the economy vehicle, Rwandans will soon be driving the Passat and the Teramont off-road vehicle — that is the ambitious goal. However, production is still limited. Only 500 to 600 cars are to roll off the production line each year.

The Wolfsburg-based company, with its focus on middle class, has a lot at stake in Africa. They must not make any mistakes, particularly because the Chinese are already waiting in the wings in this sector, too. They have the advantage of offering products with a favorable price–performance ratio, while German cars are still considered too expensive.

Beijing-based manufacturer Foton, a subsidiary of China's fourth-largest automaker BAIC (Beijing Automotive Group Co., Ltd.), has been operating successfully in Africa. In 2005, it already sold over 95,000 vehicles, mainly light trucks. This puts it in direct competition with Nissan, Mitsubishi, and Toyota. In January 2018, the company also opened a production line for large trucks in Kenya, west of Mombasa. It is operated by Associated Vehicle Assemblers (AVA), a Kenyan company with well-trained workers. "We are using it to accelerate localization in Kenya," says Sun Qingzhong, Foton's Kenya head. And African governments are now paying close attention to localization.

Who will win the African market? An Asian or even a Chinese company? Or perhaps Volkswagen or Peugeot? Since Peugeot only has an advantage in French-speaking countries, all in all, BAIC is probably the most serious competitor for Volkswagen at the moment, along with Toyota. In July 2018, the first car rolled off the production line at BAIC's new car factory in Port Elizabeth, South Africa. BAIC has invested almost US$900 million in the plant at the Coega Industrial Development Zone.

This is the largest investment in the South African automotive industry in the past 40 years and the largest in Africa. It dwarfs the recent investments made by Toyota, BMW, and Volkswagen in their plants in the Cape, South Africa. As early as the end of 2019, 100,000 vehicles per year could be produced in Port Elizabeth. The Chinese hold 65 percent of the project, with the remaining 35 percent held by a state-owned South African company.

Volkswagen has accepted the challenge. In 2019, the Wolfsburg-based company will be able to produce 190,000 cars locally in South Africa. BMW has invested around 400 million euros in a modernized production facility for the X3 crossover SUV just outside Pretoria. And at the end of June 2018, Daimler announced plans to further expand its plant in South Africa. The next generation of the C-Class is to be built there. 600 million euros will be invested by Daimler in the plant in East London. Already today, around 180,000 vehicles are exported from South Africa to Europe every year.

In the African market itself, there will probably be a price war between the Chinese and the Germans. The question is who will have the staying power. The African market is expected to grow by 40 percent in the next five years. If Africa continues to boom like this, which is very likely, there will be 10 million cars in sub-Saharan Africa as early as 2030. By comparison, there are around 25 million in China today. The future of the German auto industry will therefore not only be decided in China but also in Africa.

The Africa boom has not yet reached its peak. But because we still don't really have it on our radar, because we can't get certain clichés out of our heads, because they are repeated over and over again in the media, and because we are victims of our own prejudices, we are in danger of missing out on a development that is very important for Germany. Despite the slight decline in growth, Africa is urbanizing faster than any other region in the world. It is even possible that as early as 2035, more people will live in cities in Africa than in China. The symbol of the African boom, the 300-meter-high Pinnacle Towers skyscraper in the Kenyan capital Nairobi, was scheduled for completion in 2021.

The highest skyscraper on the continent to date, the 223-meter Carlton Center in Johannesburg, was built in 1973. It is just as unspectacular and outdated as the ailing South African state-owned company Transnet, which has its headquarters there. The Carlton Center stands for stagnation. The new "Pinnacle Towers," a double tower with 70 and 45 floors, on the other hand, represents modernity and a self-confident economic upswing.

From the top, one will have an unprecedented view of Mount Kilimanjaro and Mount Kenya. The skyscraper is being built by the China State Construction Engineering Corporation, the same company that built the UN's Africa headquarters in Ethiopia. The cost is 220 million US dollars.

The Europeans and the Americans have had all the time in the world to build skyscrapers in Africa. They could have been proud of a continent that, supported by us, is becoming more and more self-confident step by step. Of course, politics after independence was difficult in many African countries, often accompanied by civil wars in which rival clans fought for supremacy. With few exceptions, however, this phase has long since ended. It may have been a happy coincidence that China appeared on the scene just when it was time for African countries to modernize. Governments and potentates quickly realized that they could only remain in power if they created prosperity for their citizens. That's when China came calling.

That Africa has been ignored for so long remains a gross negligence on the part of the West. Only slowly are we waking up, however now it is up to Africa's leaders to decide with whom they want to cooperate. They can work with the West, which wants not only to invest but also to instruct, or they can go with the Chinese. It honors us in the West that we want to strengthen democracy, as well as uphold basic human rights, and do not want to give corruption a chance. The only problem is that no one in Africa is forced to accept our — meager (so far anyway) — offers anymore, let alone listen to us.

To sum it up, it is like this: Two sovereign partners, China and Africa, sign a treaty. Neither the Africans nor the Chinese have to seek permission for this. This may later be regretted, but it demonstrates the shift in the balance of power. In early September 2018, President Xi announced new investment in Africa of $60 billion by 2021. "We welcome Africa on the China express train," he confidently told more than 50 African leaders at the China–Africa Summit in Beijing.

At the beginning of the 21st century, the chance that Africa will become a reliably prosperous continent is greater than ever. The big surprise of this development is that the West is the big loser. We have, for whatever reason, totally miscalculated. Meanwhile, China has not only helped Africa get on its feet but has also helped it emancipate itself further and further from the West. Now, empowered, Africa is moving forward without us.

# Outlook: The Century of Global Equality

*The superior man harmonizes, but he does not make everything equal;*
*the commoner makes everything the same, but he does not harmonize.*

Confucius

Germany is facing unprecedented challenges in the second decade of the 21st century. Our concerns around the upheavals of digitization are great. Many of us feel that this fourth industrial revolution is drastic, even catastrophic. The many new technologies unsettle us, and the comparatively high speed with which developments are being rolled out is frightening. But we already know this from history; every 40–100 years, mankind is catapulted into a new age. I, myself, witnessed the end of the third industrial revolution and am now witnessing the fourth. I am confident that we will get used to the new technologies and that we will adapt to utilize the advantages and contain the excesses.

The many refugees unsettle us. We have not yet found an acceptable balance between people-friendly openness and clear rules. What makes it so difficult is that this sensitive issue is being misused for political power struggles at national and EU levels. It can be solved if we put aside the political differences.

Donald Trump's antics are also worrying. The people of the U.S. are divided into two camps and are not likely to come together after Trump. On the positive side, the U.S. are no longer interested in playing world police. This is another reason why Europe and the U.S. are drifting apart. The end of transatlantic ties, as we knew them for decades, may be painful for us. But it might do Europe some good to become independent and not look to the guardian in Washington every time we want to have a beer.

But all these are only undercurrents of a larger global epochal change. This will change our lives far more than all other developments: the rise of China. For centuries, it was taken for granted that the West set the global rules of the game. In the 17th, 18th, and 19th centuries, it was the Europeans. In the 20th century, it was the Americans. Now, we are at the beginning of an epochal, global change. For the first time, the global center of power is shifting toward Asia.

Since the Battle of Liegnitz in 1241, no non-Western country including Asia has exerted any great economic or geopolitical influence on the West. In 1241, on two consecutive days in April, the Mongols defeated the German–Polish army under Henry II of Silesia and shortly thereafter occupied Moravia. The Mongol storm was wild but not lasting. The hordes of horsemen did not advance further west. They had to go home — their Great Khan was dying.

What we are experiencing today is not a brief upset that will pass as quickly as the hordes of Mongol horsemen. We are at the beginning of a permanent shift in the global balance of power. China, the Middle Kingdom, may have been the world's technological leader a few centuries ago. But the high-tech power at that time was largely self-sufficient — apart from peaceful excursions into Persia and a brief phase as a maritime power. Geopolitically, China did not play a role. The Chinese emperors were not interested in extending their influence to the Western world. One of the best-known Chinese folk epics, at that time, is simply named *The Journey to the West*. Not "Convert the West" or even "Fight the West." The epic is based on the journey of a Chinese monk, Xuanzang, who went to India to learn. He studied the teachings of Buddha and brought his knowledge to his homeland.

But now China is no longer satisfied to be isolated. Beijing wants a say in the global rules of the game. President Xi wants global influence at this stage of China's history. He wants to go down in the annals as the first "emperor" who dared to take this step in the country's 3,500-year history. These are the dimensions in which Chinese politics thinks. Meanwhile, we are grappling to see clearly.

China is also to become the first great power in history to concentrate on conquering economic and political power in its rise — unlike the

Western colonial powers in the centuries before and the self-proclaimed world police force, the USA, in the last century. The military, which Xi keeps on a short rein, has not advanced far with Xi's strategy of "conquering" other countries without military means. As we have seen, one neighbor after another is joining the convoy of China's international rise. Here and there, with a little grumbling, but still convinced that all things considered, it is for the best. The U.S. is playing an increasingly minor role in Asia and Africa.

Beijing comes to terms with rival India, stretches out their hand to the Japanese, and eases the North Korean conflict. But Beijing can also take action when countries question them, South Korea and Norway have felt the effects of this. China dominates in Africa, the last undeveloped continent, is becoming increasingly influential in South America, and is cleverly ensuring that Europe no longer speaks with one voice when it comes to criticizing China.

President Xi is also lucky that the Americans under Trump are withdrawing as a world power. The Chinese immediately fill the vacuum, in Pakistan as well as in Ethiopia. The West's political pressure on Russia is bringing Putin and Xi ever closer together. They are not close friends, but they are convinced partners. China acts skillfully and farsightedly in the political arena and uses every opportunity, no matter how small, to expand its power. With small but steady steps, China is becoming more and more powerful.

Digitalization is also contributing to this because it is accelerating China's rise. But China's rise is also accelerating digitization. So, we need to focus on China much more in this area than we do today. China's advances in artificial intelligence will present us with huge challenges. In the U.S., the data are in the hands of influential private companies. In China, it's in the hands of one of the world's most powerful states, so powerful that it can ban American Internet giants like Facebook and Google in China and still have their founders and CEOs vying for Beijing's favor. The huge Chinese market is too tempting. In China, we are seeing that it is not Internet companies that are eroding the power of the state but that the state is setting the rules. What President Xi decides is much more important to us than what Mark Zuckerberg comes up with. Many have yet to understand that. The new abundance of power can now be felt in almost all important areas. Who is more powerful in the auto industry than Germany? Who can remain calm in the face of Donald Trump's impositions? Who, for the first time since World War II, is in a position to impose new global institutions without the West? Who is America's biggest creditor? Who is the factory of the world? Who adds to the US dollar as the world currency?

The answer is always China.

Yet the country is only at the beginning of its ascent. It's only been 40 years since China opened. What will the world look like when the Chinese celebrate 100 years of opening policy in 2078? Of course, no rise is linear, but, so far, the engine has hardly stuttered and there is little to suggest that this will happen in the near future. And because China is so adept at exporting its model of success, it has many countries on its side. Combined, they already dwarf the West based on the population size alone. This puts China on the right side of history. If we think global democracy and co-determination through to the end, only one thing can come out of it and that is one man, one vote. Every person has one vote. This is actually in line with our Western values. At the same time, it contradicts our comprehension of power and our self-image, which dictates that the West should continue to dominate.

China is now calling for nothing less than the century of global equality. If it were up to Confucius, it would be the age of harmony. But equality is now the first step. Harmony comes afterwards. This means not only that from now on the majority should rule but also that each country can follow its own path of development. No country has been powerful enough to enforce this. With the rise of China, it seems possible. Many rising countries in Asia, South America, and Africa, which have long suffered from the impositions of the West, are gladly joining China's world citizenship initiative for more global equality. And China is ensuring that there are more and more of them — with major investments in these countries and political reliability in challenging times.

The fact that China is demanding more co-determination globally but is itself not a democracy hardly matters to these countries. Even if they themselves are democratically constituted. The decisive factor is that China has the power to enforce this. Beijing routinely rejects the corresponding accusation from the West. However, the protagonists of the French Revolution were not democratically legitimized either. And it is not only the French who still shout "liberty, equality, fraternity" loudly and with conviction.

We have driven out the godly rulers. Disempowered the nobles. Deposed the emperors. We have introduced democracy, abolished slavery and racial segregation, and enforced equality for women. Now, China is ensuring that the majority rules globally. Just as in the 19th century, the aristocracy, as a powerful minority, had no chance of maintaining its absolute power against the will of the people, so too the West no longer has a chance as a global minority to impose its rules on the majority. Our monopoly is running out. That is a pity, but somehow also a good thing.

Just how objectionable it is when others suddenly take over was something the proud British Empire experienced after the Second World War. The British Empire had to hand over the baton of world power to the United States. That was inconceivable for men like Winston Churchill, but nowhere near as drastic as what we are facing today. The new change is not taking place within one and the same Western value system. We can only hope that in 20 years the entire West will not be as desolate as the United Kingdom is today.

It is ironic that Donald Trump, with his growing reluctance to continue playing the world police, is accelerating global equality. Wherever he retreats, China follows. He shouted "America first" and got "more China." It is also typical of such phases of upheaval that the established, who are being put under pressure by the up-and-comers, squabble instead of sticking together. This phenomenon can be seen in the interplay between Europe, the USA, and China. Once again, the New Kid on the Block, China is laughing.

Of course, the fact that the century of equality is being called for does not mean that it will immediately become reality. That was also the case with the French Revolution. First, there was a man named Napoleon, who had himself crowned emperor. After a good 100 years of delay, however, it did work out. For the world today, it would actually be desirable for global equality to be achieved sooner rather than later. A new world order would emerge, with several equally strong powers that balance each other out and rely on each other, perhaps, for instance, North and South America and China and possibly also India in Asia. The African states united in a kind of EU and, last but not least, Europe in close alliance with Russia. Perhaps there will even be a world parliament in which each country will have seats in proportion to its population and economic power.

So, the new world order is actually quite simple. One world with five seats of power, five currencies, five global TV stations, five armies, and five stock exchanges that constantly balance each other out in competition. They are framed by strong global institutions that allow for extensive debate and shifting coalitions, force viable compromises, and enforce them powerfully and swiftly. This would include everyone on an equal footing for the first time in history.

The other extreme is also conceivable but not desirable. It would be a China that, while probably not waging any wars, tramples around the world like an elephant in a china store and over which even the former world power, the U.S., no longer has any control. Europe certainly not. China is a power that is stronger than the U.S. in the 1990s and enforces its rules without much effort. A China that no longer needs to make friends in Africa and Asia. A China that would have the freedom to trample our values underfoot and to exploit the world's resources rigorously and without regard for any damage.

Between these two variants lies a middle ground; a duopoly of the U.S. and China, which still have a lot of old baggage, each flanked by a group of somewhat weaker states, bit like Europe today, with France and Germany in the center and more or less committed countries around them. If developments continue as they have begun, however, China will be the more powerful of the two poles. In this scenario, global institutions would be more nimble and stronger than today but nowhere near as strong and nimble as they should be.

What will prevail in the end depends primarily on how strategically skillful we are. In any case, strategy has been an integral part of Chinese culture since General Sunzi's book on the *Art of War* from the 5th century B.C., from which the 36 stratagems developed. One way or another, China will play a central role in this and we will have to redefine our position accordingly. Former Chancellor Helmut Schmidt already knew this and told us, wrapped up in a provocative statement: "I would want to risk a lot if democracy were in danger in my country. I would go to the barricades, as an old man, and swing my stick," he said, "but to introduce democracy in a developing country, I would not give a cent. I don't have the right to publicly give advice to politicians or people in other countries on how to realize human rights."

Schmidt did not mean, of course, that he did not care about how people are treated in other countries. He tried to bury our Western universalism. Only a few years after his death, it is becoming apparent that the West's claim to have developed values that are so convincing that the whole world must observe them cannot be upheld. This applies to the so-called universal human rights as well as to all rules of the game which, from our point of view, should apply globally but which we have never had to agree on globally.

With the age of global equality, hard times will dawn for the West in this respect. Everything will come under the scrutiny of the up-and-comers, and no one will ask anymore whether we think it's good or not. Let's not misunderstand each other: We are not simply at the mercy of this development. Of course, we can and should always try to convince the Chinese and others of what is important to us. For me, this naturally includes human rights. However, if we demand them by claiming that they are universal, we will quickly and rightly meet with resistance. Angela Merkel is already practicing the new modesty and has achieved a great deal, for example, the release of Liu Xiaobo's widow in the summer of 2018.

It is also undoubtedly worthwhile to advocate for the rule of law but we can no longer impose them on other countries, just as we cannot determine how private data are handled in other countries, what safety standards the nuclear power plants there have, and what their children learn. The list could go on and on.

Much more than before, decisions are now being made globally — and by the majority. And when it comes to majorities, China naturally plays a central role. For us, who haven't even gotten used to how much is already decided at the EU level, this is likely to be a tough sell. But it doesn't help to close our eyes to reality: Globally, what we in the West are convinced of, what we believe in, is becoming less important every day.

This, in turn, does not mean that hardly anything of our ideas would be adopted. But it will only be adopted if the majority of the world is convinced of it and not because we think it's good or even because it's from our universal point of view. We will have to shed the arrogance and superiority with which we have long dictated to the world what it should or should not do. And we should do this quickly; we have already wasted a lot of time in Europe because we believed that everything would always go on as it has in the past 500 years.

The decisive question we must now ask ourselves is as follows: How do we manage to retain as much influence as possible on the global rules of the game in the age of equality and to contribute as much as possible of what we hold dear? In the new world order, it is no longer enough to cozy up to a powerful ally. The times of unchangeable communities of values are over. Unfortunately, the world is becoming more complicated. We must learn to find common interests with the various players and build coalitions accordingly, tactically clever sometimes with the Chinese, sometimes with the Americans, and sometimes with the Russians: If

China is fighting for climate change, we should not hesitate to work with China. When Russia wants to free Iran from the clutches of U.S. sanctions, we should make a common cause with Moscow. If the U.S. defends the right to freedom of expression, we should cooperate with the Americans.

If we look for the common ground — and we will — we should not ignore the differences. After all, they are the very diversity that makes up the new world order. Diversity that everyone wants and that gives us the opportunity to continue to feel at home in Germany is one of the global niches. But the stronger China becomes, the clearer we must say where Beijing's path affects our interests, what we see differently, and what we want instead. If we do not deny China's own interests, China, conversely, cannot deny us that we also have our own interests. One of our interests should be to ensure that the Chinese no longer play as free a role in the world as they have in the past. We must accept the challenge of global competition. We need a major European Africa initiative and we must fill the New Silk Road with our values and ideas. And we need to do it quickly. It is naïve to believe that what we think is right will prevail on its own.

We must learn to change perspective and see the world through the eyes of others. We will all become little ethnologists. This will become one of the most important virtues in the age of equality. This is also the big difference from the era of post-colonialism, which came to an end in November 2008 at the latest, when the global community switched from G8 to G20. Only if we see the world from the new perspectives will we be able to act strategically and wisely. This will have to be more about consensus than about bare majorities.

There are three sentences that we Europeans must remember.

First, only a Europe that speaks with one voice is a strong Europe. Moreover, we will not be able to avoid working together with our neighbor Russia. Only with Russia is Europe complete and powerful enough to play a weighty role in the world. This will not be possible without painful compromises on both sides. But those who have understood how powerful China is becoming will be ready for it.

Second, it must go without saying that our political system can also always be improved. For example, it makes little sense for politics to have to take into account a state election every few months. It might also make sense to extend the legislative period in the federal government by one year or to limit the re-election possibilities of a federal chancellor.

But we also have to think in large political dimensions again. How about, for example, a "Chamber of the Unborn"? In it sit people who make sure that we live sustainably. After all, future generations should have the same scope to shape the world as we do. This is not something we need to talk about with Trump. However, it is a topic that we could discuss with the Chinese, who always plan 100 years ahead.

Third, we are no longer automatically seeded in times of globalization. We have to give the other big players a reason to let us play. Or we can do what Great Britain did and opt out. On the island, they will soon be able to do whatever they want, but they will no longer be relevant. Of course, we can also opt for this option. Then, we can sit in the bar for a while and think about how we want to live and complain about what impositions Facebook and Google are for us. We can employ ethics committees, appear on talk shows, and write lots of books. But whether anyone will still listen to us is another question. So, if we still want to have an influence on the values of the world, if we don't want to play to empty seats, then there must be reasons why we need to be listened to.

There are two more reasons why China is still in talks with Germany. One, the Germans are comparatively reasonable. Some Chinese politicians even consider German politicians to be the most reasonable in the West. The second and much more important reason is that they talk to us and they listen to us because we have the technological know-how that the Chinese desperately want. As we have seen, the phrase *"Vorsprung durch Technik"* (progress through technology) now belongs more to China than to Germany. So, we have to make an effort to remain interesting. If we want to have a say in the values of the new world order, we must therefore put an immediate stop to our creeping technological decline. China has alternatives to Google and Facebook, Germany does not. Neither did Europe. That was the first major setback. The second will be e-mobility.

Basically, we have to start all over again: We need to focus our children's education on creativity and inventiveness. We need an industrial policy that is worthy of the name and as strategically oriented as China's. We need politicians with foresight. We in Germany must set a good example and convince our European neighbors to follow suit. It is worth the effort because there is too much at stake. No other country in Europe is as dependent on exports as Germany. If our products hardly find any customers, if we miss out on future technologies, and if entire industries collapse, Germany will be torn apart and Berlin — one of the most exciting and diverse cities in the world — will cease to exist. The diverse neighborhoods in Berlin with their subculture and the hidden champions in Swabia are two sides of the same coin. Only if we stand together in Germany and Europe will we be able to preserve this diversity and compete with China and many other countries for what are then truly universal values, in the age of global equality.

# Afterword: The Constructive Compromise

## China's Global Movement Profile at the Beginning of the 21st Century

Innovation and technology are now crucial to China's expanding position as a rising world power. Above all, the combination of politics and technological innovation is now China's outstanding strength by international comparison.

The politicians of this authoritarian political system have realized how important innovation is in global competition, more important even than armaments and a strong army, more important than the United Nations or the World Bank with its Western-style structures. In global competition, innovation now stands side by side with the trade business that China dominates as the world's factory. Innovation will soon become more important. China's neighbors will then become the factory of the world.

Beijing knows that innovation only emerges if there is decentralized, market-based competition among conflicting, diverse players. On the one hand, the state now limits its economic planning to good starting conditions. Individual competitors are provided with money, staff, and infrastructure. In case of doubt, this also applies to state-owned enterprises, which, however, no longer even account for 30 percent of China's economy. At the same time, the state makes sure that central areas in which innovations seem necessary are covered, even if success seems to be in the distant future.

On the other hand, it ensures a balance of power in the end. The companies should not form monopolies and thus unhinge competition. Then, as in the case of the Alibaba trading platform, the state intervenes as a competition watchdog and ensures via anti-trust law that the group does not squeeze the air out of the up-and-coming new companies. Unlike in the West, however, this happens abruptly, angrily, and with a big hammer. There is no legal recourse.

The innovation push managed in this way has been surprisingly successful. It has put Beijing in a position to establish global development directions and rules of the game. The batteries in electric cars, the drone industry, and 5G are just a few examples of areas in which China has become more advanced than the West and can, for the first time in China's long history, play a decisive role in determining the direction of global development.

The global triumph of the e-car, for example, began when Beijing had the power to oblige all companies in China, including foreign ones, to produce an increasing proportion of e-cars. Manufacturers were forced to follow. The Chinese car market is too important. It is now the largest sales market for most. Well over 40 percent of German manufacturer Volkswagen's profits already come from China. And what's more, the Chinese market is so important that it no longer made sense for foreign manufacturers to continue relying on combustion engines in their home markets. This applies to Europe, the Mecca of the automotive industry, to a greater extent than to the USA. China's strategy worked.

The government made the tactical smart decision just at the historic moment when China took the global lead in a key area of the auto industry of battery technology together with South Korea and Japan. In fact, the new generation of LFP batteries for e-cars is now produced almost exclusively by Chinese companies worldwide.

And China is now also setting global standards in the digitization of cars, especially autonomous driving. They are technologically the furthest ahead and are now able to generate more data much faster in the densely populated country of 1.4 billion people than in the West. This is also thanks to an even less pronounced awareness of data protection among the population — data that the artificial intelligence algorithms need to learn quickly and use the collective knowledge to make driving a single car much safer than when individual people drive.

This is a steep learning curve that China has completed in 40 years. Coming from a Maoist-planned economy with self-destructive elements, and going through the phase of being the world's factory after the opening policy, China is now at the beginning of a revolutionary innovation push with global impact. The still low per capita income, at about the level of Romania, indicates that there is still much room for growth.

While China is rapidly adapting to global challenges, the West's image of China, on the other hand, is only sluggishly moving away from two clichés: The Chinese are copying. And a country ruled authoritatively by communists must collapse sooner or later.

From this point of view, the West has just missed the tipping point in Chinese development. It is the point at which China's catch-up modernization, at least in its most advanced provinces, can be considered complete. Above all, the provinces in the coastal regions now have a similar — in some cases better — infrastructure than the West, a similar per capita income, similar levels of education, and similar industrial structures. Thus, the time was ripe to address innovation.

China's image in the West is shaped primarily by the second half of the 20th century, by China's position during the Cold War. Initially, it was on Moscow's side but soon seeking a third way.

Viewed from a greater historical distance, which is quite common in China, the innovation surge does not mark such a big surprise. Basically, it is the return to a certain normality of the old Chinese empire. China has been considered a prosperous and innovative nation most of the time — and China has existed as a nation since 200 BC. However, the past 200 years have been marked by a major crisis. China, due to a mixture of arrogance and lethargy, underestimated the importance of the European industrial revolution. At the time, the imperial court simply could not imagine that another country — especially such a small one from the Chinese perspective — at the other end of the world could be capable of inventing anything meaningful for the course of world affairs.

But the world had already moved so close together in the context of colonization that one can already speak of the first globalization push. China had little to offer in this global competition, fell behind, and became economically weaker.

Beijing had no longer the power to counter natural disasters, traditionally a key sign of political strength.

Crises became more frequent and economic growth declined, eventually leading to collapse. This resulted in social unrest led by religiously charged saviors who promised an easy way out of the dilemma, while Beijing slogged through and eventually fell into shock. It became an easy prey for the colonial powers, who plunged China deeper into crisis by unfairly trading opium for silver.

The unrest turned into riots and civil war-like conditions, to which the imperial court had no effective answers. Its monopoly on the use of force eroded until the empire collapsed at the beginning of the 20th century. It left behind a power vacuum that initially none of the dominant opposing forces, i.e., ultimately nationalists or communists, was able to fill and that the colonial powers were also unable to contain.

It seemed quite likely that this great empire would disintegrate into smaller parts in the face of power struggles, until, through a mixture of luck, courage, and tactical skill, Mao Zedong managed to expand his power and unify the country into one nation again in the mid-20th century.

However, Mao underestimated how weakened the Middle Kingdom was. Above all, he did not want to admit that China could not get back on its feet on its own, independent of the rest of the world. His unrealistic, ideologically masked, brutal campaigns left millions dead and brought the stumbling country to the brink of collapse again and again.

At least, however, he succeeded in maintaining and consolidating national unity and making China once again a power factor to be reckoned globally.

His efforts were crowned after two decades by U.S. President Richard Nixon's visit to Beijing in the early 1970s. This was a great satisfaction for Mao, after the humiliations by Joseph Stalin in the 1950s. The president of the most powerful nation in the world paid his respects. The fact that the Americans' domestic politics were up to his neck and that he was desperately seeking foreign policy success took a back seat. Nixon wanted to win Mao as an ally against Moscow, true to the motto, the enemy of your enemy is your friend, and thus turn the upcoming elections in his favor.

The visit gave Mao face, but it hardly helped the people economically. Effective economic reform became possible after Mao's death in 1976. His successor Deng Xiaoping was given free rein to develop "socialism with Chinese characteristics," which was later more accurately called a "socialist market economy."

Nevertheless, this was not easy for Deng: Deng first had to confront his compatriots with a bitter truth: China, which had been a leading world power over the centuries, was so weakened that it could no longer manage to rise again under its own steam.

It was no use, Deng revealed to his compatriots, and China had to let the capitalists, the imperialists, and the class enemy help. This message was diametrically opposed to the ideological consensus. Quite a few cadres at the time thought Deng had lost it when he tore down the familiar ideological railings with the sentence "No matter whether the cat is black or white, if it catches mice, it is a good cat." Deng was already quoted as saying this sentence in the 60s, but it was not enforced until the 80s.

They quickly changed their mind when refrigerators, televisions, and other consumer goods suddenly became available. As it turned out, the opening-up policy was the decisive step that enabled China's economy to run smoothly again, and, to the West's surprise, even to become the world's factory, producing everything from plastic buckets to smartphones to cars in a mix of low price and quality that was unparalleled anywhere in the world. In the past 20 years alone, China's per capita income has increased by 700 percent. Beijing has also succeeded in exchanging economic power for political capital.

This phase of China's resurgence, spectacular in itself, is now complete in large parts of the country. In 100 years, however, not only the past 20 years but the entire 40 years of reform policy will probably be regarded as a comparatively boring phase, in which the Chinese learned economically what is already common in Western economies.

The next 40 years, which have already dawned, will probably be incomparably more exciting, when China and its innovations will help determine the direction of the world's development. Now, it is no longer just about goods for the world but about the rules of the new world order.

These are at least the dimensions in which Chinese politicians think, and large parts of the population have no problem following them — at least as long as growth rates are stable.

In China, it is still quite common to view the world in the time frame of dynasties. The reign of the Communist Party, which has just turned 100 years old, marks the beginning of a new dynasty.

And, of course, each dynasty also has its own ideology in a certain sense. What we think of as Communism or Marxism–Leninism — that is Marxism: What is the essence of the economy? And Leninism: What is the best politics? — has little to do with what we know from the Soviet Union or the German Democratic Republic (GDR).

Instead, Chinese policy is characterized by constant trial-and-error — also in the relationship between the free market and civil society participation and state control.

This pragmatism has created a major dilemma for the Communist Party: China's politicians have realized that only the free market economy can create enough prosperity to prevent people from rebelling against the party.

But they have also understood the price they are paying. The party is losing influence to the extent that the economy will regulate itself through market forces.

That is why it is responding to the movement towards a market economy with more control, thereby exacerbating the contradictions.

In addition, the self-controlling forces of free-market competition and pragmatic experimentation with various development paths are not well-suited for a fascinating ideology and certainly not for a communist one. But the more successful Chinese pragmatism is, the louder the communists insist on their creeds, and each new party leader builds another dazzling edifice of thought for eternity to legitimize the party in the booming country, while the majority of the population has long since been absorbed by the shopping malls or, more precisely, by the endless stream of online shopping. Currently, it is the "Xi Jinping thinking on socialism with Chinese characteristics for a new era."

This can certainly be described as an attempt at re-ideologization, without having to face the accusation of viewing China through Western glasses. Most Chinese, however, have already solved this issue for themselves in a stubborn way: They have concluded an informal social contract with their government: It creates prosperity, and in return, the people leave the party alone, even if the ideologies fit less and less into China's lifeworld.

That is why only 95 million people out of the more than 1.4 billion people are party members, nowhere near 10 percent, and the lines are not long to join the party.

The party's birthday in 2021 proceeded accordingly. No holiday. No parade. No large groups of people in front of the mega screens in the shopping malls, where instead of the Louis Vuitton advertising, they switched to Tiananmen Square, nor was everyone staring into their 5G smartphones when party leader Xi Jinping gave his keynote speech. For the majority of Chinese, this was not an important day. Instead, most people met Xi's remarks with the attitude of self-confident citizens: Xi has delivered sufficient growth. The country is stable and secure. People can be proud of China again. So, let the man make his speech.

As I said, this sovereignty is certainly a success of the pragmatic policy initiated by the CP, of which it is proud, and at the same time, this success worries the party. It is literally terrified of losing control and no longer being able to break through in the roar of the consumerist frenzy. The top cadres are afraid of losing out to the market in this contradiction between more and more market and the desire for control.

President Xi embodies these two conflicting movements like no other state and party leader before him in the People's Republic. Movements that are also fed by two collective conflicting historical traumas: The fear of losing control versus the fear of missing out on a surge of innovation. Every politician and most people have learned at least one thing from recent history. What happened to China's rulers in the 19th century must never happen again: That China underestimated a surge in innovation and lost political control. The resulting humiliation to national pride was unimaginable at the time: In just half a century, the leading power in the world economy shrank to a large but globally marginal country that played virtually no role in the global economy.

The deep-seated desire to leave the feeling of humiliation behind has given rise to the two great contradictory movements in their tenseness, which are so incompatible with the ideas of the West.

Control is increasing in parts of civil society, the rule of law, religion, the media, subculture, and social sciences. At the same time, the scope of start-ups, scientific research, business, and everything to do with innovation is increasing.

If one wants to illustrate the extremes of these developments with two city names, then it would be Kashgar in the western province of Xinjiang, directly on the border with Pakistan and Afghanistan. And on the other hand, deep in the south, the mega-metropolis Shenzhen in the Pearl River Delta with its 25 million inhabitants.

But in no other city are the extremes so densely and tragically packed together as in Hong Kong, with a synchronized, censored, and in some cases imprisoned protest movement and a growing ultra-modern financial market. The third most important in the world after New York and London, which is based on the rapid, free flow of economic information, has no equal on the Chinese mainland and finances China's innovation drive internationally via its stock market — a financial market that is at the beginning of an upswing, because the Chinese financial market is now opening up in the area of asset management for foreign, also American–Chinese, joint ventures with Western majority participation.

In the West, the captivating part of the development, which blatantly contradicts the values of the West, is perceived more forcefully than the unleashing part. The unleashing undermines important moral standards of the West, which have been laboriously fought for, especially in Germany — the unleashing challenges, the innovative power, and the competitiveness of the West. In a sense, described in binary terms, the situation is simple when viewed from the West. In the unleashing movement, China is bad and the West is good. The question of what one prefers to deal with in the West is thus answered for the time being. And likewise, it is not a question of what one prefers to deal with in China.

Nevertheless, it is a risky choice for the West. The West now tends to underestimate China's unleashing in much the same way that the Chinese underestimated the surge in innovation in Europe in the 19th century, with quite comparable risks.

It would therefore be important for the West to correct the imbalance in perception between unleashing and shackling in China's politics. In fact, Xi Jinping also stands for unleashing, also due to biographical reasons. Xi's father, a politician in southern China in the early 1980s, played a central role in the development of Shenzhen and spent his retirement there. Today, Shenzhen is one of the most open, youngest, and most innovative cities in China. A city where even NGOs have been allowed legal status for the first time. Xi's daughter Mingze studied at Harvard in the U.S. until 2014, earning a degree in English and psychology.

On the one hand, Xi obviously knows exactly how important innovative strength is for the country's rise. But he also knows from his own experience during the Cultural Revolution how it feels when the state loses control. And he knows that in this increasingly pluralistic society, the party must fight for its influence anew every day if it does not want to expose itself to the competition of a multi-party system. Hence, the spurts of stronger control, which are disturbing for the West.

That is the dilemma of a successful, modern, and at the same time authoritarian one-party system.

The big question is how long the party, politics as a whole, can balance these contradictions between freedom and control. How long it can afford to focus on competition when it comes to the economy and innovation but not when it comes to political freedoms.

This can probably work for a few more years, at least as long as growth conceals the contradictions. In the long run, however, it will become increasingly difficult for Beijing to explain that political freedom and innovation are not one and the same pair of shoes. It is also clear that the party will not be able to maintain the balance forever but will have to choose one of the two directions, control or innovation, at some point.

If it pushes the balance toward control, that means less progress. If it pushes towards innovation, that means less control and thus less power. Still, it is very likely that it will choose the latter. After all, more control does not create more growth. On the contrary, however, in case of doubt, the party needs growth even more urgently than control in order to survive politically because without growth, control becomes much more difficult, precisely because people then cancel their social contract with the party. It loses the mandate of heaven, so to speak.

The domestic movement of restraint and unrestraint in turn has its counterpart in foreign policy. There, it is a movement that can be described with the simultaneity of retreat and opening. However, much of Beijing's policy, which is summarized in the West under the heading of retreat and perceived as ideologically influenced, is actually normal behavior on the part of large emerging economies. This includes, for example, the tendency of every large country wanting to generate as much economic growth as possible in its own country because this makes it less dependent on the ups and downs of international power struggles.

So, when China's policymakers decide to strengthen domestic consumption, this is far from decoupling and certainly not remaoization but rather a development that the Americans also carried out a few decades ago and that the Germans would also like to follow. However, Germany's population is too small for this strategy, which is why a good 40 percent of the German economy depends on exports.

China's growing desire to be less dependent on the West in the area of the international economy is also quite understandable, since the experience with former U.S. President Donald Trump, more than ever. Trump, at the latest, has shown Beijing what the power struggle between the West and China can look like: The established world power is trying everything to thwart the rising world power. It is not surprising that Trump has unintentionally intensified Beijing's retreat, with the aim of preventing dependencies on the West. That this is to the detriment of the United States and will not allow America to become "great again" can be seen as one of the most lasting proofs of Trump's short-sighted policy, in the wake of which EU sanctions against China were also announced.

As a result, Beijing is now buying less from the West. In 2021, the Chinese sold around 25 percent more to the US than they bought American products for China. Trump's policy of forcing China to buy more from the U.S. has thus failed resoundingly. At $676 billion, the trade deficit between the U.S. and China is higher than ever.

The movement with regard to the EU is even more pronounced. China sells as much as 57 percent more products to Europe than it buys goods from Europe.

This withdrawal movement by China in one part of the world corresponds to an opening movement in another part of the world. In short, China is not buying less but now buying elsewhere, from politically more grateful suppliers. Imports from ASEAN countries, now the largest trading partner ahead of the EU, rose by over 22 percent in 2021. And even from Australia, with which China is locked in a bitter political dispute, imports will rise by almost 20 percent. Imports from Belt and Road Initiative (BRI) countries are also rising. So, the term for this movement cannot be decoupling but must be diversification toward Asia, where there is greater gratitude for the exchange of goods. And diversification, by the way, is part of a movement of China's stronger trade with the world, which crossed the 6 trillion threshold for the first time in 2021. China's exports and imports worldwide grew by about 30 percent. That doesn't speak well for the decoupling thesis either. Never in history has a country run such a large trade balance surplus. If not for semiconductor shortages, power outages, and closed ports due to COVID-19 outbreaks, the figure would be even higher.

However, the most important trend is Beijing's opening toward Asia, and this movement will increase. Since January 1, 2022, the Regional Comprehensive Economic Partnership (RCEP), the world's largest free trade area, has been active, involving all of Asia, including Australia. Only India is still hesitant, but they have not slammed the door shut.

The goal is to build a single Asian market — without the help or mediation of the West and certainly with the common goal of less dependence on the West. What is unique about this free trade area is not only its sheer size, accounting for about 30 percent of the world's population and about 30 percent of global GDP, but above all its diversity. Never before in world history have so many countries with such different levels of development, such different sizes, such different political systems, and such different religions joined together to form a single market.

A unique laboratory of openness and cooperation in globalization has emerged. A laboratory that was initiated, led, and negotiated with great tenacity over eight years by China, whereby quite painful compromises were necessary to get the signatures of 15 countries under the treaty. The movement is supported by the Belt and Road Initiative (BRI), which was founded back in 2013, and extends to Africa and now has around 70 member states. Imports from BRI countries are also on the rise. Even trade with India, which is not part of either RCEP or BRI, has increased despite serious political tensions. It increased by more than 45 percent in 2021 and cracked the $100 billion mark for the first time. Most notably, China has been buying a lot from India: Imports grew by a good 38 percent.

It will certainly not be easy for RCEP to maintain stability, as can already be seen in the development of the EU. However, it cannot be ruled out that the pragmatism of cooperation is greater in Asia than in Europe, since in Asia the relationship between the individual and the community traditionally leans more toward the community, making implementation easier.

China's reorientation between unleashing and shackling on the one hand and withdrawal and opening on the other is taking place within the framework of the three major challenges we have to deal with at the beginning of the 21st century — climate change, digitalization, and precisely the pluralization of global economic forces and political powers in the direction of Asia.

The risks of climate change have now become part of everyday global political trade. The opportunities for digitization are higher in Asia than in the U.S. and higher in the USA than in Europe. The third major movement is shaping political action in Asia, but in the West, the idea is deeply entrenched that it is a temporary phenomenon that is, in a sense, reversible. A movement that will ebb away if only enough toughness is shown. Yet this movement is also profound and powerful. Its direction is clearly emerging: an epoch that lasted several centuries is coming to an end, in which the white, global minority of the West had the power to determine the rules in the world in a binding way. At first, Europeans held this power in their hands. 100 years ago today, the British Empire still ruled a quarter of the world. Then, from about the middle of the 20th century, the Americans became powerful enough to challenge the Europeans for the position of power. A turning point was the establishment of the U.S. dollar as the world currency at Bretton Woods in 1944 and the founding of the World Bank, in which the U.S. still plays the central role today.

In the early nineties, the USA reached the peak of its power. The Soviet Union had collapsed. The energy-sapping, global Cold War seemed to be over, and China was still too weak to stand up to the United States. But this plateau of power lasted only a decade.

Already in the first years of the 21st century, it is clearly visible that China is beginning to relativize the power of the USA and the West as a whole. The important date of this development is China's membership in the World Trade Organization (WTO) in 2001.

Since then, the West has been losing influence on a daily basis and the world is on its way to a true multipolar world order, to quite the same extent that digitization is playing an ever greater role and climate change can no longer be denied and is forcing action.

The COVID-19 pandemic has exacerbated this trend, as China and Asia have been much better at managing the crisis and it has left much less economic damage, the extent of which is still hard to assess in the West. Inflation in the USA of 7 percent is a harbinger of this development. On the edges of Europe, for example, in Turkey, it is already 30 percent. In the UK, it is 5.4 percent — the highest value in 30 years. Asia is a long way from this. In the developed Asian countries, inflation is on average two-thirds lower than in developed countries in the West. In the emerging markets in both regions of the world, inflation is still half as low. This development should not be underestimated.

The fact that the West underestimates the pluralization of global power compared to digitalization and the fight against climate change is astonishing in that these two issues can now only be addressed together with China and not without or even against it.

In the process, the West is becoming entangled in peculiar contradictions. The global development that we see today can certainly be compared with a development surge in the European nation states. The nobility, too, was a minority that ruled over the vast majority. And over time, the bourgeois majority developed an irrepressible desire to be allowed to decide for itself. Thus began the decline of the nobility, which was slowed down here and there or temporarily reversed but in the end could not be stopped in favor of more co-determination.

What took place in the European nation states in the 18th and 19th centuries is now developing with considerable speed at the global level. While the shift of power from the aristocracy to the bourgeoisie is naturally seen as positive, the opposite is true of the global shift of power from the West to Asia. To a certain extent, this is understandable; in this development, the West is seen as the aristocracy of the world, so to speak, and thus as the relative loser.

Not only the Western relegates but also the Chinese upstarts are becoming entangled in contradictions in these major movements. While Chinese politicians at the global level demand co-determination in accordance with China's population size and its economic power in shaping the new world order, they do not like to grant their own population this form of co-determination. In the end, 95 million party members rule over 1.4 billion Chinese.

As China grows economically and becomes more innovative, this contradiction will become greater. Beijing may be able to endure it for a few more years, perhaps even more than a decade. Domestically, growth makes people more lenient with their political elite, and in terms of foreign policy, China's growing economic power contributes to the fact that Chinese politics has to put up with less and less internationally.

Already, the West is no longer in a position to force Beijing in a direction in which China does not want to go. Sanctions against China are a political tool that has been overtaken by history, and their application only makes it clear that large sections of Western politics have not recognized the dimension of the development, as can be seen clearly in Europe in the existing EU sanctions against China and in the U.S. by the failed attempt to reduce the trade deficit. It reached an all-time high again in 2021 at around $40 billion. Overall, global dependence on China grew even more in 2021. China's trade surplus with the world reached its all-time high of around 700 billion US dollars in 2021.

The West can no longer assert and force. It must now act more and more in an exemplary and convincing manner. This means a major transition. But the sooner the West adapts, the greater its room for maneuver in view of the challenges that lie ahead in the context of the shift of power.

The upstarts will convert their economic power into political power and challenge most of the rules of the game that the West has installed globally and insists are universal. This universality, even if there are good reasons for it, is already doubted by Beijing, since China was not really consulted in agreeing to it. When the UN Charter on Human Rights was adopted, a Chinese man sat there and co-signed it — but he was not really allowed to have a say.

At the same time, Beijing is increasingly attacking the traditional power structures of global institutions. In the International Monetary Fund, the U.S. still has *de facto* veto power. Beijing is less and less willing to accept this. Beijing has already very successfully founded a competitor to the World Bank: the Asian Infrastructure Investment Bank (AIIB), of which 87 countries are members and 16 are candidates. Among them are the most important EU countries — against Washington's expressed will.

And Beijing is making its own position increasingly clear when it comes to the major global challenges of our time.

There will be heated debates about who consumes how much $CO_2$. The West is already accusing China of being the biggest climate polluter in absolute terms. Beijing replies that the $CO_2$ emissions of a single American are twice as high as those of a Chinese. And both are true.

The Chinese accuse the West of not being able to make important globally relevant decisions because of co-determination. The West accuses China of being able to decide quickly, but that civil society has not been involved and that the decision thus lacks democratic legitimacy.

There will probably be a much more intense debate about whether the various human rights should simply stand side by side or whether the world should agree on a ranking. First, enough to eat, enough doctors, enough education, enough prosperity, and then voting, the rule of law, and freedom of expression, Beijing demands. So, first economic and social human rights and then civil and political. The West will insist that free elections and the rule of law are precisely the best way to establish economic and social human rights in the long term. There are examples of both ways. Not just for the one in each case. Whatever the outcome of this debate. What is important to see is that the West can now be forced by China to engage in these debates. They can be fruitful and constructive. But they can also become destructive. To prevent that from happening, the West should understand that it can no longer decide alone, even if it feels so much in the right of its own historical experience. China, in turn, should not overestimate its new power and resist the temptation to go it alone, even if it now seems possible.

In the new, more diverse world order, there is a greater chance that the right decisions will be made on the important issues. But this requires all nations and their citizens to moderate obstinacy and focus more on public spirit in the interest of the individual.

Dialogue, at the end of which is constructive compromise across different cultures and social systems, is thus the most important global virtue for the new world order at the beginning of the 21st century. Reliably practicing it will take a generation or even two.

Frank Sieren
*February 2022*

# Acknowledgements

This book was written in many places and in conversation with many people whom I cannot mention here or who do not want to be mentioned. I have passionately discussed the theses of this book with all of them, which has brought me decisively further.

When you write a book, it is an imposition on your own family. I would especially like to thank my wife Anke for her patience and endless support. And I would like to apologize to our twins Tim and Leo that there are so few pictures in the book. They are still wondering how the letters from the computer get into the book. And when asked what their dad does for a living, they reply, "He types."

I would like to thank Sophie Pugstaller for always keeping an overview and a cool head and not letting her good mood be spoiled.

I thank Zhang Wei, who patiently sat through most of my books with me, and Fabian Peltsch for his tireless, qualified, and precise opposition. I thank Aline Schmittmann and Sophie Schmitz for not only researching thoroughly but also making sure that I always remained understandable, and Jessica Aishan for taking care of the interviews.

I would also like to thank Donata Hardenberg and Soundararajan Raghuraman for their help and valuable feedback on this English translation.

Thank you, Daniela Vogel, who, heavily pregnant, competent, and in a good mood, proofread the book and gave valuable input. This is the second time she has been on board. In the meantime, little Moritz has been born. The century of global equality will be his century.

I thank my brother Andreas for the Africa expertise and my parents who always support me selflessly. Also Barbara and Ray for their generous help on the home stretch at Lake Neversdorf, Ray I thank especially for the hints to Google and the South China Sea. The final point then I have set with Sabine and Bernward at the Üdersee.

I am grateful to Britta Egetemeier, the publishing director of Penguin, for the very stimulating conversations.

I would also like to thank Julia Hoffmann, who manages the non-fiction section — for her patience, her good advice, and her long-suffering when things got tight again towards the end.

Above all, however, I would like to thank Heike Gronemeier, who, as always, edited the book with as much rigor as sensitivity and showed strength of nerve not only on the home stretch.

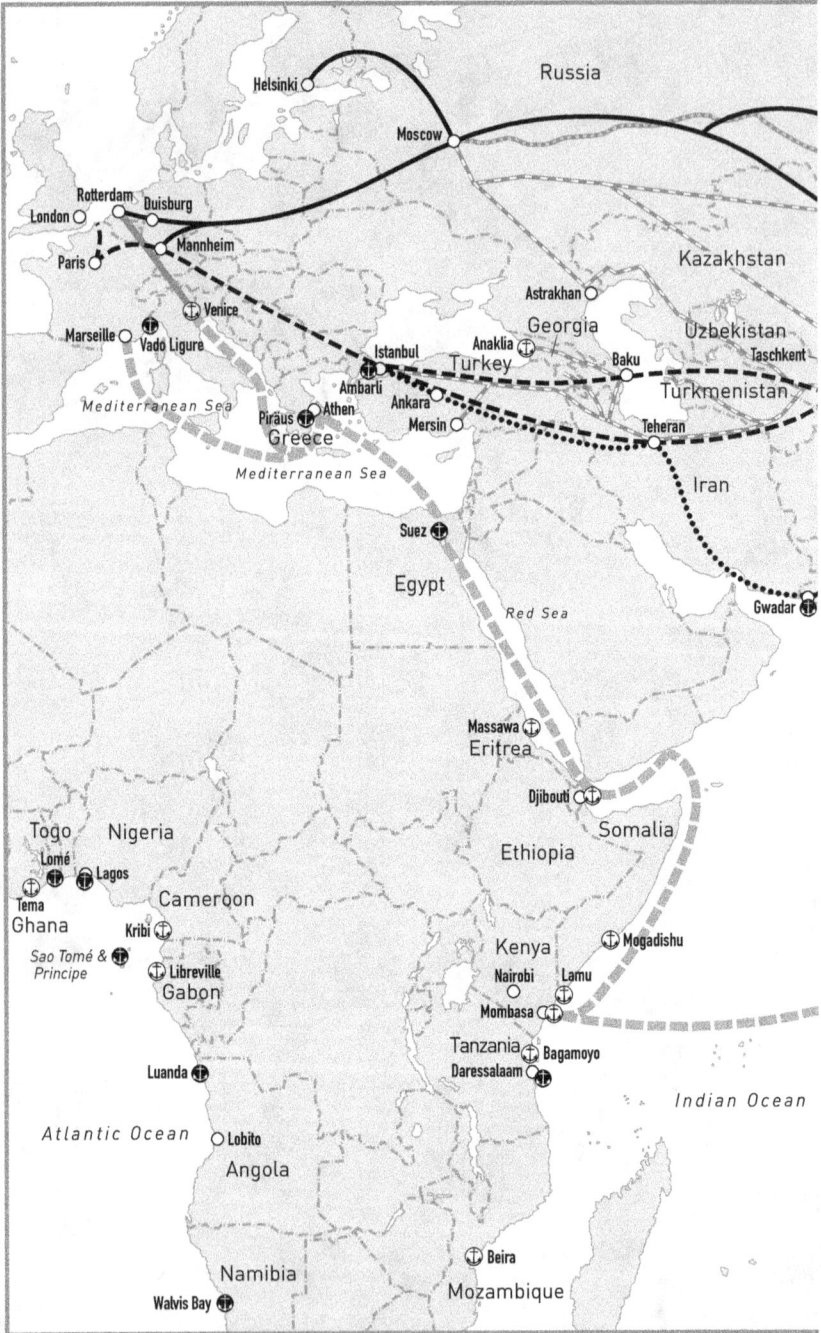

The different routes of China's New Silk Road

Russia
Nowosibirsk
Krasnoyarsk
Omsk
Irkutsk
Astana
Ulan-Bator
Almaty
Mongolei
Harbin
Bischkek
Hunchun
Kyrgyzstan
Shenyang
Rajin Vladivostok
Samarkand
Kashkar
Urumqi
Beijing
Chongjin
Duschanbe
Dandong
Afgha-
Lanzhou
Xian
nistan
Islamabad
Zhengzhou
North Korea
China
Schanghai
Chongqing
Pakistan
Yiwu
Fuzhou
Karatschi
Dhaka
Nanning
Quanzhou
Chittagong
Beihai
Kalkutta
Guangzhou
Pacific
India
Bangladesh
Kyaukpyu
Hanoi
Haikou
Ocean
Myanmar
Arabisches
Meer
Rangun
Paracel-I.
Thailand
Vietnam
Kambodscha
Sihanoukville
Spratly-I.
Sri Lanka
Colombo
Hambantota
Malediven
Malaysia
Malé
Kuala Lumpur
Kuantan

Maritime Silk Road
Singapore
Land extension of the Maritime
Borneo
silk road
Sumatra
ECONOMIC CORRIDORS
Northern Corridor
Jakarta
Indonesia
Central Corridor
Bandung
Southern Corridor

Railway lines
Silk Road Routes
Indian Ocean
Trans-Siberian Railway

Ports with Chinese participation
existing
planned/under        0    500    1000    1500 km
construction

www.ingramcontent.com/pod-product-compliance
Lightning Source LLC
Chambersburg PA
CBHW061238220326
41599CB00028B/5467